LEFT FOOT IN THE GRAVE?

LEFT FOOT IN THE GRAVE?

Garry Nelson

A VIEW FROM THE BOTTOM
OF THE FOOTBALL LEAGUE

CollinsWillow
An Imprint of HarperCollins*Publishers*

First published in 1997
by CollinsWillow
an imprint of HarperCollins*Publishers*
London

© Garry Nelson and Anthony Fowles 1997

1 3 5 7 9 8 6 4 2

A CIP catalogue record for this book is
available from the British Library

ISBN 0 00 218773 6

Printed and bound in Great Britain by
Caledonian International Book Manufacturing Ltd, Glasgow

CONTENTS

VALLEY FAREWELL

They expect you to look up to them at Anfield. Literally. Overhead at the end of the stud-clattering corridor that leads from changing rooms to pitch hangs that famous sign reminding you whose turf you're about to have the nerve to tread on – as if reminder were necessary! The clear intention is to psyche you out.

Certainly I found it impossible not to let my eyes stray upwards. But I fought gamesmanship fire with fire. I didn't miss the best by much, I told myself. Nice to have got this close to the real thing (which would have been me playing at Goodison). Then I was out into the roar of the 37,000 crowd and blinking my eyes used to the unnaturalness of the floodlighting. It was 28 February; the fifth round of the 1995/96 FA Cup, Charlton away to Liverpool, and a game that was surely going to be my last opportunity to touch the hem of big-time greatness.

That was a cast-iron prediction no-one at William Hill would have quarrelled with. Charlton's brave and classy Cup run had secured them this nice little earner against a team who, we kept nervily reminding each other, had twice recently crumbled at home to 'inferior' opposition. But none of us, I fancy, believed in his heart of hearts that it was going to be a case of three in a row and, in the event, with Roy Evans and his Syncopated Millionaires calling the shots to the tune of 2–1, it was to prove a form-book result. Charlton played quite prettily at times and the game was certainly far better value for spectating money than the eventual Final. But, even with Liverpool not quite bothering to engage top gear – if he hadn't been in prodigal son mode Stan Collymore would have had a hat trick – the result was never too close to call. The best we could claim was to have come a goodish second.

For all that I wasn't too cast down. I'd been determined to deliver some kind of performance and came off believing I pretty much had. True, my most vivid moment was totally negative: sliding in to tackle Sir Stanley right in front of the Kop, I bought his dummy hook, line and nutmeg to end up closer to Birkenhead than the ball. But otherwise, unlike some of the more touted names in the Charlton side, I didn't let the big-match occasion get to me. In terms of the yardstick which I'm reduced to measuring personal performance by these days – error-free competency – I had one of my best games of the season. When Nelsonian contribution gave way to substitution I felt I'd earned the hand I got from the Charlton faithful.

Too much so, it seemed. On the coach ride back south I had to take a lot of stick for doing a self-granted half lap of honour milking applause from the away end. Automatically I became a serious nominee for the squad's upcoming Yellow Jersey – the visible garment of shame and ridicule that Charlton's wally of the week is obliged to wear. I had to admit I could only cop a guilty plea for waving to the Kop and hogging more than my fair share of the Charlton limelight. But in mitigation I argued that umpteen of the Merseyside Nelson clan were in the ground and, if I had seemed reluctant to quit the stage, well, I was never going to have a bigger, more famous one to bow out on.

When two days later and back to humdrum training-ground routine I was told that manager Alan Curbishley 'wanted a quick word or two', I was more than half expecting those words to begin 'Sorry, Nelse, but …'

'Sorry, Nelse. We'll have to make do in here.'

The hallowed grass of Anfield one moment, the Charlton Youth Team boss's 'office' the next. Curbs had invited me into this cupboard because his own command module was occupied by first-team coach Les Reed re-running the video of an old game whose words he was in danger of forgetting. And indeed, as if responding to our surroundings, Curbs did go through a few ice-breaking moments of picking my brains over a couple of minor YTS problems that needed sorting. But this was just the warm-up. I knew that uppermost in both our minds was the awareness that my one-year contract expired in June; that the transfer deadline was already casting its intimidating shadow back from the future's already visible horizon; that my soccer pensioner status and years at Charlton combined to give me an automatic 'free'.

'You're a dilemma, Nelse,' Curbs said. 'A real dilemma.'

His eyes slid away from holding my own look to inspect the emulsion on the wall behind me.

'You've always done it for us, Nelse,' Curbs said, 'all the time you've been here. You've done it for us this year, too.'

A bit over the top, I thought, but, well, not by too much.

'You haven't let us down in any way, shape or form,' he concluded.

'But …' I said.

His eyes came back to lock on mine.

'But – your contract's up at the end of this season and … well, the way Kim's been banging them in lately … you can see I've got a problem.'

At Anfield, out of the blue, Kim Grant, one of my rivals for an upfront berth, had chipped over David James' basketball player's reach to score a once in a lifetime goal. If I thought hard about it I could think of a couple more nuts and bolts strikes he'd converted over the last eight or nine games. Kim is about 12 years younger than me.

'So I could be looking at a free,' I said.

'Well …' It was wall inspection time again. 'If we make it to the Premiership then – it's only fair to let you know now – you won't be figuring in our plans.'

So. I was never going to play in the country's top division. OK. I could live with that. I'd been doing it for the past 18 years.

'Fair enough,' I nodded. 'But what if we don't get promotion?'

Yet another shift. Again I had his undivided attention. I steeled myself. I've learned from football, as I have from life, that whenever people look at me openly and frankly in the eyes they are always about to be less than frank and open.

'If we don't … well, that's still to be decided. This is where you're a problem. Thing is, there's been a couple of clubs enquiring after you.'

'Such as?'

'Well, they're only preliminary enquiries.' But Patsy Holland at Orient fancies you and there are a couple of others I think'll be interested. If you could pick up a two-year contract somewhere else before the deadline … well, I wouldn't want to stand in your way. But with us still going to the play-offs, really, I still need you here as well.'

His look went back to the wall. I resisted the temptation to turn around and look at it myself.

'Thanks for letting me know where I stand,' I heard myself say, even as I began to wonder where the hell I was.

I got to my feet.

'Wish I could be more positive.'

I smiled and nodded. As I closed the door I found myself pondering the logic of dropping your senior pro in the event of graduating to the most senior division but keeping him on – maybe – for the Young Turk dog-fighting of a lower. Surely in the stiffs, in the dressing room … Well, forget all that. The line had to be drawn one day. More to the point was whether the tickles Curbs had mentioned were from the same sources as mine. Or if, indeed, he'd had any at all. It didn't matter. The point wasn't that Curbs was being a touch devious; it was that he was being kind. He'd been telling me to be sure that the tyres on my bike were pumped up. Which they were. Resisting the impulse to turn to look at the wall behind hadn't been that difficult. I already knew too bloody well what the writing on it said.

Sunday 21 April

If I'd still nurtured any lingering hopes-cum-suspicions that the merry-go-round of the transfer market, a revisionist tactical theory or plain old boardroom penny-wise, pound-foolishness might deliver a stay of execution on Charlton showing me the door, a little social exchange this evening has blown them clean away.

The setting was a testimonial dinner. The richly deserving beneficiary was the no less richly gifted midfielder Colin Walsh, his disintegrating knee finally crippling him out of the game. *Le tout* Charlton faithful were there amid the splendours of the Swallow Hotel, Bexleyheath – among them Chairman Martin Simon's effervescent wife, Lee. In the depths of the coldest spring in living memory she was sporting a sun-tan as impressive as her cleavage. When we came *tête-à-tête* at the bar the night was still young. I thought it more prudent to acknowledge the former attribute.

'Seychelles?' I asked.

'No,' she smiled. 'Skiing. All that lovely smog-free altitude. Of course, being a player you're not allowed anywhere near the slopes, are you?'

'I've not skied since I was on a couple of school trips,' I said. The kids love it though. And Carole was really getting into it when she was living up near Aberdeen. It's all a bit harder, though, when you're living in Essex and you're married to someone in this game.'

Lee smiled again.

'Well,' she said, 'they should all have plenty of time for skiing next year. And you, too.'

Wham! Ultimate confirmation! From the chairman's wife. To this moment I'm not sure whether Lee was being charmingly indiscreet or considerately intent on giving me advance warning. The evening progressed into the heady mix of scintillating repartee and high romance that has made Bexleyheath a cause of deep despair for Vienna and Biarritz. In its course a lot of nice things were, most properly, said about Walshie. He's collected the insurance on his knee and is probably going to stay on at Charlton coaching the youngsters. As for me? Lee had said quite enough. That evening, with the night, like myself, no longer quite so young, I found myself maudlin to a fault as I contemplated the prospect of soon finding myself indeed tackling the lower slopes. Of the Football League. The Conference. The ICIS.

Saturday 4 May

The last Saturday of the season. But there is no game for us today. Once again television is calling the shots. Our home game against Wolves has been re-scheduled for tomorrow to ensure the cameras maximum couch-potato ratings. It's not only a home but a crunch game. Our destiny, as the cliché runs, is in our own hands. Outright promotion having slipped steadily through our fingers, we need a win to give ourselves a mathematically guaranteed spot in the play-offs. It's not a climax to the season we should ever have allowed ourselves to be facing.

As per recent tradition Charlton went into the last quarter of the 1995–96 season with outright promotion there for us to lose. During our last dozen games we have displayed more generosity than a lobbying agent on the Commons' Terrace … Our consistent territorial domination of games has seldom been converted into three points. School of science? We've been strictly headless-chicken kindergarten, hustling and bustling down one blind alley after another. What we've so conspicuously lacked is a cutting edge up front, the ability to slice through or bypass defensive road-blocks. Further, whoever the opposition, whichever players injuries were causing us to field, with relentlessly unimaginative predictability we've played a two centre-back 4–4–2 formation. One Charlton game seen, an opposition scout has seen them all.

I can write this with a measure of detachment, because for most of this period a combination of injury and selection policy has kept me largely an interested bystander – on the subs' bench at best. When I have got on it has been usually, I think, for the marginal better. I've not given the ball away much, nor hit those impossibly ambitious long balls that desperation triggers. Restoring a bit of shape and rhythm to our side, I've made runs that have been to the point and drawn defenders. But, although my lifetime first-class goal tally stands at 149 – and it would be nice to round the figure up – I haven't supplied that missing edge. I've not scored or often even looked like scoring. Mind you, knowing I'm playing on borrowed time and that the various numbers I've lately been sporting on my back are all about to be simultaneously up hasn't been the greatest aid to precision finishing.

Tomorrow, though, the fat lady will still be singing her Nelson aria. With Charlton's rivals for promotion play-off places also bottling out down the straight, one of the season's paradoxes has continued to apply. The player who won't figure in next season's Premiership plans is still getting the nod for this one's crunch games.

Sunday 5 May

Drove up from darkest Essex this morning in a thoughtful mood. The win is a must. Playing at Portman Road, Ipswich – our nearest challengers – should be able to steamroller relegation-haunted Millwall with something to spare. Not all bad, mind you. Knowing this the Charlton fans will be 100 per cent behind us today. The role of worst enemy will go to Wolves. They've nothing to play for but bloody-minded pride, but that could do it.

As for me, I was coming over the Dartford Crossing to take it easy. My mission, should I choose (choose!) to accept it, was to put my bum on the subs' bench. When we bundled an untidy, blissfully welcomed, goal midwayish through the first half, I thought I might get on for the last quarter as fresh (old) legs helping out our holding action. We did, after all, have as good a defence as any in the league. Yes ...well ... Glen Crowe hadn't heard about that. Winning a ball that shouldn't have been his, Wolves' Northern Irish prospect hammered a shot of Van Basten power and precision into our net. 1–1. Not good enough. Destiny was again slipping through our increasingly sweaty fingers. And fast. The Wolves had got into the Valley pen and the headless chickens were running around in ever-decreasing, panic-stricken circles. The time had come. Twenty minutes to go and Curbs was nodding at me. Time to throw the old rooster into the stew to see what he could cluck up.

'Wide up front on the left,' Curbs had told me. But while there was the inevitable stutter of attracting the referee's attention, wise old reserve team coach Keith Peacock was whispering in my other ear.

'Nelse, don't worry too much about holding your position. It's a goal we're after. All the best.'

For the good pro to hear is to obey. But whom? Let instinct decide, maybe. Meanwhile I got into stride quickly and knocked a few 'keep it simple' balls about. But it was still all blunder land. Instead of picking locks we were blindly surging forward trying to beat the doors down with our numb skulls. With time passing I erred more on the side of Keith's lack of caution and started to wander. I saw the ref take that heart-stopping first of his last looks at his watch. The Wolves' fans in the south stand were shrilly anticipating his final whistle. Another surge forward. Anticipating its shape I went on another run. Not wide on the left but on a diagonal that took me down the inside right channel at and through the heart of the Wolves' defence. Ball at his tricky feet, wits about him, Mark Robson was alive to what was on. He slid an inch-perfect pass through to me. I was roughly on the corner of the six-yard box with about a yard of space to work in. The angle was difficult but with the keeper advancing to make it still harder, defenders closing me down, I had only one option. I gave the ball a firm side-footed clip with my right (wrong) foot. It was a true strike. Beating the keeper to his own right hand the ball flashed sweetly across the face of the goal to kiss … the outside of the far post and go out for a goal kick. My heart sank with all hands. With my last kick of the game I'd had the chance to put Charlton incontestably into the play-offs. Instead, with what would now be my last kick in a Charlton shirt, I'd blown it. Yes, final kick. The whistle was sounding and cold, sickening despair was causing the Valley stands to spin round as much inside my head as out. I saw John Robinson holding his own head in his hands, Shaun Newton stretched out face down on the turf … Someone, Stuart Balmer, possibly, was racing over to the tranny-tuned in crowd to get an update on the other scores. He was turning … his habitually saturnine Scots face was beaming … other idiotically smiling faces were hurtling onto the pitch from the dug-out. We had made it! We were in the play-offs! Like the 97.45% of football that never gets reported, my non-goal was fast fading from collective memory. A no use to anyone horror of a result at Portman Road (a draw consigned Ipswich to another year in Division One and Millwall to relegation) had handed us the sixth play-off place.

Laughing, crying, the squad embarked on a lap of honour. Cheers, ringing applause. Next year, surely, Newcastle, Blackburn, Spurs … I joined in this Valley parade, but my grin was pasted on. Heartsickening remorse was preventing me from joining in the jubilation. I'd had that gilt-edged chance and blown it. So near and yet so far. My career summed up in one strike.

Friends at the game, most critically Keith Peacock, later told me I had nothing to be ashamed of. It was my run that had set up the, at best, half-chance. I'd only had a split second to pull the trigger and I'd not hesitated. Anywhere closer to the goal and the keeper would have made the ball his. Whereas I'd had every right – in Alan Pardew's days of ghosting forward, the certainty – to expect a team-mate to be sliding in and toe-poking the ball home at the far post, the actual follow-up had been half a mile and half an hour adrift.

All the same, had Fate spun it my way, the obverse side of the coin would have been the stuff of fairy tales. The old man had come on and with his last kick in his last league game notched his 150th goal: the goal that had earned the Valiants a place in the play-offs and himself a place in Charlton folklore. '*I was there the day Garry Nelson got that injury time winner that meant …*' Dream on.

Monday 6 May

Life likes to be cruel but, even more so, Life likes to be inconsistent. Life therefore sometimes has to be kind. Minutes after the final whistle yesterday the beer began to flow like Fosters for the rest of the lads. But not for me. Today being a bank holiday I had long ago pledged myself (a touch unofficially, be it said, for a member of a play-off squad!) to play in a Plymouth fund-raising friendly – an anniversary match between the current promotion-seeking side and those who 10 years earlier had achieved it. No celebration for me, then, but, instead, right after a match – which I'd not anticipated being put off for 24 hours – a five-hour drive. I'd never felt less like undertaking such a marathon stint but way back I had given my word I'd take part in the reunion game. Now it was time for a man to do what he'd promised he'd do. And for his wife thereby to suffer. Too canny to offer consolation, Carole sat beside me all that long way as I played my unlucky strike over and over again in my cringing mind's eye.

The 7–5 scoreline indicates what sort of game it was. But deeply satisfying a result though it proved, it was – well, it might be – only a forerunner to a far more substantial result.

If I hadn't forced myself to make the long trek down to the Devon-

Cornwall border for the friendly, I'd have missed a potential turning point in my life.

It started after the game and, inevitably, at the bar. I was with my old mate and once mirror-image winger Kevin Hodges. My own age, give or take, and still boyishly slight enough to make a bus pass application stick, Hodgie currently has the dubious prospect of finishing his career on the books of the Football league's lowest club, Torquay.

'What's happening with you next season, then?' I asked him.

'I was just about to ask you,' he said.

'I'm not entirely sure,' I shrugged. 'But it looks like Charlton are going to release me. I'm toying with the idea of going self-employed and playing part-time.'

Hodgie looked at me.

'The thing is, Nelse,' he went on, 'Our chairman, Mike Bateson, has been speaking to me about how I would do things if I were in charge.'

'Really,' I said, thinking that they could do a lot worse than upgrade an intelligent old pro like Hodgie from his present position of looking after their youth team. And it might be only Torquay but it was work. In this day and age, never knock that.

'If it happens,' Hodgie was continuing, 'you'd be my number one choice for first-team coach. What d'you think?'

I'm not sure what the expression on my face conveyed at this moment. The truth is I had half seen this coming. A couple of times during 'keep in touch' phone calls Hodgie had speculated aloud about us teaming up, about how a job needed doing at Torquay.

'Who's likely to be manager?' I asked. I knew that if Eddie May hadn't been shown the door already his job must be hanging by a thread. Last season Torquay achieved a 1–8 result in the League and a 4–8 defeat in the Cup.

'There won't be one,' Hodgie was saying in his country boy burr. 'Coach, assistant coach … whatever labels are on the door, it'll actually come down to you and me, Nelse. It'd be us picking the side, deciding on the way we play. We'd be running it.'

I tried to get a handle on the swirl of thoughts pinballing about in my brain. Surely I was mad even to consider it. Bottom club out of 92 last year. That court case with Stevenage still outstanding, which, if they lost, could see them relegated to the Vauxhall Conference. I shouldn't touch this one with a barge-pole.

'Well … I've got to look at every opportunity,' I heard myself saying.

'I'll give it some thought.'

'You and me, Nelse,' Kevin said eagerly, beseechingly almost. 'We've always worked well together. Always been on the same wavelength.'

That was true. We may not have been Kanchelskis and Giggs, but as a twin-wing strike force we'd hammered in 30 goals during Plymouth's promotion year. And, as mates, we'd complemented each other just as well off the field.

'I'd still be playing?' I asked. That could make the difference.

'Nelse – no way Torquay can afford you *and* a player!'

'Look,' I played for time, 'other than probably being on the way out at Charlton I don't know where I am just now. I've got about seven balls up in the air and two of them are my own. But an offer from you – that's serious. Put it this way, if it works out for you, then, yes, I'd definitely be interested.'

'Listen, I know for a fact the chairman's going to be down at the ground tomorrow. I could fix up a meet for the two of you? You know – just for an off-line chat.'

The plot was thickening rapidly.

'Well, seeing as it's on the way home …'

Tuesday 7 May

From what I could make out from the corner of my eye, Plainmoor is a neat little ground these days. Three of its four sides seem well up to snuff. I was no less impressed with my first sighting of Torquay Chairman Mike Bateson. He is a tall, dark and forceful looking man with a touch of Robert Ryan about him. It's not hard to see how he made a fortune during the double-glazing boom, I was much struck by his frank and open manner.

'Well, Kevin obviously thinks highly of you,' he said.

'We're old mates. We do tend to see things the same way.'

Mike Bateson nodded.

'That's a start,' he said, 'But we're looking at a long road here. I've got plans for this club. Ambition. I see last season as a one-off blip.'

'How about the July court case, then?'

Every fan knows that Torquay are part of the 1996/97 Nationwide Division Three season by default. Stevenage Borough strolled their way to last year's Conference title. Not many would put money on Torquay holding them in any head-to-head encounter. Only their sub-standard ground (to the Football League's thinking) has prevented Stevenage from becoming a 'League' side at Torquay's expense. And they don't think it's all over. They have taken out writs against the Football League and the Devon club for denying them their, as it were, constitutional rights.

Mike Bateson had frowned at my question and then grinned.

'Oh, I don't think Stevenage will get a result there,' he said. 'They didn't get their priorities right. Other clubs spent their money on getting the ground right rather than strengthening their squad. Besides, there's plenty of precedent for other non-League clubs losing out on promotion because of their grounds. Macclesfield, for one ... Kidderminster. Let Stevenage in, what do you do about them? Besides, by the time the case is heard this coming season's fixtures will all have been scheduled. Is all that going into reverse? We'll be there when the new season kicks off. The question I'm interested in right now is, if you were here, how'd you go about getting us up off the floor?'

I found myself trotting out one of my pet theories: that any half-decent side should be able to vary its formation to confront and confuse varying opponents. I said that if we went a goal down early on we ought to be prepared to throw a big defender forward, Joe Royle Oldham fashion, just to stir things up. Since it's goals *scored* that count these days, not goal difference, it made sense to do the same thing if we were 3–0 up with 15 minutes to go.

Then we discussed my marketing qualifications – more on-paper than tried in the work-place but, all the same ... I started to get the feeling that Torquay were after not two but three for the price of one. Time maybe to back off.

'Look,' I said, 'I'm still officially contracted to Charlton and I'm going back into a play-off situation. I mean, you haven't made Hodgie a definite offer yet, have you?'

'No. Not yet.'

Money was mentioned. Not a lot. I'm not that high in the Charlton wage packet pecking order but this definitely seemed like an offer I could refuse. If I'm going to fetch up at Plainmoor as coach, player and bottle-washer, there will need to be further negotiation.

'Well, you've got the picture,' Mike Bateson was finally saying. 'Give it some thought.'

'I'll do that,' I said, giving him my open and frank look. We shook hands. Socially.

On the drive back to London Carole and I sat silent for long miles.

Conversation was redundant. We were both trying the same forward-looking scenarios on for size. Who might first break the silence was beside the point. As it happened, I did.

'Well … we've always enjoyed living down in the West Country.'

'Yes. But the kids – it's only a year since we uprooted them and changed their schools.'

'And their friends.'

'Carly's not a million miles from having to think about her GCSEs. We know nothing about the schools down there.'

'We can always find out.'

Now that I'd heard what I'd said I was interested to find that I was thinking positively.

'One thing's for sure,' Carole sighed. 'The house prices down there aren't any better than the South East. If at all. It's all posh retirement territory.'

Commonplaces, I know. Countless other couples have the same conversation every week. But the accelerated career path of the pro footballer means the upping your roots shocks to the family system (and sometimes to his form) come with far greater regularity than to your average accountant.

'One thing,' Carole continued, 'it would be lovely to have our own place again and not rent. To be in somewhere I can get to work on.'

'Hang about!' I said, well able to hear the sudden edge panic had given to my voice. 'Player-coach. First time of doing it. To the bottom club in the four leagues. If any of this happens at all it could so easily go pear-shaped in six months. Less. There's no way we should think about buying. We have to rent.'

'Hmmn.'

Hmmn, indeed. A regrouping silence on both sides. This was one that would run and run. I put my right foot down harder on the accelerator of Carole's newly bought second-hand Fiesta and, at the moment, our only car. Soon I became aware that, with nothing to do on this fast stretch, my left foot was beginning to twitch. Coach, yes. But I'd still be a player. That 150th goal might not be so elusive after all. Not at that level. I could sure as hell still do a job on the Division Three park. What a kid I still was, though! The little boy in me still wanted to be out there stroking it around in search of that golden, totally perfect goal.

When we got back to our little brown home in darkest Essex there were about 412 messages on the answer phone. I kicked them into the next day.

It was past my bed time. Other players would be unwinding now, their feet up on the recliner beside some holiday pool. But by virtue of our side-door qualifying for the play-offs, I still had a couple of hard weeks to put in at the funny farm. I probably hadn't taken my last kick at a ball while wearing a Charlton shirt. What would be, would be. We might be going to Wemberlee. Or, if we didn't get past Palace, not.

Thursday 16 May

The morning after our second semi-final play-off leg against Palace I know I will be going to Wembley. If I decide to buy myself a ticket. Come last night's final whistle Charlton had lost their chance of formal participation in the final to an aggregate score-line of 1–3. On merit.

With hindsight I'm tempted to think that the slapstick goal that Leif Andersen gifted us within two minutes after the start of the two-legged tie was arguably the smartest move Palace could have devised. Allowing ourselves subconsciously to believe we were home and dry, we played the rest of the half with verve, flair and complacency. Just as we had against Wednesday in the Cup we stormed forward to demonstrate this time – that's right – we had no cutting edge. Palace's more uncompromising, forthright and directed game was to see them dominate the next three 'halves' in general and, in particular, come away from the first leg not only a goal up but also with two close-to-priceless away goals in their credit balance.

Mountain to climb time. And now, curiously, the man being chosen to lead the assault that might yet claw us up into the Premiership was the one not deemed sharp enough to start for Charlton most of the season and already told he would be surplus to requirements if his efforts should contribute to the winning of promotion.

As it happened my recall from no-man's land was only the prelude to my achieving 'missing in action' status. Palace killed off the semi-final with a goal coming nearly as early as our first leg opener and as they relaxed into a confident holding action I found myself living off scraps. My last contribution in a Charlton shirt was one of my most anonymous. Substituted seven minutes into the second half (why bother to wheel me out for it at all?) I could have little complaint. Before quitting the pitch I gave the already disconsolate and, thanks to Mr Noades' un-neighbourliness, sparse Charlton faithful a farewell wave. But I don't think that many clocked it was my last hurrah and I certainly had no sense

I was getting one back. Like the lads still out on the pitch.

'... *We're going to Wemberlee.*' Maybe I can get a comp.

Friday 17 May

The end not of an era – that would be far too heavy a word – but of ... something. A watershed day for me. My last one at the Charlton training ground and my last employee-boss chat with Curbs. This time the venue was his office. I sat in the same chair I'd sat in on umpteen previous visits. In the time-honoured fashion of all executives he shuffled a token couple of papers across the top of his desk.

'Well, then, looks like this is it,' he said.

'Looks like it.'

'I'd obviously have preferred it if things had worked out differently but ... well, not to be.'

'No. And fair enough. Obviously I can see it your way.'

Now he did look at me.

'Thanks for all you've done, Nelse,' he said.

It was a good moment. We'd had the occasional fierce flare-up over the years – his jagging at me relentlessly after my putting in a 'mare of a performance; my telling him he was more concerned with what his directors thought about him than his players. But we were both happy to let sleeping set-to's lie. I hope his respect for me matched mine for him.

'All the best then.'

We shook hands and I went down those stairs for the last time. In the reception area were the mixed bag of Charlton likely lads who were about to become my former team-mates. I said a few quick farewells and found myself outside walking to my car in that 'it's the end of a chapter, I'm leaving here for good' daze we all come to encounter. It was a bright spring day on which you should have been starting something, not finishing. Away in the mid-distance the posts and nets were still up. Cones still strewed the grass. But there was my car. Here I was somehow inside it. I let the clutch out and drove down the twisting approach road away from the fields where for the past five years I'd laughed like a loon, sworn like a trooper and, most of the time, run my heart out. There was no fanfare, no roll of drums. It was just another day.

TORQUAY OR NOT TORQUAY

Saturday 18 May

One door closes, another prepares to slam in your face. A day later here I was in Fowey, and there was Hodgie, and here we were face to face discussing the same possible future in not quite the same bar. Hectically enjoyable throughout though today has been, its most significant element has unquestionably been this meeting – itself the coincidental outcome of a good deed in a naughty world bringing its reward.

As long ago as last February yet another former Plymouth team-mate, Leigh Cooper, had invited me to the annual bean feast of the club he's now honorary president of, Fowey United. It would be like singing for my supper. I'd do a variation on the little party piece that has evolved out of *Left Foot Forward* and in return the Nelsons would get an all-expenses-paid weekend in a delightful hotel in a smashing spot.

The timing had been excellent. To make the most of this weekend Carole and I had long since planned to drive down on the Friday. Consequently, after my 'thanks, but no longer thanks' chat with Curbs yesterday, the immediate thing I had to do was zoom off lickety-spit to outer Essex, then, wife, children and luggage rounded up, turn the car round again for the long eyes-squinting run towards the evening sun. With all these logistics and the 'how much longer, dad, I'm bored' mantra from the back, I hadn't had time or even inclination to brood over my coming to the end of the other, the Charlton, road.

Then had come a rush of old mates, new friendly faces and handshakes, the evening, the dinner and, after dinner, the, er, after-dinner speech. That had seemed to go down well enough and after various people had bought me several drinks (so as to earn the right to pin me down on this or that remark!) here was Hodgie buying me yet another.

'He still hasn't told me the job's mine,' he said.

'I'm sure he will,' I said. 'He made it crystal clear to me he's going to.'

'Well, OK. But if he does, I've still got a problem. No way am I prepared to take it on by myself. No way I could. And if you don't come in with me … well, putting all my cards on the table, Nelse, I haven't got anybody else in the frame.'

I winced. I seem to be a problem to a lot of people these days.

'One of my problems,' I said, 'apart from all the relocation hassle, is simply money. What he's currently offering … it's nowhere near enough.'

'Aren't you going to take that up with him when you see him tomorrow?'

'I'll have to. After all, I do have one or two other irons in the fire.'

Hodgie's' face fell to an even lower level than Torquay had managed.

'I wouldn't say any of them were hotter than this one,' I tried to cheer him up with.

'Thing is, you, me … We'd all be doing what we do best.'

Maybe, I thought. Sometimes. I could feel myself wanting to yawn. It wasn't from boredom but sheer fatigue.

'Look,' I said, 'if I'm going to impress him I'd better get some beauty sleep. I'm off upstairs. Soon as I'm through with him tomorrow I'll give you a call.'

'Fair enough. Good luck.'

Tired as I was, I didn't go to bed straight away. I was in that too tired to sleep state with too many thoughts, possibilities, fantasies spinning round in my head for me to have any chance of drifting off at once.

It has been a funny old year. I've had more publicity as a player than in most of the others combined. This hasn't been anything to do with my form. It's been the knock-on effect of my being – what? *who*? – a best-selling author. The book I started purely off my own boot, so to speak, as something of a corrective to all those bland superstar production-line jobs and a salute to all my also-running fellow pros has made me, as a friend sweetly put it, a division two media personality.

As a result a few radio and television spots have come my way along with invitations to write a few articles. One card I *could* play now is to opt for some kind of a writing-media career. But I think that might be premature. Garry Nelson media pundit? Not sure about that one. I don't have the 'previous' and hence street-cred of an Alan Hansen. And it's scarcely credible that I'm going to have Hugh McIlvanney or Beryl Bainbridge looking nervously over their shoulders whenever they start handing out the prizes. Besides, that little boy still wants to go on playing football. All that said, though, I'm determined to confound those who have said *Left Foot Forward* is a one-off, nine-day wonder. Hence these new and, for the moment, very self-conscious pages.

Curiously my first writing effort has served to earn me not only artificial prominence but also a couple of tangible playing offers. I wasn't trying to bluff Hodgie, wasn't hoping he'd be right on the phone to the Torquay chairman, when I said I had a couple of irons in the fire. The offers are there all right. In one instance 'fire' might be the operative word. A team in the Lebanon is after me. Since they are backed by some serious Arab banking money this is possibly a gift camel I shouldn't look in the mouth. But as the father of a family for whom a possible move from Essex to Devon threatens to come close to trauma, I feel I've got to.

The other offer – one of the tickles helping to sustain me in my 'on your bike' meetings with Curbs – is much harder to respond to. It comes from Leon Shepperdson, chairman of St Leonards Stamcroft, a progressive semi-pro club – one many would say is better set up financially than Torquay. With his senior pro, my former Brighton team-mate Mike Trusson probably whispering sweet somethings in his ear, Leon has told me he won't take no for an answer. The money would be useful and we'd be back at Worthing easily able to pick up all kinds of schooling and social threads. But I don't know … The allure of League football, of crowds still in the thousands rather than the hundreds, still glitters seductively. I'll have to give the Stamcroft offer more thought. But also Torquay's. Fast. Past midnight already. I'm now technically into my second day of unemployment. There's one thing I must be sure to get across to the Torquay chairman: my conviction I can still do a job out on the Division Three park.

Sunday 19 May

I've crossed the Rubicon. The Tamar, anyway. Five hours of sustained negotiation and talking Torquay with Mike Bateson have concluded in reasonably mutual accord and I am now on a two-year contract as the club's assistant coach. My suggestion of a fairly modest escalation to the offer originally on the table didn't seem to make his nose bleed too much. And there's going to be a relocation fee. Throw in some media-generated pin money to subsidise my Torquay take-home and I reckon we can survive. So finally I said 'yes' and we shook on it.

In terms of title there's going to be no manager. A delighted Hodgie's appointment is 100 per cent in the frame, but his official designation will be head coach. 'What's in a name?' as Shakespeare said. Very tasty player. Oh yes – I'm player/assistant coach, be it noted. The little boy can still go after his 150th goal.

I'll cling to the detail of that hope for the next day or two. Like all major decisions, this, now taken, seems the wrong one. A commitment to catastrophe. But it is a commitment. So let's look on the bright side, Brian.

Like … Torquay's on the coast and we all like to be beside the seaside. Put it this way: when you're between the devil and the deep blue sea the ocean's bound to seem the lesser of two evils. Even if it does mean fetching up at the last resort.

A little too late in the day to be comfortable, Carole, the kids and I found ourselves once again sampling the delights of the eastbound M4. This time Carole was the first to break a sustained silence on our trek homewards.

'Of course, Torquay Grammar would be ideal for Carly,' she said.

I got a distinct impression of more cornflour being stirred into pot and plot.

I also got a fleeting sense that I'd not really made a positive decision: that some kind of a music box had long ago been wound up and I'd been powerless to do anything other than dance to its predestining tune.

'And bottom club,' Carole continued, 'you can't really go wrong, can you? If it all goes rotten, everyone will say you never had a chance. Finish 91st next year and you've got a result.'

I was quick to knock this one on the head.

'Don't you believe it. Mike Bateson won't consider one away from the drop any kind of result. He's looking for a mid-table finish, at least. Top of table, even. He regards last year as a one-off blip.'

But I wasn't being completely straight. I was aware that part of me had been attracted to that dangerous last place glamour. In footballing terms 92nd has a higher profile than 82nd or 72nd. Which clubs had finished in those positions anyway? *Ninety-second* is a sort of negative bench-mark. All eyes regularly turn to it. A lot of players in my position, give or take, have gravitated to useful semi-pro sides as a way of cutting their managerial teeth in relative obscurity. A big turn around at Plainmoor would be much more in the limelight. As would failure. The argument, I reminded myself grimly, was very much double-edged …

'What's the betting,' I resumed, 'now I've said yes that when we get home there'll be a message from Curbs saying Juventus or Barcelona have come in for me?'

'Or the National Youth Orchestra.'

We kept on down the motorway.

Saturday 25 May

Today I exorcised a ghost. I went back to Wembley. It was only as a spectator but I was there in person, one-on-one against the venue which for five years I had allowed to embody all the minuses, all the littlenesses of my career as a pro footballer. In 1991 it had been my then team, Brighton, that had fought its way through to the sudden death of a last play-off game. A fight in which I'd punched my weight. Although on the fringe of the team for much of the season I had been included in the Seagulls' Wembley squad of 16. Foolishly – I had scored goals in the season's run-in – I allowed myself to build up my hopes. Perhaps ... for all my 'sensible' attempts to stifle them at birth, the Roy of the Rovers fantasies grew. With hindsight – and not, I think, too much paranoia – I can now see that I'd been set up. I didn't even make it to the subs' bench. Instead my inclusion in the Brighton squad gave the manager the opportunity to kick me into touch. At the last possible moment, in the most humiliating circumstances – I can still visualize every last tile in that bloody toilet – he delivered the death blow to our long rancid relationship by announcing to me in the classic formula: 'You're not involved.'

Since that kick in the guts – I wasn't going to run out on to that pitch where Moore and Puskas, Law and Eusebio had worked their magic – Wembley has represented to me all the honours and rewards I wasn't good enough to win from the game. For five years the name had been an instant depressant.

Not any more. Today I had the best of antidotes for banishing all sour spectres for ever – the presence at my side of my nine-year-old son, Christopher. Not even the downer of the fried onion, junk food stench pervading the approach to the stadium or the growing realisation that the 'Venue of Legends' has become the venue of logos could begin to dampen his bright-eyed enthusiasm.

Treasured memories began to flash onto my mind's eye. My grandad taking me to my first Goodison game. My own father leading me up this walk toward the twin towers of an Everton final. Champagne moments? Don't you believe it. When years later I first tasted some fizz it was flat

25

anti-climax by comparison, nothing like the bubbling fountains of expectancy with which I approached the prospect of seeing the demi-gods in live action. The intervening years have turned my own rites of passage through the turnstiles into imperishable memories. And, as we took our seats today, I inevitably found myself thinking that, God willing, 30 years on it might all be happening again: Christopher might be leading his son towards a key fixture. Perhaps not at this obsolescent, poorly laid out stadium – who wanted to play here anyway! – but at some field of heroes worthy of my grandson's anticipation. As this sense of the rolling continuity of things came to me, on the instant the tarnished veil between me and Wembley magically dissolved away. All the clichés shone new-minted. If you can't lose, you can't, sometimes, win. There's no triumph if there's no despair. Being remembered for living each day with the prospect of defeat and despair and still coming back for more was not so bad a legacy to pass on.

To the eye Wembley might have been half-empty but when the teams came out it sounded as if it had been filled twice over. Chris even stopped noshing on his Marathon for a few seconds and, as the teams stood frozen in those last few seconds while the ref checked with his linesmen/ assistants, I could feel almost first hand that wash of ice-cold adrenalin I knew each lad out there would be suffering. *Peep!* With an accompanying wave of the arm the whistle got the game under way and, like the players delivered back to dealing with the familiar, I could relax into it.

It was less than a classic. Half-time came with honours between Plymouth and Darlington edgily and scorelessly even. I sat wondering – another ironic, if minor and past, connection – with what dressing room sermon my erstwhile (Notts County) boss of 26 playing minutes, Wembley play-off wizard Neil Warnock, was trying to ensure the Pilgrims' progress. Whatever it was, it had been preaching to good effect.

In the 65th minute, it was Plymouth midfielder Ronnie Maugé who had the forward momentum. He was driving into Darlington territory and to Pilgrim fans it must truly have seemed like the coming of the Lord as he made the net bulge. Wembley was suddenly a passable facsimile of Celtic Park when the home team goes one up against Rangers.

In front of 43,000, Plymouth hung on at the venue that is now part of their own legend. As they took a lap of honour, I whooped and hollered with the best of Warnock's green and white army. It was going to be the class of '96 that through going up went down in Argyle history. But good luck to them. And always look on the bright side. If I do go to Torquay, they'll be one less thing to worry about.

'What did you think of it?' I asked Christopher as we made our way towards the exit. 'Not bad. Been better if it'd been Charlton.'

'Come on,' I said to reward his backhanded loyalty, 'only one way to finish off a day like today. We'll go to Football/Football.'

Football/Football is located half-way down The Haymarket in the middle of the West End. As the name tells you right away it's a themed restaurant and, the first time you go, a pleasant surprise. The food may be fast but it's also good. Tonight there was another surprise. As Chris and I walked in who should be the first people we saw but also visitors to the Wembley game, Alan Curbishley and his family.

'Come on over and join us, Nelse,' Curbs said at once. 'Hello, Chris. Enjoy the game?'

We sat at their table. Soon Curbs and I were talking relaxed shop. This time there was no self-conscious trouble with eye contact. All the constraints of the boss-employee, manager-player relationship were gone for good. We were just two long-in-the-tooth pros who had a few instances of soccer agony and ecstasy in our respective pasts and countless examples of the workaday humdrum. Between us we'd been to most places, high and low, and come away with most of the sweat-drenched T-shirts. The meeting was quite by chance but it couldn't have been planned for the better. It gave me an opportunity to tell Alan about the Torquay job. A little later as Chris and I got up to leave Curbs insisted on picking up our bill. 'All the best, Nelse. I hope things really work out for you down there.' I knew he meant it.

Sunday 9 June

Earlier this evening we drew a line under four days of madness at Nelson Towers. We waved (a thankful) goodbye to Mr and Mrs Hodges and their daughter Holly. Nothing personal, you understand – just gratitude that we can now lapse back into our own version of bedlam.

Starter for 10 is having two wives and mothers under the same roof answering to the same name – not a negligible factor when the house has rocked to the patter of juvenile egos incessantly demanding attention, food, drink, spending money and instruction as to the whereabouts of the most recently acquired video game. Such diversions from the real business of the stay had been exacerbated no end by the hammer blow of the unseasonable heat. The temperature has been up in the high 80s and sultry with it. It's the sort of weather that sandpapers your nerve ends and where humidity condemns you at night to hours of being unable to escape into sleep. At least Hodgie and I were still talking to each other when he left.

Object of our exercise was to get our Torquay act together. To create an act in fact. We've talked ourselves hoarse going round and around, back and forth over how we'd run the team. We've racked up more notes than Bradbury Wilkinson's.

Part of this brainstorming has been discussing the pros and cons of playing formations. Setting up Christopher's ProAction Soccer table and, happy as two field marshals over plans for a Somme attack, moving the little figures around for hours, we've thrashed this one to temporary death. It has kept us happy but I'm not sure how meaningful our variations were. Last night fielding a 3–5–2 formation we notionally took on the Doncaster Belles and lost 0–3.

The main reason for our up in the air hypothesizing has been our considerable ignorance as to whom we will have on our books. You have, no question in my mind, to deploy a line-up that plays to the natural strengths of your squad. To make the point through exaggeration, if you've got Robbie Fowler on your books you don't ask him to play as a centre back because you've also got Shearer and Ravanelli and are wedded to 4–4–2.

But with fairly natural wastage having pared the Torquay squad to a less than sufficient nucleus we don't know *who* we have got. Or are going to get. That's what these frantic four days have been mainly all about, the two of us trying to come up with do-a-job players we might by some miracle attract to the bottom club.

A litany of names has swirled around my overheated brain, this one or that occasionally breaking loose to pinball across my skull, take a different place in the circle, dislodge somebody else. If we *could* get A, then there's no point in pursuing B – although B would cost us only half as much and maybe give us a line in to C. It's been an education. I've learned two things overnight.

First, I don't know nearly enough about the players in the bottom two divisions. I've been able to name several old lags, whom I'm sure would still make the Division Three grade, and quite a few wannabe youngsters who, the grapevine has whispered, are being let go despite showing genuine promise. But calls soon whittle this list down. Another club's got in first. We couldn't begin to match the terms being asked for ... A typical instance of an interesting player saying 'thanks but no thanks' was Stuart Munday, a fast and tenacious defender still only in his mid-20s but now finished with Brighton. Stuart could have supplied defensive strength exactly where needed but his final verdict can be easily summarised: remote, lowly, impoverished, Torquay isn't to be taken seriously. Soon, I realise, my not very long short list of potential recruits is all but exhausted.

That's lesson number two. If all this goes ahead, Hodgie and I have got to put in place some sort of scouting network. However half-arsed it might be to begin with, we've got to spin some sort of scouting web that takes in the North East, the Midlands, all the key footballing forcing grounds. This isn't just with a view to the rare possibility of nipping in to whip hidden gold out from under the noses of 91 other clubs. It's going to be essential if we're to get accurate intelligence about the tactics and form of our week-in, week-out opponents. It's obvious that such card-marking input as has hitherto been coming into Plainmoor has been much more miss than hit. As is rather the case right now. Hodgie has a crop of names we might get somewhere with. Like two novice monks with worry beads we click through them: Ian Chapman ('We're hurting for left-sided defenders'); Stuart Myall ('He's looking for something better, too'); Christian Taylor ('Blackpool...We could do with his height'); Martin Ling ('Dream on, Hodgie'); Graeme Power; John Vaughan; Tom Pearce ('Last time I saw him he had a 'mare') ... Incoming calls, outgoing, the phone is never at rest. It's soon as hot to the touch as the ambient temperature. More often than not, as we rapidly learn, it's a source of disinformation.

One of the names above has been recommended by a business acquaintance friend, the sort of mad-keen fan you can enjoy a footie chat with in any pub. 'He's magic,' he told us. 'They're fools to be letting him go.' Or are they? I call a player mate of mine who's been out there on the park with the lad in question. 'Well, he has got something to offer coming forward,' he tells me. 'But for the job you say you're looking for him to do ... well, he's not it.' Lord protect me from enthusiasts.

And from agents too. Disinformation is what they are entirely about. Not too long ago Curbs told me without a second's deviation or hesitation (there was much repetition of one adjective) that agents were the biggest bugbear of his life. At the office, at home, by phone and fax they were constantly ambushing him to rob him of hours of his precious time.

29

Low in the pecking order as we are, virgins in fact, Hodgie and I have already had our ears cauliflowered by several 'price 'em high, sell 'em hard' sales pitch calls from various of these caring faces of football.

'I've got just the player you need, Kev.'

'Nelse.'

'Right. Nelse. He's a 6ft 3in striker just come back from China. Been a monster success. All we're asking for is a signing on fee ...'

I cut him short. The idea that Torquay can afford a signing on fee is nearly as gross a fantasy as the description of his meal ticket. Sorry, player.

Tunnel visioned (the light at the end is a neon pound sign) agents are probably the game's worst enemy in the shameless way they extol their wares. They are certainly their own worst enemies. One of the smaller fry, to illustrate this point, has been instrumental in translating two former Charlton employees to Torquay in the not so distant past. In horticultural terms neither 'took' in the Plainmoor soil and have been rooted out. Now, already two strikes to the bad, the same agent is singing the praises of another of his clients as though he were a young Ruud Gullit. But, again, an independent and objective source tells me the lad isn't right for us. The agent seems blithely unaware that his point of departure shouldn't be the names on his client list but our specific needs. More damagingly still he seems blissfully ignorant that with three strikes you're out of credibility for a long, long time. It's clear that I'll have to set up some kind of screening process at Plainmoor to keep the whole tribe at arm's length.

' ...OK. Where were we? That lad at Dulwich – '

Hodgie and I battle on.

Friday 14 June

I'm scribbling this while waiting for a cab to take me to Gatwick. For the second summer running I'm off to America. There's an iron in the transatlantic fire I'm determined not to allow to cool down.

Last year on a very modest scale I became involved in setting up some summer soccer schools for young American kids. Supervising all the shooting matches was immensely hard work (a lot of the support facilities needed instruction from Page One of the manual too) but as rewarding as enjoyable. Now, I'm about to repeat the exercise coaching and supervising other coaches on a somewhat enhanced scale. This could be my old-age pension, I tell myself.

For the next month my mind, I hope, is going to be wiped clean of all Torquayesque thoughts. I've told Carole to contact me only if it is Juventus. I wonder if there's such a thing as a national 'Old Gits' Orchestra?

PLAINMOOR PRE-SEASON

Sunday 14 July

Bastille day. But not here in Rhode Island where it is merely the last day of my four week States-side coaching stint. Perhaps by its end there will be dancing in the streets at the manner in which Nelson practice-session theory has irresistibly progressed to tournament victory. Attracting no fewer than 186 boys and girls teams from as far away as Indiana and South Carolina, South County's heralded Seaside Classic competition should provide the perfect show-case for my stuff-strutting Under-13 girls side.

Ah, a slight procedural problem here. A first round-robin kick-off of 8 am would do few favours for a coaching maestro who had welcomed the same morning in demonstrating himself to be a gambling incompetent in a nearby casino. No matter. An initial absence would bespeak confidence. And a bright-eyed and bushy-tailed – *you betcha!* – presence for the 11 o'clock game should preserve my touchline credibility as the Eisenhower of the prepubescent game.

Not exactly. In what proved something of a Battle of the Bulge all the technique training I had laboured to instil throughout the previous week dissolved away in the heat of a 0–2 defeat. An unjust defeat. A farcical penalty decision and a blatantly offside – honest! – goal gave me a plausible case with which to counter the surfacing hostility ('This guy is a coach, Myrtle?') of the natives.

Flexibility in football is everything. A two hour interval gave me ample time to fine-tune tactics and formation. Taking it in their tiny strides my young ladies lined up for the next game in unbeatable 3–5–2 mode. They lost 1–2.

In football trust is everything. Assuring the muttering non-believers that – trust me – the thinking game always took time, I forced through a vote of confidence in myself and a 3–4–3 line up. The girls gave their last game their best shot – and again lost 1–2. Recalling that I was in the land not only of the free but of the original 'three strikes and you're out' I did a lot of deeply sincere smiling and said I had a plane to catch tomorrow, a hired car to return, packing …

'We're missing you already, Nelse.'

Hmmn. Regard it as a learning experience, I told myself. It may serve you in good stead when you start coaching the young gentlemen of Torquay. Or get sacked.

Monday 15 July

I put through a quick call to Hodgie prior to boarding at Logan Airport.

'How's it been going?' I asked.

'Pretty good, Nelse. Just a couple of hiccoughs.'

'Oh?'

'Mark Cooper – after shaking hands on a deal with the chairman, he's signed a three-year deal with Hartlepool.'

'Ah.'

'Those two other trialists we targeted …'

'Yup …'

'They aren't coming now.'

'… Right.'

'And talking of the chairman, he's due in the High Court tomorrow over the Stevenage appeal to take our place.'

'Ah, yes …'

'Pitch is crap, by the way. All dirt and no grass. Oh – our chief scout has just walked out on us.'

'Chief? Isn't he our *only* one?'

'More or less. He was.'

'Er … look, Hodgie, better talk about all this tomorrow. I'll ring you from Paddington.'

'OK, Nelse. Have a good flight.'

Tuesday 16 July

Cradled amidships by one of Mr Branson's Ladies in Red, I miraculously managed several hours of cat-napping on the flight back to Gatwick. At times it came close to sleep. But not enough.

The next several hours were a whizzing blur of trains, saying hello to wife and kids, unpacking, present giving, mail sorting, phone calls, repacking, waving goodbye to wife and kids, trains and somehow – how did I do that? – eventual red-eyed arrival at Plymouth North Road Station. There to meet me was a smiling Hodgie.

'Great news, Nelse. The training kit has arrived.'

'Terrific. How many sets?'

'One.'

Wednesday 17 July

The dawn of possibly a new era for Torquay United and quite definitely a new one for G Nelson, began far too early for the latter's liking at seven this morning.

'Up and at 'em, Nelse.'

Looming through my bleary focus was the face of an insufferably keyed-up Head Coach Hodges. I tried desperately to fetch my brain back from somewhere out over the mid-Atlantic.

'Piss off,' I wittily riposted. Churlishly, rather. The Boss was being kind enough to bring the chief officer breakfast in bed. Come on, I must make an effort. Shaking the ongoing drone of plane engines out of my ears, I swung out of bed.

'What time of day is this to launch a new career?' I said.

'The right one.'

Three-quarters of an hour later we were quitting the house where, such are the economic realities of both Torquay and myself, I shall be imposing on Kevin and Carole until the Nelsons can sort out their own place. A few random clouds creamily clotted the Devon sky as we began with a westbound detour to pick up the now confirmed third member of Torquay's new back-room triumvirate, Steve McCall. His joining us now drove the BMW's driver-passenger combined age total up over the century mark. Three months older than I am, Macca is a veteran of sustained campaigns at the top (or thereabouts) with Ipswich. Dark, saturnine, he has all the canniness you'd expect of someone born in Carlisle, that old heart of border skirmishing. Monday to Friday Steve will be the youth team coach. On Saturdays, though, his midfield play-making is going to be central in every sense to our attempts at upward mobility. Artful in the extreme, he's an old fox of a player who never quite runs but always seems to have stolen a yard on his marker. He doesn't concern himself with brilliant passes; he's all about a constant stream of telling ones.

Already talking shop, we drove on. The scenery was a good deal more picture-postcard than the M23 but commuting is still commuting, I sourly began to remember – all the more so than when our rushing progress down the picturesque B-road short-cut was abruptly halted by the tractor occupying the entire width of the solitary lane. We were late arriving at the ground. I couldn't have complained if instead of making a good first impression I'd copped a first day fine. I reached the inner sanctum of Plainmoor Control, the manager's office beneath the 'main' stand, as unhindered as unrecognised. The paint on the office door is a bit uneven. Ten managers in six years has left its mark on quite a lot of things at Plainmoor.

Not least, I suspect, the players. Within the hour I was meeting them. Astutely Kevin had arranged for this to take place over the doling out of the squad kit – one (count them) shirt, one pair of shorts, one pair of socks. There was thus a nicely tangible bit of routine business to despatch and a need to keep things moving which drove away any artificial formality. I tried to put names to faces – any teacher will tell you that if you don't know the names of the kids you haven't reached square one – but I was as much concerned to note how each of the 15 (count them) players responded to the introduction. Some came forward with a broad smile and a firm handshake. Some with a furtive mutter and the barest meeting of palms and eyes. I didn't detect any masons but I've not been involved in any safety-committee meetings yet.

Each player had to sign for his staggering weight of gear. All did so without so much as a glance at the form.

'Pity they didn't have the same attitude to last season's bonus sheet,' Mike Bateson tersely remarked when I mentioned this later. Since he's seeking ways and means to improve this year's incentive bonus – however marginally – it was a dig I think he could fairly be allowed.

Second ice-breaking item on the routine agenda was the ritual day-one weighing-in. I was charged with overseeing a process arguably falling short of the standards expected of Her Majesty's Department of Weights and Measures. In the absence of state-of-the-art digital technology I was stuck with a pair of bathroom scales that Carole, for one, wouldn't have given house room to. Temperamental as an Irish midfielder they stubbornly refused to register any weight at all for several of our heavyweights. This demanded a high-tech solution. We pooled ideas. What should have been a five-minute job had extended way beyond when – eureka! – a flat bit of changing room floor was discovered and readings of a sort collected. For me, coming in at a three-year low of 12 stone dead, the delay had a happy ending. Stress beats diet any day.

Housekeeping now gave way to ceremony. The chairman delivered himself of a 'welcome back' address that ensured by its end that, as theatricals put it, there wasn't a dry seat left in the house. Follow that. Hodgie did. A motivating speech that he'd honed to perfection over whole seconds ensured that there wasn't an undrooped eyelid. That concluded the preliminaries. The call now was: 'Gentlemen, start your engines.'

The warm-up lap consisted of a gentle jog through the classier part of town to the heights of the Babbacombe cliff tops where we could simultaneously take in the view and the fact that in regulation fashion the sun was marking English football's return to the grindstone by beating down unrelentingly. In this heat tourist-amusing stretch exercises came easily and I was pleased to detect laughter and an absence of any kind of psychological strain. Then the semi-serious slog began. We put in 10 two-minute runs with not too long an interval between and followed these with a dozen 30–40 yard power runs. Nobody shirked.

Not to snuff out this enthusiasm I didn't let on that the pace will quicken. The pattern of training over the next few days will bear a distinct resemblance to the one I've come to know if not love in SE7. We'll agree to draw a veil over their finishing, but Charlton's starts in the past five years have been consistently impressive. I'm not too proud to borrow.

Right, then. Finish. Quick shower and off. Ah, not quite so fast. I've crossed that great divide. I can permanently forget the luxury of a short, sharp session.

Still damp from the luke-warm douche droplets (the hot water was in short, metered supply) I returned to my desk and, sifting through the PFA 'free' list and the umpteen letters and faxes from displaced players, resumed prospecting for hidden gold. The chief requisite for the job is a heightened ability to read between the lines. I'm getting nowhere slowly when club physio Damien (no, it's not a nickname, I'm not joking) enters with ominous news calculated to keep me at it. Injuries have reduced our vast squad of 15 to precisely 11 fit bodies. No sooner has Damien thus caused my cup of cheer to run over when very fit body, Paul Baker, is knocking on the door sadly seeking to lower the count to 10.

Both Paul's fitness and attitude were admirable this morning, but he does present a distinct drawback in terms of the overall Torquay scheme of things. He lives in Newcastle. Upon Tyne.

Two children, another on the way, negative equity and the inflated property values of the South-West all combine to rule out any realistic possibility of a move to Devon. He trains in the North-East and most of the other players recognise him when he shows up on a Saturday.

'Bakes' purpose now was to remind us that given his circumstances he was still hoping for a 'free' that would enable him to move to a club closer to home. A dilemma as Curbs would say. Technically Paul has one year remaining on his contract. But sometimes there's more to football than contracts. Now 33, this hard-working and honest player has always been a good value for money, work-for-his-team-mates pro. Believing we've been there ourselves, Hodgie, Steve and I know where he's coming from and where he wants to go. With no small measure of reluctance we tell Paul we're willing to help him: we won't stand in his way. In the next breath though, we make clear that should he see his way to staying, he'll figure prominently in our plans. When he thanks us for our understanding, I suspect he hasn't always been treated in such a grown-up way.

To emphasize this solidarity I stroll back with him to the changing room. Numbers here are low but spirits momentarily high. The rest of the lads are leafing their argumentative way through a boot catalogue. Choosing a pair of match-boots, training boots and trainers is a morale boosting task when the tab is being picked up by the TUFC (aka Mike Bateson). Mind you, the gear will need to be well looked after. One pair of each is it for the season. Any replacements are down to the wearer.

I've got a stake in this. I sit down and start clocking the brochure. Gradually I become aware of a less than natural silence. The noisy, mickey taking back-chat is no longer bouncing off the bare walls. Why has everyone clammed up? … Idiot! Trying not to blush, I muster an excuse and go on my way. As I close the door I'm angry, embarrassed and sad. The anger is at myself. I've just committed a page one error. I must stay in after school and write out 100 times: 'You are no longer one of the boys; no longer a squad number.' The initials on your shirt label you as one of Them!

The embarrassment is at my own stupidity. But it's the sadness that registers most. Of all the great pleasure I've got out of football, the below-decks changing-room banter, the oneness with the rest of the lads, has always been the keenest. Now I'm cut off from that. I know now that every time a player talks to me, a bit of his guard, at least, will be up. A faint shadow of constraint is always going to hover between us. Ah, well … I got myself into it.

I certainly did, Stanley. The players gone, there was still desk work awaiting the three wise monkeys. Highly frustrating desk work too. Three calls to verify suggested players' credentials petered out when I couldn't reach their referees. Now there's a first. Then, out of the blue, good news. For me. We can't attract a player but the Nelsons can sell a home. Carole was on the line, her voice positively beaming. The *War and Peace*-rivalling saga of trying to unload our Worthing home had reached its final page. Contracts had been signed. Not only had I one less thing to worry about but also we now have some chainless manoeuvrability to buy down here. Mind you, that's going to be a worry …

Half past five. Quitting time. We trooped towards the car park with the sagging shoulders of players walking off from a 0–4 drubbing. Now came a telling moment. Chalked on a board hanging on the exit gate was a simple injunction: 'Last one out, please bolt the gate.' The task fell to me. As I slid the bolt home it came to me that in 17 years-plus of pro football this was the first time I'd ever been last away. Welcome to the future, Nelse.

Which continued remorselessly. Chez les Hodges there was homework to do. Class left-sided act Ian Chapman conscientiously returned my calls to announce he had just signed a two-year contract with Gillingham. There was little more joy to be had from ex-colleague John Vaughan. Leery though he feels about being asked to goal-kick 80 yards minimum, a two-year deal with John Beck's Lincoln looks like an offer too good to reject. Matt Jackson gave me my hat-trick. His fee has just been cut from £1.2 million to £600,000. I was foolish enough to fantasise that our passing acquaintance at Charlton during his loan-signing, and my lifelong support of Everton, might be enough for Torquay to secure him after a matching second reduction.

Dream on. Before Trevor McDonald was giving out with the news, that's exactly what I was doing.

Thursday 18 July

More 7 am room service to start the day. But this time executed by a host-waiter with a face of doom.

'Nelse – a 747's gone down in the Atlantic.'

In nothing flat I'm wide awake, the pit of my stomach lined with icy ulcers. Mark Barham's wife, Maxine, had been due to travel back over-night on the same Virgin Jumbo flight I'd taken. Hodgie is ahead of me.

'It's all right,' he says. 'It was a TWA flight. To Paris. Makes you think, though.'

It does indeed. There but for the grace …

A little later a ring on the doorbell has me thinking less universally and more positively. On the threshold is a trialist we've actually got our mitts on, Paul Adcock, formerly in the Argyle side with Kevin and currently in the Conference with Bath City. Another commuter for the Plympton Express. As we travel Paul and I compare American notes. He too has just returned from a coaching stint.

Straight to some more ear-bending exercises. First call is to Geoff Twentyman, recently appointed assistant to Ian Holloway at Bristol Rovers. Through our PFA duties we have come to know each other well. After thanking Geoff for writing to wish me well at Plainmoor I get to the meat of the sandwich.

'These two lads you've had on trial from QPR, Geoff … How have things – '

'Forget it, Nelse. We've signed them both. Ian knew them from working with 'em at Rangers.'

'Oh. What about the lad Wright?' Not Mark but another centre back just released by the Pirates.

'Signed for Hull.'

'Oh.'

'Don't despair, Nelse. Keep at it.'

Who says it's good to talk. Progress is not quite what I'm making in this Search for a Star game. I'll put it down to being new at it.

But the endless switchback soon manages a small climb. I'm not so new as to fail to recognise that most of the Torquay squad turning up well ahead of the designated start time is a plus. Positive indicators continue to register through a morning of training in blistering sunshine. The pace was no less blistering but the collective attitude never wavered – not even in the face of the news that an afternoon session would keep everyone at it until 3 pm. I can permanently dump one romantically down-beat, constantly recycled, Hollywood-derived scenario. This isn't going to be Dirty Dozen/Heartbreak Ridge time – grizzled top-sergeant has to be cruel to be kind to whip motley crew of malcontents and incompetents into shape. Whether or not the talent is weak, the spirit here is willing. What lies ahead will be more subtle than a Clint Eastwood cliché.

'OK, lads. Let's be having you.'

'Commitment' is the second most overused word in football. It's got to be there but, like a player having two legs, it should go without saying. But I'll say this now. If Torquay United make fools of themselves again this year it won't be for lack of fitness. Back to the desk … And no messages, no developments. As we left I had the pleasing realisation that for long periods of the day I had not felt self-conscious. I was settling into a routine.

Friday 19 July

A genuinely upbeat start to the day. Jon Gittens – a central defender who has gone the rounds with Southampton, Swindon, Middlesbrough and Portsmouth – phones to declare his availability and tentative interest. Pompey reserve team manager Martin Hinshelwood (first-team coach in my Brighton days) had bridged him through to us on another strand of the old pals' network. Tough, fast, Jon could certainly do a job for us. We ask him to join us next week for our four-day training jaunt to Winchester, a coincidentally convenient 20-minute drive from his home. That he doesn't turn us down out of hand seems almost a result. It was in good spirits, therefore, that the Three Wise Men departed for *La Manga*. Sadly passports would not be required. The Iberian sobriquet ('doesn't he play for Real Sociedad, Nelse?') is the moniker of Chairman Mike Bateson's hacienda. This homestead, spread over several acres of the endless pampas surrounding Torquay, is our training ground for a day on which, while the temperature is very much Mediterranean, the experience is anything but holiday-like. Asked to run several laps of the largest field in thoroughly brisk time and then put in a score of thrust runs up a slope, the squad shed sweat by the bucket. Where once cows had madly grazed, a different breed of dangerous animal – the pre-season pro-footballer – now roamed through thickets of discouraging words. Finally, though, came the day's most encouraging syllable. Lunch. We made our way to La Casa Grande and the broad vistas of the buffet lunch the chairman was standing us.

The body language of several players was now worthy of a silent movie. *En route* to the food stood a massive tub of iced beers. To booze or not to booze. This was the question. Careful, mate, could be a set-up to spot the playboys. Restraint that could just about described as commendable was exercised until, with a broad grin, the man of La Manga signalled the beers were on limits. The ensuing sprint, fastest by far of the morning, was so fiercely contested I nearly didn't get one.

You won't find this exercise recommended in Charles Hughes' *Book of Invincible Soccer*. But footballers cannot live by dread alone. Running close to dropping is a need. Putting in the crunch tackles is a must. But so is bonding, so is differentiating between all the individuals in your team. Who's insecure underneath it all and needs the occasional quiet word of 'spontaneous' encouragement? Who thrives on the needling put-downs that make him bounce back harder? Now, as the beers flowed, some early season doubts began to evaporate almost visibly and possibly permanently. The new lads were good news after all. The demanding training, face it, did make sense. Maybe the Three Wise Monkeys did know a thing or two. Ninety second out of 92 last year – so what? Things could only get better.

One day some of the YTS lads would be running out for their first game in a first-team shirt. No bad idea, then, to get them over stage fright. Oh look! There's El Presidente's karaoke system, the Del Trotter 'Pro' model. OK, lads, you're on!

Credit Mike Bateson with canny, even delicate timing. There was a diversionary dimension to all of this. As I wandered across to the nearly empty tub for a top-up, I had a moment to remember that, even as I drank, 200 miles away in the High Court, the QC appearing for Stevenage Borough would be giving it his mercenary's best shot. It was a sobering thought. Almost.

Saturday 20 July

A watershed day in the annals of Torquay United. Following my footsteps another venerable Charlton relic has migrated Westward Ho. The yellow jersey – not the *maillot jaune* worn by the leader of the pack but its infamous soccer counterpart worn by the wally of the week. The democratically elected wally. After I'd explained the mechanics of the ritual the nominations flocked in.

Thirteen in all. The charges ran from bad dress sense (too close to call, this, with any football squad) to bad training performance. In between were such crimes as the spooneristic 'The ground is only two miles from here as the fly crows.' And my own nomination of, inevitably, Hodgie for his welcome back mumble. No one, however, could really argue with the judges' final decision.

A recent addition to the footballing workface has been the persistent warbling of the mobile phone. Without a state of the art example no player has street cred. That makes me incommunicado wimp of the Nationwide League, because the trend has otherwise widely infiltrated its bottom club even down to the trialists. As witness, Joe Davey, brother of our physio Damien.

Joe was watching television the other evening when the conventional phone rang. On the line was established player Mark Hawthorne.

'Damien there?'

'Afraid not. I can give you his mobile phone number though.'

'Fire away ...'

Twenty seconds later Joe's couch potato viewing is interrupted by a warbling sound.

'Damien?'

'No, It's Joe.'

'Joe – you've just given me this number.'

'Yeah. Damien's always forgetting his mobile when he goes out.'

A place in Torquay history, Joe. First recipient of the yellow jersey. Emblem of wallyhood – and of enormous use as a safety valve when the ambient pressure is on too steep an upward climb.

And now for something entirely different. Maybe. Once a series of calls to the council offices had determined where we would be training today, we all set off for Uncle Garry's first coaching session. Successfully refraining from a Deborah Kerresque rendition of *Getting to Know You* I put my little dears through a keep-ball session. Prime object of the exercise is to (a) retain possession for as many passes as possible and (b), once the ball is lost, to organise regaining it as quickly as possible. Not easy today. The bone-hard bobbly council pitch didn't make for pretty passing patterns – especially, since, as it was their effective reintroduction to the game's most central piece of equipment, the ball, all the lads were fired up and out to impress. They went into the exercise at break-shin speed. I slowed things down and corrected a couple of page one errors of my own making. I had made the playing area too tight and neglected to have enough back-up balls to replace those that got wellied over the council railings.

Soon I was enjoying it. I've always been a closet thespian and here I was in the lead role on a stage of my own devising with the captive cast as my captive audience. I vividly remember my debut game, my first league goal, my first hat-trick, and I'll certainly always remember today.

Monday 22 July

Another peg in our underpopulated changing room is being put to use. 'Where exactly is Torquay?' Lee Durrant asked us, when over the phone we nipped in on the rebound of Ipswich releasing him on a 'free'. Now, after an exhausting eight-hour journey from Suffolk, he knows. Good news: he's that rare commodity, a natural left footer. Bad news (as I privately think): it looks as if he's enjoyed a good summer. Too good. I'm amazed that a player let go by a club in May, allegedly desperate still to be involved in League football (his livelihood, after all) come next August, should ignore the need to keep himself fully fit. How else can he expect to make the maximum impression during any trial period? I try not to be too prejudgingly censorious. He's got touch, know-how. If he can shed those excess pounds he may have something to offer.

Definite good news now: Jon Gittens has agreed to join us for our Winchester week. We revise the accommodation arrangements upwards. Our little band of brothers will now consist of a massive 22 players (including myself and Hodgie) plus physio Damien and Mike Bateson. The chairman has earned himself a king-sized gold star by making an injury-time decision to book (and personally pay for) a 53-seater bus. We can thus count on a positive contribution from one coach at least. Instead of travelling in a job lot assortment of cars, we'll journey like true professionals, our self-esteem and our bonding that little more enhanced.

I almost wrote '23' players – something that would hugely gratify Damien Davey. Still only in his mid-20s and with the looks of a prettier Gerard Depardieu (he turns ladies' heads as easily as he manipulates joints), Damien is clearly extremely capable professionally. But then again he was very close to enjoying a career as a professional player. The heavy-duty injury which sidelined him had more than one knock-on effect. It triggered his coming back to the treatment room as healer rather than patient. Now, though, so to speak, the physician has all but healed himself. You can sense the urge to play bubbling away there just under the skin. I have just the faintest worry that this may soften Damien's focus on just where his precise professional priorities lie – with the lads? the management? – during the season ahead. Well, we'll soon see.

Tuesday 23 July

The gleaming 53-seater proudly sported the official Torquay United Team sign as it inched its way towards Winchester. We could all read it. To avoid three hours of non-stop taunts from passing motorists, the driver had turned it inwards before leaving Plainmoor. We sat trying to look like Benfica on their way back from a friendly with Cardiff. Journey's end was not the Stadium of Light, though, but Sparsholt College, set, appropriately for an agricultural institution, in beautiful Wessex countryside.

The rooms were spartan, but they were more than compensated for by the training facilities. The flat, lush grass contrasted with the uneven, tinder dry slopes of the Torquay parks. Very gratifyingly this didn't go unappreciated. An enthusiastic, keenly contested keep-ball session demonstrated most participants' ability. Early days, I know, but I began to have an encouraging sense of confidence returning to the egos so severely demoralised just a few weeks ago.

Time to put my own ego and confidence on the line. I took the first 11-a-side coaching session since my full coaching license course at Lilleshall four years back. Not altogether unaware that last year Torquay conceded 84 League goals, I concentrated on organising or possibly inventing a defensive strategy, working from the forwards backwards. All the squad were attentive, eager to learn, anxious to put things right. I knew from years of being on the other end that the session had gone well.

Wednesday 24 July

A landmark day for the club and its new set-up, with several highs and one unexpected low.

Any fresh arrival at a club can always be counted on to maintain a suitably modest low profile as he plays himself in over the first two or three days. Imagine, then, my annoyed surprise when, mid-morning training in full blood-pumping, sweat-pouring swing, I hear new-boy trialist Jon Gittens tearing a mega-decibel strip off first-year professional Michael Preston. Several potential team-mates raised ruffled eyebrows at the vehemence of this so-called 'advice'. Being a stranger hadn't in the least inhibited him. Must get across to him that too many chiefs on the warpath spoil the Indians. But not all bad. If we can channel him to assume responsibility, it could be very useful ...

'Cheep, cheep.'

The warble of the chairman's mobile formally halted proceedings. Part of me was now subtly amused. I could see the incongruousness of Mike Bateson surrounded by silent men in the middle of a noiseless landscape shoving an index finger into one ear, the better to hear with the other. But my inclination to giggle was symptomatic of my tension. We all knew what this call had to be about. Simultaneously with our pressing on regardless towards the new season Stevenage's appeal to the courts had been building to a climax. Today was decision day. We might not have a new Nationwide season at all. Holding our breaths we stood trying to read meaning into the chairman's deadpan expression. He grunted. The finger came out of his ear … and vanished behind a thumb jabbing triumphantly at the sky. *Wa-hoo!* Rebel yells invaded Hardy's landscape. Forget malignant Destiny! God was in Her Heaven! On our side! As had been the judge. Later we learned it had been a damned close run thing but we had got our result. The huge, silent weight which, despite the chairman's outward air of confidence had been on all our shoulders, was lifted. We positively fizzed as we went back to our work.

And anticlimax. After 10 minutes of re-underlining what was expected of the team defensively (the retentive powers of players' minds for tactical drills are notoriously short) we set up some shooting practice. From it came the worst hour in the 60 making up my first working week. On our hands and knees two-thirds of the Torquay coaching complement spent sixty minutes – *sixty* fruitless minutes – trying to find the misdirected training ball buried deep in a Hampshire thicket. One hour. A long time to be playing silly buggers in the sort of game it's hard to image Alex Ferguson and Brian Kidd being asked to take part in. A misguided sense of priorities? No. That's the point. For Torquay, footballs are a significant cost item. If two or three more had gone permanently adrift, there could well have been talk of the bus being sent packing and the squad thumbing its way back west. Mercifully the scenario wasn't realised. The rest of the shooting practice was on target.

As, glory be, it was at Wimborne. In gaining a thumping 6–0 win the team delivered to the two non-playing coaches exactly the performance we had asked and hoped for. A pre-season friendly against part-timers is not the ultimate trial but Wimborne are no mugs and we were a side that managed no more than 30 League goals last season.

Moreover, whoever the opposition, this was our first game in charge, the first time all our theorising, great expectations and, yes, self-doubting, had been put to the acid, pragmatic test of a game played in anger. The outcome – six past their keeper, none past ours with Matthew Gregg keeping the defensive record blemish-free thanks to a wonderful penalty save – was such sweet relief. Our feet couldn't be entirely made of clay.

Less euphorically, it had to be said that, on later reflection, the jury was still out on three of the trialists. Jon Gittens, though, positively impressed both Hodgie and me. The chairman, the man who might have to foot the bill for him, affected to be less than convinced.

The great sound of laughter in a winning changing room, wide smiles in the Wimborne bath. Skipper Alex Watson came over and asked if it would be all right to buy a few cans with which to continue toasting this famous (well, rare) victory on the coach trip back to our base. Flatly I reminded him of what was what.

'It's pre-season,' I said. 'Get them to drink up. On the bus for 10.'

He choked back his expletives with professional diplomacy but dark sarcasms audibly pursued the schoolmasterly coaches as we boarded the bus. A few minutes later, as per instructions, the bus turned into the car park of the pub the same pedants had clocked *en route* to the game. 'Coaches welcome' the board said and as jeers turned to cheers, it temporarily applied to Hodgie and me as well. Even more sweetness and light suffused the atmosphere when we made an announcement. 'The chairman's sorry that he had to shoot off. But he said to say 'Well done' and by way of showing he means it, the drinks are on him.'

Hodgie and Nelson's big night out. To good effect I hope. The alternation of whip and carrot may be a touch mechanical but if we're going to turn things around we must put the restoration of self-belief, self-respect at the top of our unending rehabilitation programme.

Thursday 25 July

A brief, serious chat with Jon Gittens. He's interested but all future negotiations will be with his agent, who will doubtless open from that lofty height somewhere in cloud cuckoo land. That's not a coaching problem. After establishing a few parameters we pass the ball into Mike Bateson's court where it comes to rest alongside the buck.

Saturday 27 July

No weekend peace for the wicked. The coaches sit down to review the Torquay talent profit and loss columns. It's a task I feel qualified to contribute to now that I've started to get a handle on our squad members as individuals.

To be sensibly taken for granted for immediate working purposes is a narrow band of thoroughly competent pros – central defenders Alex Watson and Lee Barrow, midfielders Charlie Oatway and Steve McCall – who may lack a yard of pace here or power in the air there but will essentially do a good and consistent job for us.

A big brave defender, Alex is the archetypal pro, as you might expect from a player who in the course of several Anfield seasons represented Liverpool in the Charity Shield. As reliable off the field as on, he's the ideal skipper, good in the changing room and everywhere else as well.

From the long to the short. Midfielder Charlie Oatway is diminutive but, one of nature's 100 percenters, he has programmed his tiny frame to run for ever. As with many bantam weights there's a lot of in your face strut about Charlie socially. You're always likely to hear his voice first. I suspect there's a deal of over-compensating. Blush though he would to admit it, Charlie has got his sensitive side. He wouldn't be slow to blame himself for dropping an on the field ricket.

Steve McCall is another midfielder but is the cheese to Charlie's chalk. Quiet, not missing a trick, where Charlie bustles and gets a foot in, Steve will be our man for running the game. His long years at the top have taught him not only how but also when to put his foot on the ball to slow the game. There is the air of assurance about his play which you might expect from someone who has graced a UEFA Cup Final.

Lee Barrow is not an immediately eye-catching player but after 90 minutes always likely to be a Man of the Match contender. Neat, self-contained, he does his defending good works by stealth allied to consistency. He's not unduly tall but good in the air and – a bonus for us – a long-throw specialist.

To these 'plus' names we can add those of Jon Gittens and Paul Baker if their personal plans allow them to become and to remain fixtures respectively. So far, so good. But it's not what you can call a long list. We slide sideways very soon into grey areas.

Goal keeping is a problem. Veteran Rhys Wilmot is clearly some way from recovering from heavy-duty spinal surgery. When he stretches to take a high cross he's in pain. He's here on a month-to-month contract which, in all fairness, is the most we dare commit ourselves to. Rhys is unlikely to start the season for us. More likely to play is Ray Newland, a former understudy to Nevil Southall. But he has a shoulder injury. He's making lighter of it, we suspect, than he should. Further, the punishment he shipped last season seems to have impaired his confidence. He has a tendency to be in three minds over whether to come for the ball and communication between him and the back three or four is still at the four-lettered stage. Our third keeping choice is Matthew Gregg, one of our YTS lads. He's exactly what you'd suppose from that – promising but self-evidently inexperienced. The trick will be to give him positive experience.

'Promising but ...' is a descriptive tag that could fairly be tied around several of the squad's necks. Ian Hathaway is a 'cheeky chappy' on and off the field. He's stuffed with footballing ability but unfortunately with too many calories also. Not a good sign at 28-plus and one raising a question mark over his, yes, commitment. If his wise-cracking masks an attitude problem I hope it's a legacy from the humiliation of last year and, as such, temporary.

A more serious case, I'm beginning to believe, of threatening to flatter short term with his technical ability but deceive long through his attitude is young left-sided wing-back, Scott Stamps. Having not caught the eye during trials at Derby, Stampsie finds himself part not of a Premiership but a Division Three squad and his feckless attitude towards training may well be attributable to his ongoing disappointment at having failed to bridge the huge difference in status and reward. That former team-mate Paul Trollope succeeded at the Baseball Ground precisely where he blew out may be prolonging this disenchantment. A harsh accusation. Is this the sour, disgruntled judgement of a plodding, over-the-hill pro jealous of the flair a young gun carries lightly and casually? I don't think so. Whatever the shortcomings in my own game, I always worked hard, I still do, to minimise them. And I've certainly trained alongside immensely talented players who never took either their skills or eventual success for granted. What they did well, they constantly tried to do better. I think my assessment of Stampsie is reasonably objective and measured. It leaves me with an obligation – to bring home to him that he'll be a fool to himself if he doesn't recognise the need to develop a wholehearted, work for himself, work for everyone else, professionalism. If we can get this response out of him or, rather, persuade him to get it out of himself, he'll be a massive plus to us.

'Professionalism.' Another of football's – of life's! – most often abused words. How do you define it? Recognise it? It's certainly not a case of being a dull, grind it out clone. People are different. The player who wise-cracks his smiling way through the training day may well be the most serious. You wouldn't find a funnier man in football than my former Brighton team-mate Russel Bromage. Or a better pro. That word again. I suppose I'd have to fall back on conveying what it implies by repeating the old insight. 'A professional is somebody who can deliver his best work when he's not feeling his best.' The professional, for working purposes, is the one who, when crisis threatens and a team-mate blurts out 'Christ! What do we do now!' replies, 'The best we can.'

But back to the stock-taking. Three promising youngsters whose best is yet to come, Hodgie and I feel, are Stevie Winter, a right back who has come to us from non-League Taunton, Mark Hawthorne, a central midfielder and Ellis Laight, a striker who has banged in his non-League hat tricks but found Division Three defenders far less generous. The latter two are with us on three-month contracts, which I'm coming to feel should be extended. Closer to realising his potential, perhaps, is trialist Paul Mitchell, a right back joining us from West Ham on the strength of a strong recommendation from Harry Redknapp, a manager who didn't think twice about snapping me up – he didn't! – when I was long ago up for modest grabs. Solid, composed under pressure, Paul looks the part. One part. He's a defender first and a venturing forward *wing-back* a distant second. We'll probably have to work on his speed. But haven't I already banged on about how players' abilities should determine formation, rather than shoe-horning players into what for them are unnatural positions …

Finally – for the moment! – there's Torquay's international, Rodney Jack. He too, I believe, earns a 'very promising, could do better' assessment on his report card. We'll lose him on several occasions as St Vincent and the Grenadines mount their World Cup challenge, one the soccer world will watch with bated breath. Well, the Windward Islands, anyway. At first glance Rodney seems a smaller, thinking man's version of Franz Carr, quick, tricky with the ball at his feet, possessed of a hefty shot. There's still a question mark in my mind about his savvy, whether passing the ball or moving to receive it, in linking in with the play. Hodgie tends to rate him higher in this department. Let's be positive: work on the training field can produce marked improvement in positional sense relatively quickly.

As Hodgie and I conclude our chat feeling that we've a reasonable nucleus to work on, I find myself thinking of the way in which my casual entry into the changing room reduced the atmosphere to a strained silence. I've got to get this right. I must work it so that the lads continue to come to me for informal advice. Dutch uncle, yes. Father-figure ... OK. Headmaster, no way.

Our mini mini-break does the intended job. The team reconvenes for the evening friendly in good mental shape. Our 3–5–2 shape on the field is a success too. The three central defenders look solid and, as per instructions, we get plenty of midfield bodies forward as we beat Stoke Gabriel 6–1. All right, they're not Stoke City. But 12 goals in two games has to be a confidence booster to the lads up front, a reminder that it can be done.

Sunday 28 July

Reunion day. The Nelson family regroup at ruinous high-season expense in a posh Torbay Hotel. Object of the brief stay is not only to remind each of us what the others look like, but also to give the much put upon Carole some tender loving care and then – taking back with one hand what I've just given with the other – provide said Carole with a base from which to launch her next high priority assignment, namely finding Carly and Chris schools and all of us somewhere to live.

Monday 29 July

A heavy day. It begins in the office with renewed participation in the player pursuit race. With two Blackpool lads in mind I put through a call to Sam Allardyce, the manager sacked when, at the end of last season, Blackpool – first in their last league game and then in the play-off against Bradford – twice snatched defeat from the jaws of promotion-conferring victory. Wishing me well, Sam is goodwill personified. But he brings no joy. Andy Gouck has been snapped up by Rochdale and Scott Darton has re-signed, not for the Musketeers but at Bloomfield Road.

As I put the phone down the radio news delivered a bombshell. I'd just been a geographical fraction out in my prospecting. Down the road a promising lad was up for grabs and I've missed him. Newcastle got there first and Alan Shearer at £15 million is this month's world's most expensive player. Curses! So near and yet so far! Just £14,900,000 out.

No time to grieve. Our pre-season campaign is taking several steps up in class tonight. We've got Pompey at home.

Against whom – glory be again! – we get a fine result. A 2–2 draw. Again the 3–5–2 system holds its shape and does a solid job limiting Portsmouth to few scoring chances. Our two goals came from midfielders getting forward, Charlie Oatway and Stevie Winter, a double bonus in my book in that neither has a league goal to their credit.

It's even better than that. Victims of an atrocious penalty decision, we are moral 2–1 winners. As the referee pointed to the spot I was up from the dug-out pointing out no less explicitly to him the errors of his ways and his birth certificate. And now came a pleasing exercise of privilege. Immediately substituting myself on, I was able to continue the lambasting at breath-scorch range. I had no qualms about thus indulging my wrath. We'd been a goal down and equalised. The penalty put us behind again. If we'd *not* equalised a second time the egg-shell thin surface of Torquay's slowly re-building confidence might have been irreparably shattered for a second season. To huge universal credit, though, we didn't buckle. We worked a second equaliser and came off with the protective layer a significant degree stronger.

The old man? He still remembered his way round the park.

Tuesday 30 July

The papers are full this morning of the Shearer return to the scenes of his childhood. On our way in Hodgie and I discuss the implications of this not entirely sentimental journey for the Torquays of the game. Neither of us begrudge the man his fortune: he's operating so far out of our sphere no comparisons are meaningful. (For the record, though, Shearer earns more in a week than I do in a year; Vialli's weekly tax liability would run Torquay's entire operation for the same seven days; Ravanelli's National Insurance contribution would pay the wages of our top three players. But who's counting? Mine's a very large Murphy's.) However, as Shearer's fee is 15 times Torquay's 1995/96 *turnover* this does give us pause for jaundiced reflection. Torquay are not the most direly strapped club in the Nationwide by any means. That the millstone of a massive, interest-gathering debt is not round our necks is due in large part to the chairman working full time as an unpaid chief executive and constantly subbing the club out of his own pocket. And, as current non-events are proving, when it comes to competing in the transfer market, we're hamstrung to the point of being crippled out of the game. Not merely as buyers but as sellers too. In 1993/94 the two bottom leagues' share of transfer monies realised £7 million. A single year later, precisely one-tenth this sum was generated. This is pre-Bosman. As the Sir John Halls and Martin Edwards of this world pour money into buying guaranteed membership of the European Super League, and so into buying assured access to the funds Murdoch is spewing into his B Sky B-Premiership flagship, it makes less and less sense for an Arsenal or a Tottenham to buy a promising youngster ripe for development from, Carlisle, say, for £200,000. The better bet, as Eric won't be slow to point out, is to get a proven international from Ajax who will deliver ('My life on it!') a monster instant return for the shareholders. R&D is not a boom sector in Premiership soccer.

It is at Torquay, though, where the club's youth scheme is alive and kicking. By the end of the century, whatever League we find ourselves playing in, we'll have a far less synthetic team than Manchester United and Chelsea have long been and Newcastle and Middlesbrough have now become.

No more poignant, moral-pointing contrast between the game's 'haves' and 'have-nots' could be contrived than the encounter Kevin and I had on arriving at Plainmoor. One of our trialists approached us with a small request. He's been motoring in from Plymouth every day. Could the Club run to his petrol money? Reasonable enough, surely. Only, such is Torquay's petty cash position we had to trot out our informally sympathetic version of that old, establishment hand-washing: 'We have not been given authority to make any such disbursement.' Alan Shearer, £30,000 per week? No problem. Simon Dawe's £30 petrol expenses. No way.

And yet – as so often in football – I find myself immediately required to adjust my thinking. Reacting positively to his coaching team's insistence that Jon Gittens is a defender who could answer a very real need, Mike Bateson is an authority who on this occasion is prepared to make funds available. What's more, although it's traditionally not part of the coaching brief, he asks us to join him and Jon in open four-way negotiations.

Terms remain a problem. But as we had already pointed out to the chairman, JG was on a free not because his form was on the slide but because of the considerable wages he was costing Portsmouth. A no-win situation had arisen. He didn't figure in Terry Fenwick's future plans. He was, meanwhile, getting bored out of his skull training with the kids. To cut their losses quickly – the more so because were they to demand a transfer fee they would be legally obliged to offer Jon the option of contract renewal at a matching level – Pompey were prepared to let him go on a free.

This was the background to the talks that, training even more of an imperative, Hodgie and I had now reluctantly to absent ourselves from. We left Jon and the chairman to an ongoing, open and frank discussion of their respective positions.

When, hot and tired, we returned to Plainmoor it was to a result. The chairman eventually going so far as to offer him a two year contract, Jon had eventually agreed to trade income for time. He'll now get from us in two years what Pompey would have coughed up in one. Mind you, that will still make him our highest paid player. So! Our first significant signing! However it turns out – two years is a sizeable commitment – the first sensation was a great buzz. I couldn't help but feel bucked by the chairman's 'go for it' pro-active decision.

Proactive has to be the word for this very busy day. Hodgie and I are soon two on one in a 'ways and means' chat with Paul Mitchell. He makes it clear that he has no interest in our run-on-the-spot suggestion of a three month contract. Why should he? With his West Ham pedigree and Brentford plucking at his sleeve, he knows it's a refusable offer. It looks like we're going to have to do better. If not, a useful player is going to slip through our penny-wise fingers.

As could another. The phone rings and it's John McGovern on the line. Can we see our way to allowing Paul Baker to train and play at Millmoor for a couple of weeks while Rotherham run the rule over him? Faithful to our promise we say 'yes'. The move northwards would add immeasurably to the quality of Bakes' life and we don't want to find that the price of retaining him is having a disgruntled and resentful player in the changing room.

Two injuries from the night before are now confirmed. One is to Lee Durrant and I have no doubts that it is a direct result from him reporting for his trial over-weight. A less than match-fit body can't go on playing above itself and improvising for 90 minutes. On the same topic I have a long, off-line chat with Ian Hathaway. Most people at Plainmoor would nominate Ian as the most gifted player on our books. But the same people would also say that for long periods of last season he went missing. All right, he might argue that there wasn't anything much to let down in the first place or, more accurately, the last. But I would counter that there was. Himself. I now stress the importance of the coming season to Torquay and his own importance in our scheme of things. I ask him to bear down on the other, the 'boring' side of his game, the nose to the grindstone side, the hard grafting for his team-mates when it's all going pear-shape. I point out that the more surplus weight he's carrying, the less paradoxically he can pull. To a part of my brain it all sounds a bit schoolmasterish but it's got to be said. It's vital. Ian looks me in the eye and gives me to understand that the message has been received and understood.

The day ends on a downer. I drag myself back to the Torbay hotel to find Carole depressed and on edge. With good reason. She's been the rounds of every house-letting agency in Torquay. Only one house was available on a long term let but her immediate inspection dashed the hopes she'd naïvely allowed to build up. It was totally unsuitable. The problem is that short lets to holiday makers are far more profitable. Visibly, I'm afraid, I got depressed too. We may be looking here at long-term separation, long-distance commuting.

Wednesday 31 July

No training today in view of our glamour pre-season friendly home to West Ham. I can relax all the way to joining Carole in an ever tenser, house-hunting sweep of the greater Torquay-Exeter area. Wider still and wider, our bounds are being set. Around midday a faint gleam starts to lighten our gloom. We draw up outside a large, modern-but-pleasant house in Chudleigh, some 20 minutes from Plainmoor by car. It's right on the edge of Dartmoor and has superb views matched by an attractively planned, splendidly maintained landscaped garden. As soon as we cross the threshold our two walking litmus papers, Carly and Chris, silently signal approval. I can see why. The decor is excellent: this is an ideal family home large enough to boast an enormous spare bedroom – no small consideration given the far-flung nature of a footballer's circle of acquaintance. Owners of this des res are a deputy headmaster (transferring to a headship of his own in East Anglia) and his wife. They tell us with their inside knowledge that Chris could go to the excellent new school just 500 yards down the road. Carly's requirements present more of a problem but the teacher's own school, a 10-minute drive away, enjoys a first-rate reputation.

Just as I start to believe that after being kicked up in the air by the centre back of Life we've landed on our feet comes the catch that always seems to follow when I get that feeling.

'I should tell you,' the deputy head says, 'that you're the sixth couple to show a definite interest in renting from us.'

'Ah …'

'We've not committed ourselves to anyone yet. We feel the only thing to do is ask people back in the near future for a formal vetting. Then we'll decide.'

'Yes … Naturally … Well, we've absolutely no objection to that, of course …'

So near. Still so far. Well, he is a deputy head.

As it later strikes me, so am I. One whose heart in spite of all my dressing room pep- talking cannot but sink as I see Futre, Rieper, Dani, Dicks, the full Upton Park monte taking the field against my largely anonymous pupils.

What followed was both a triumph and a disaster. As always, it was the negative of these two imposters that ended by dominating. What should have been an unqualifiedly champagne moment in our fledgling career had been soured. The taste the evening finally left was bitter in the extreme.

The statistics first. The nobodies won! Ninety-second Torquay beat the League of Nations superstars 3–2! Two stunning long range strikes from Ian Hathaway and a penalty saw us home. But the result was about to be rendered irrelevant.

Coaches are allowed to ball watch. I didn't see the incident live but a roar of shocked disgust from a section of the crowd and a linesman's urgently waving flag had me turning my head away from the main action. There had been an incident. Way off the ball, as I subsequently gathered in ever more precise detail, and with totally cold-blooded cynicism, Jon Gittens, the player who on his evening arrival had boosted everyone in the club by signing his two year contract, had thrown a punch to an opponent's head. It left Harry Redknapp's latest top-drawer import, the Romanian Raducioiu, stretched out on the ground. The £1.5 million investment could well be out for the season's opening weeks. Harry – the same Harry who earlier in the evening smilingly accepted my thanks for the steer towards Paul Mitchell – is out of his dug-out in nothing flat. So great is his whirling, stomping indignation he's scarcely able to stay on his own feet. His face is as red as the card everyone expects to see any second and the air around him is as deeply saturated a blue. But this game being a friendly(!) the ground rules have already been established that a 'sin bin' will take the place of bookings. Hodgie and I exchange a quick glance and quicker nod. To defuse the situation, to pre-empt the referee making it official, to pre-empt Julian Dicks getting involved, we substitute Jon Gittens. But it's the pits. The ink on his contract is still wet and I'm wondering as he approaches the touchline whether I'll have to physically restrain Redknapp Senior from attempting GBH.

The aftermath of the game is very schizophrenic. On behalf of the club I try to apologise to Harry but my words fall on understandably disgusted, largely unhearing ears. His pre-match promise of a sympathetic ear to loan-signing requests now seems very far in the past.

As I drive home, I find it's the incident and not the win that stays in the mind. What to do? That contract. The ink may be dry now but the document still hasn't been put in the post. We could just tear it up! Deny it had ever existed! ... Give me some credit. I nurtured the fantasy for only 3.7 seconds. A contract, first and last, is a promise. Promises are what you have to keep.

Thursday 1 August

We sit down with Mike Bateson. West Country TV have been on to him, we learn, to confirm that they have last night's incident on tape and it's every bit as damning as reported. Harry Redknapp has been on. Raducioiu hasn't sustained any fracture but West Ham are considering lodging a formal complaint with the FA ... We sit and talk. I try not to let the knowledge that we need the man out there doing a job for us on the field unduly influence me. At last we agree. The point is not to over-react. Jon Gittens will spend his first weeks as a contracted Torquay player on the receiving end of a very considerable fine. It's a lot of money out of his just agreed salary. All the same he's getting off comparatively lightly. A red card in a League game would have cost him a three-match ban, a fine on top and, very likely, an away fixture at Lancaster Gate.

Since we're convened, any other business? Yes, and very pleasing business, indeed, that goes a long way to lightening our mood. Once again backing our hand, the chairman approves offering Paul Mitchell a one-year contract.

Later, it's my turn to be on the end of an assessment. Carole and I drove up to Chudleigh to 'audition' before the deputy head. We smiled, nodded a lot and majored heavily on the fact that we had let our own last house out and could deeply and sincerely empathize with all the misgivings he and his wife must be feeling. Yes, of course our children were house-trained. Perfect angels. Christopher was thinking of entering the church … Don't call us we'll call you. It's going to be a tense old time until they make their decision early next week.

An enhanced sense of momentum by late evening. Arguably the biggest plus of the new job is Steve McCall's Youth Team. In thrashing their Swindon counterparts 5–1 at Dawlish tonight they showed great cohesion and individual promise.

Their elders, but not necessarily betters, may be tapping into this potential much sooner than is ideal. With Paul Baker at Rotherham and Jamie Ndah (at 25 the game's oldest 'apprentice') injured, we're conspicuously short of conspicuously tall target men. And we've stretched Mike Bateson's inclination to invest for the future to the limit. Unless Bakes moves on and frees up some pay-roll monies, we're up to capacity on squad numbers.

Somebody who won't be going on the weekly pay-roll is Lee Durrant. He came in today and took us by surprise by announcing he was off.

'Hang about,' we said. 'We're really pleased with what you've done. There are still a couple of friendlies coming up and we're certainly planning to feature you.'

'No, sorry. That's it. I'm away.'

'All right,' we say, 'we won't stand in your way.' We wish him well, but if he's set on staying in football he's going about things the wrong way.

Friday 2 August

A tough-talking start. Kevin calls in Jon Gittens and spells out the size of his fine. No prizes for guessing that he's not overjoyed by the news, but he knows when he's comparatively well off and comes quietly. I point out that our decision is designed in part to head off formal FA action. I also try to underline the invaluable role that an example-setting senior pro can play among so many youngsters. He nods. Well, we'll see …

Mike Bateson is now able to relay what we have done to Harry Redknapp in a personal call. It's not a moment, apparently, for rejoicing but at least the gesture is appreciated and civilised dialogue is resumed.

Not altogether for me though. I'm immediately involved in another terse exchange. One of our trialists, Simon Dawe (here on a free from

Plymouth for whom he managed only a handful of first-team games), has a short-sighted attitude to being coached. It's not a case of everything going in one ear and out the other. It's that he always talks back. It's always somebody else's fault or would have been better done his way in the first place. All in all, given his credentials he's a silly boy to come on so strong. I don't put it this bluntly as we speak but the scarcely hidden agenda of what I say is 'shape up or be prepared to ship out'.

Other players rotate to the forefront of our stock-taking. Both Paul Adcock, the lad let go by Bath, and Paul Sykes, once with Wednesday, are naturally anxious to know where they stand. After all, they're well aware our purse is far from bottomless and that we've already committed ourselves to two signings. The answer is that they're still in limbo: we need to see more. Hodgie feels that Paul Adcock is a talent waiting to emerge. I still have my doubts. He's certainly worked hard in training but he woefully lacks confidence where he needs it most, in front of goal.

Pushing through the pen and phone work I clear a space on my desk by three. No training today on account of our having another match this evening. Significant for me. It will be my first full 90-minute outing. I shoot off from the ground. If I burn rubber I can expect to spend half as long touching base with my family.

It's not the best example of quality time. Nor is it only the rubber that gets burnt. Eating Carole's cannelloni against the remorseless clock I remove about eight layers of skin from the roof of my mouth. The last sheds as I hurtle out again to renew acquaintance with Leigh Cooper and do battle with the tasty side he steered to the Jewson South Western League championship, Truro City.

The game turns out to be a classic example of how a scoreline, hastily glanced at in next morning's paper, can mislead. Once again we won 6–1. Nelson, a report would have said, scored Torquay's first goal and made three others. A group and personal doddle of a triumph, then, obviously. Not a bit of it, as it happens. My own most telling contribution was not with my boot on the field but with my mouth in the changing room.

Despite our doing all the pressing, the score at the interval was the same as at the kick-off. We'd spent the time between showing small sign of being able, willing even, to translate our territorial superiority into chances taken. At half-time I deliver myself of a few home truths and an insight born of my experience. Core of my sermon was that I'd played in dozens of matches where team A had dominated without breaking into a sweat only to see team B break away to the other end of the field and score the only goal. 'Just think of United at St James Park last year, lads,' I said. 'Believe me, I'm old enough to recognise the signs.'

After five minutes of our resuming the seige of their six-yard box, what did Truro do? Exactly. Break out and score. Sheepish glances were turned in my direction as my street cred went up several begrudged notches. But so had the team's concentration and application. Moving up a gear, finding that cutting edge, we banged in six goals in the last third of the game.

In the dressing room Hodgie and I gave our captive and cowed squad short shrift. A right bollocking, in fact. My remarks were intended to be as blistering as Carole's cannelloni. The one thing I hadn't expected at Torquay was complacency.

When at the end of this long, long day I at last got back to the hotel, it was close to midnight. Carole was waiting up but not entirely for me.

'It's worrying about the house,' she said. 'What they'll decide. I knew I wouldn't be able to sleep.'

The joys of power.

Saturday 3 August

All work and no play. The three amigos and their senoras go out on the town in Plymouth. Yes, Plymouth. It was a great unwinding evening. But what a goldfish bowl the place is! Everywhere we went people came up to give us the benefit of their expertise. Some time in the small hours we flagged down a taxi. The driver looked us up and down.

'Bit late for a managers' meeting,' he said. 'Another crisis?'

Monday 5 August

A red letter day! We've come first in the Great House Handicap! Carole phoned through with the news at 9am. It's ours for the renting! It seems that what swung it for us was Carly and Chris, bless their designer trainers. The owners felt that theirs was a *family* house and should continue to be put to such use. Further, they did pick up on our having been in their letting shoes ourselves and so that little more likely to treat their property with respect. The biggest strike against us, they revealed, was my profession. The deputy head thought I might not be around to see out a full year's contract. He may not be a bad judge!

A huge weight lifted. Happy as a sandboy with a winning lottery ticket

I seek out Mark Hawthorne and Stevie Winter both of whom could pretty obviously do with a bit of good cheer brushing off on them. They're well aware that neither look like starting the season in the first team. That's not the end of it, I assure them. It doesn't mean they don't feature in our plans. Keep up the good work, I urge them, the break will come.

Then Hodgie and I flip the coin to its dark side. We call in Simon Dawe. We're letting him go, we inform him. He's not best pleased. He clearly feels he hasn't been given a proper chance to prove himself. We beg to disagree. We believe we've been more patient than most managers would have been. And, if he cares to look, there is a positive side to his Torquay experience. Yes, he can, if he chooses, go away calling us every name under the sun. Alternatively he can take the good out of the situation, namely a focused awareness of those things in his game he needs to work on – certain boot to ball and positional things and, above all, his attitude.

Another incoming call – possibly a straw in a wind destined to become a force 10 gale. It's Mick McGuire, Gordon Taylor's colleague, seeking to confirm that Rhys Wilmot is still the PFA rep at Plainmoor.

'Yes, Mick, he certainly is. He's down the road right now getting a spot of treatment.'

'Right. Could you just let him know that the strike ballot papers are going in the post today.'

'Will do.'

As yet a cloud on soccer's horizon no bigger than one of Rhys' gloves, this is one that could run and run, grow and grow. Its single issue is clear cut. What percentage of the seriously rich monies coming to the Football League from the BSkyB deal should be allocated to the PFA, the organisation which has set in place the most comprehensive and tangible education, accident and benevolent player benefits the English game possesses? The PFA receive a flat-rate sum of £565,000 a year from the £9 million per annum coming into the League from television. They are now asking for a 10 per cent share of the revised television monies of £25 million per year. Or rather, asking for the 10 per cent tranche which was long ago negotiated and agreed upon to be restored. When TV revenues were slimmer and times harder, the PFA volunteered to commute that 10 per cent for a lesser fixed sum. Now, in an age of ever fatter footballing cats, the differential is clearly unjust: £2.5 million would seem a modest enough request on the face of it. This season it adds up to appreciably less than Man United's insurance premium. But the League's first reaction has been dismissively negative. Strike action as a means of applying pressure has been mooted. It is (so far) only being discussed in terms of players outside the Premiership (whose officials, though, are monitoring all this with an extreme interest) and would only be deployed in the context of games scheduled to be televised. But the nature of strike solidarity tends to escalation – as witness America's 1995 baseball World Series, which, since strike action prevented its being held, nobody in fact ever did. We – and the Football League – will see.

Good God! A window in time! A chance to nip out for a haircut before I resemble the goldilocked slip of a lad ancient Plymouth fans remember flitting down the wing. The barber is just round the corner and, in Central Casting fashion, Italian. We get through the weather. Then the inevitable 'day off from work today, sir?' has it all coming out.

'Ah,' he says, 'another Torquay manager. You're not exactly my first ...'

Tuesday 6 August

A knock at the Command Module door.

'Come.'

Algernon, the club's ventriloquist's dummy mascot, entered closely followed by a beaming Mike Bateson.

'Grilliant news,' Algernon croaks forth, 'Stevenage have lost their replay. Their appeal has been turned down. The gattle has gone our way again.'

'Fan-gluddy-tastic!'

'I'm off for a gottle of gear.'

Although expected, the news still came as a relief. The lads have been working hard on the training pitch but this was the sweetest dummy I'd seen all week.

Wednesday 7 August

Anti-climax. What should have been a highly-charged encounter with Plymouth in the Devon Bowl (Exeter v Plymouth v Torquay round-robin fashion) has been cancelled at the last minute.

In a hastily drummed up alternative fixture, we play non-league Dawlish at Plainmoor.

But it's an ill wind. The step down in class, with respect, certainly won't be doing us a favour. The afternoon had found us confronting a problem that threatens to recur throughout the year – putting out a side from the slim pickings of a skeleton squad. We're down on numbers now. Nearly, but not quite. Paul Sykes, for one, is off to try to catch the eye at Darlington. John McGovern at Rotherham has reportedly shelled out £25,000 for striker Richard Landon. If that's true, no way he'll be taking on Paul Baker. That, though, does not mean his return. On an 'on approval' basis he too has coincidentally moved to Darlington. He's working his way closer to home all the time. None of this helps us solve our problems up front but our promise to help him relocate still stands.

Jamie Ndah is finally niggle-free. He deserves and needs a run-out. But he's not match fit. A half is the most he should be asked to tackle. And I'm not fit either, having picked up a flu bug. About as much as I can manage is to distance myself from everyone else in the stand and, wondering whether the doubled work-load has undermined my constitution, watch the game in the splendid isolation of quarantine.

It's another let-down. There's no spark. Playing 3–5–2 in the first half we did take a 1–0 lead through Jamie but it was all listless, going through motions stuff. A switch to 4–4–2 after the break brought greater fluency. The players were back to operating in familiar territory. We looked a lot better going forward. But we were going forward against a semi-pro side beginning to run out of steam. Not so heartening, then, that we added only one more goal.

Is my bug dragging me down or am I indulging in pre-season paranoia? I find myself thinking that the season proper hasn't started and we're already going off the boil. We've peaked too soon!

Thursday 8 August

A day off. Not for husbands, though. I drive Carole and the kids to Plymouth Station to wave them off. Carole is far from being the happiest chappy. Schooling arrangements for Carly and Chris remain up in the air and, while the house problem has been resolved overall, it transpires that we won't be able to move in until the 28th. That's another three weeks of separation, during which all the hassle of organising our move will fall on Carole's shoulders.

Stop-press end to the day. Dean Wilkins has agreed to join us for a week's trial. Joining Plymouth is Bruce Grobbelaar, also to await the outcome of a trial.

Friday 9 August

A lesson learned today – one that goes some way to explaining our dip in form. While away at Winchester, I took the squad through a series of exercises – pattern of play, shadow play, phase of play – which while bog-standard for many sides were fairly new to Torquay.

Pattern of play is essentially setting up two sides (or subsets of a side, 8 v 10, say) in a situation you want to walk and talk them forward from as you tactically develop it. Shadow play is, as in boxing, having no opposition. In this unreal but streamlined mode you can build up moves with maximum clarity so that everyone knows who goes where when.

These five finger exercises, so to speak, are helpful in organising defences, demonstrating how midfielders should look to get forward in support and on into the box, or explaining the gentle art of showing the opposition inside where they can be not so gently jostled out of possession. They are intended to make a player's awareness of what his responsibilities are at any given phase of the game's ebb and flow become second nature.

That's the theory. In practice such awareness hasn't been too conspicuous. At Winchester we got a good, quick understanding of what we were trying to communicate. In the welter of (too many?) matches since, however, these lessons plainly haven't stuck. We've seen the disciplines melt away in the heat of battle to be replaced by scrambling, hand-to-mouth improvisation. And the reason's clear. Now. It's been clear since Kevin had a chat with Neil Warnock, current masterbuilder at Plymouth.

Neil's advice had all the credibility of common sense. Players in the lower divisions, he told Hodgie, tend to share a common characteristic. They don't remember things! To lodge a tactic in their memory, he insisted, you have to repeat and repeat your drills. What squads have pat by the end of week one can disappear from their minds by the end of week two. Exactly our case. We haven't lost yet but we've come close to getting caught out. We obviously need to work hard at re-enforcing as well as refining.

Suiting our actions to Neil's words we put in what, considering it was the day before yet another match, a long session. On balance, though, fresh pre-season batteries should not have been drained by it.

Then more man to man management. This time it fell to Kevin to take Ian Hathaway off to one side. We're disappointed by his contribution in the two games that followed his stunning performance against West Ham. He mustn't fall prey to the temptation of thinking he's a big match specialist. He's got to rise to the small occasion too. But he won't be doing that tomorrow. We're going to 'rest' him.

Saturday 10 August

A tediously useful dummy run for the brain-deadening trials by monotony we will soon be enduring on our coach journeys to far away places with such strange sounding names as Wigan, Hartlepool, Scunthorpe. Today we have to cover no more than 70 miles or so but with the M5 bumper to bumper in both directions the two and a half hours of the resulting crawl is made up of end to end yawns. When we arrive at Clevedon a pleasant surprise and a tiresome nuisance greet us. The plus is the excellent standard of Clevedon's new ground. The minus is that Jon Gittens, given permission to make his own way from Winchester, is conspicuous by his absence. He shows up 20 minutes before kick-off.

Technical question: can you fine a player already in non-receipt of salary due to a previous fine? You bet you can. What's more, giving a young lad a game, we leave him on the bench.

With a strong wind behind us we surge into the attack from the kick-off. Within 25 seconds I put us 1–0 up. That'll do nicely – as will the quality of our passing for the remainder of the half. Far less pleasing, though, is our failure to increase our lead and downright worrying just one week before the start of the season is Rhys Wilmot's discovery that he's experiencing a severe reaction to yesterday's sustained practice session. At half-time he has no choice but to give way to Ray Newland.

Things don't improve. Cause for immediate concern in the second half is how we dramatically lose our form. There's minimal sign of midfielders coming through to support our increasingly goal-shy strikers. Our shape and organisation are off blowing in the wind.

Lucky winners at the end, we remain unbeaten but my nagging impression that the last week has seen us sliding backwards has been nastily strengthened.

Meanwhile, 200 miles away a game had taken place that I would have welcomed a walk-on part in. Ten thousand Charlton faithful put their money where their applause had long since been and turned up for my old mate and archetypal pro Colin Walsh's testimonial match against Spurs.

The receipts, richly deserved to the last penny, will help set Walshie, Shelly and the kids up nicely.

Lee Sharpe also picked up a cheque this week as he moved from Old Trafford to Elland Road for a £4 million fee. Once he was at Plainmoor. Torquay then sold the then promising youngster to the other United. The fee then was £185,000. And no sell-on clause. This gave me cause to raise my own eyebrow in Mike Bateson's direction.

'You're joking,' he tersely replied. 'A cash-strapped club being offered a 185K in readies ... You ask for a sell-on clause as well, all they'll say is, "There won't be one, son". What you going to do?'

Monday 12 August

The start of a crucial week for us and a full stop for Bruce Rioch. After much snapping at his players over their pre-season form, he's bitten the dust at Highbury. For us it's six days to the 'off' and counting. There's still no definite news from Darlington on Paul Baker. What began as a favour to him is turning into a nightmare for us.

But one boil is lanced. Kevin and I have a long talk with Jon Gittens about all the bad vibes he's encountered/created in the first 10 days of his Torquay existence. We agree that he's very much got off on the wrong foot and the best thing is to make a psychologically 'clean slate' fresh start. He doesn't make petty excuses and as our meeting ends I feel distinctly that things have taken a turn for the better. He is important to us.

So is the little matter of what formation we are going to adopt. Or formations. 3–5–2 or 4–4–2? The 'to be or not to be' of contemporary soccer. If it's going to be the former, we need to get our back three playing closer together. Reflection has convinced me that the deterioration from solid at the back to loose and panicky is the product of as simple a cause as their drifting too far apart in recent games.

If we go for a back four we've got problems with our wide men. They're defensively sound but ineffective at getting forward into crossing positions. Our hand may be forced somewhat anyway. Paul Mitchell has an injury that's a concern, as has Charlie Oatway.

Another game this evening. It should only be a jog, we believe, as it's against minnows Tavistock. We're taking the opportunity to play a clutch of our youngsters. Plus the two old know-alls. Neither Kevin nor I feel that three games in the bank apiece is enough preparation for Saturday. This will be a labour-unintensive doddle, anyway.

In football never carry pre-conceptions around with you. As events transpired, the Tavistock game constituted an object lesson in how not to manage. We won 3–0 and I made all three. But that was about all I did. I had two nightmare misses and I couldn't get into the game any more than the rest of the side. A very underachieving Jamie Ndah limped off after an hour.

Solitary ray of hope – well, Dean, actually – in my book was the contribution of latest trialist, Mr Wilkins. I was embarrassed he should see us like this, but I rate him better in his position than anything we've got. Kevin and Steve, however, are likely to find signing another mid-30s midfielder too much to swallow.

Tuesday 13 August

Good news of a sort and for some. We're getting Paul Baker back. Bottom line of the talks he's had with Darlington is – even taking into account that, as he would be working on his Newcastle doorstep, he'd be prepared to take less – they can't get anywhere close to the wages we pay him.

Three days before our league game, it's worth noting the manner in which we are obliged to set about training every day. At moderately successful Charlton we worked at our game on the club's superbly appointed, dedicated training ground. Torquay have nothing like this. We don't have anything. Every morning we have to go through that hand to phone rigmarole of calling up the council to see which square on their threadbare recreational chessboard they've allocated us. Then the Fred Karno's capers really start.

Wherever the despatcher sends us won't possess any facilities. There won't be any goalposts. We take our own. Collapsible ones. Metal. We strap them lengthways along the roof of the ailing mini bus which, food for worrisome thought, can hold our entire first-team squad. The cross-bars extend proud of the bus's front like a seven foot high battering ram. This to the fore, we career down the narrow lanes of Devon like a run-away rhino with a David Attenborough film unit up its backside. *En route* we snap the occasional protruding branch away from its trunk and, in my case, sit tensely anticipating when contact will be made with the fuel tanker round the next bend. Are you watching, Man United?

Back on the bus today was a fit again Scott Stamps. Let loose, he looked excited and exciting. I revise my estimate of him several points upwards.

Two executive coaching decisions by close of play today. One: we're going with a back three. Two: soccer realpolitik will continue to rule. Normally, we'd be offering Rhys Wilmot a two-year contract. But such is the unknown quantity of his injury and the club's bank balance we don't dare. His month to month arrangement will continue. The timing is harshly unfortunate. Yesterday saw the birth of Rhys' second child. Just when his playing career and, hence, income hang in the balance, there's another mouth to feed.

Wednesday 14 August

We might well have given everyone a day off. With team-spirit still in mind, however, and on the theory that a change is as good as a rest, we took the squad for a fun work-out session at the English Riviera Leisure Centre, a magnificently appointed complex – weights, jacuzzi, rowing machines, you name it – that physio Damien Davey has been using to treat various of our walking wounded. Good intentions! The intended fun day brought a serious issue into the open and eventually sparked a nearly explosive confrontation between Damien and me. Starter for ten here was the highly visible profile – and silhouette – of various very shapely damsels also using the Leisure Centre – young ladies on first name terms with several of our still unattached lads. Though perhaps more stimulating, the ambience was distinctly more relaxing than a slog your guts out training field on a wet and windy day. Hence my concern.

If you've got a long-term injury, then a break in routine on top-drawer remedial equipment is very much to be encouraged. But a contact injury that should clear up in a week, or at most two … In the context of such amiable surroundings, well, it could take three or four – especially if the team is doing badly and emotionally, politically, you want to distance yourself from it until there's a soft-looking fixture for your comeback. One of Torquay's ongoing problems during last year's disastrous campaign was the tendency of several players to go missing when the going got tough. Swinging the lead, in fact, rather than pumping the iron.

Damien's view is well meant and he has a right to fight his corner. He wants the best gear for those he's treating. My more jaundiced view is that it comes back to the age-old need to know your players: know who will knuckle down to the business of getting back as soon as possible, who will take advantage. It's harder, I suggest to Damien, to separate the sheep from the goats when you're almost one of the lads yourself. My heavy-duty bottom line is that we shouldn't establish the leisure centre as a to be taken for granted routine response to injury. It should be the exception rather than the rule and directed at longer-term problems. You shouldn't, I submit, convert injuries into meal tickets.

Thursday 15 August

The Thursday before the first Saturday and the injury list is almost blank. Everyone is 'up' for the watershed game that's surely going to kickstart their henceforward brilliant career.

By the end of training there can be no real doubt in anyone's mind who are this Saturday's upstanding heroes and who its wilting willies. As near to dammit as makes no difference the team is announced ahead of schedule.

Naff cause for this is the Clennon Valley training pitch the council have stuffed us up with for this morning. It's narrow, bumpy, uneven – utterly useless for a professional side pledging to live or die in pursuit of a 'to feet' passing game.

The only way to emerge from the session with a profit is to walk through a series of pattern of play exercises. As we set them up there could be no prizes for guessing who was in the frame for Saturday and who could slope off to the back of the bike sheds.

The Paul Baker situation continues to have knock-on effects. Now he's back there's no pay-roll leeway for signing anyone else. For this, if for no other reason, I found myself having a farewell chat with Dean Wilkins. Putting it politely, he feels that he's been buggered about.

'What was the real point of getting me down here?' he asks.

He's more right than wrong, I believe, to feel that we brought him down here on a wild gull chase. Liking him a lot, knowing what he's got to offer, I feel bad about this. This is the first judgement-call difference of opinion I've had with Hodgie and I'm sorry that another good mate should be the unwitting occasion of it. That the two of us disagree doesn't worry me at all. If Torquay are to thrive we'll need to come out fighting from opposite corners from time to time. Former mates are taking on increasing importance in my scheme of things. Torquay possess virtually no scouting system. We've got to do something about this. Short term – 'Help! You didn't really have any plans for this Saturday, did you!' – I've eventually managed to tee up three blasts from the past to clock forthcoming opposition tomorrow.

Friday 16 August

The success of one small motivating exercise pleases me. According to their position we set targets for each player to reach by January – so many goals, so many clean sheets. Odds of 5–1 are then set clear across the board. The lads are asked to stake a fiver they'll hit their personal target. Miss, and that's all they'll be out by. Make it and the club will see that it's their little pony. Camelot it's not but I'm chuffed to see there's 100 per cent take-up. If they all turn out to be winners no one will be happier than me.

Current wearer of the yellow jersey is none other than Hodgie. Among the many items of unanswerable evidence brought to bear at his trial the most damning was the verbatim text of his proud claim to be inscrutable: 'I keep my cards pretty close to under my hat.' The prosecution rests, m'lud. Hodgie wasn't the happiest of head coaches on suffering the full rigour of the law, but he knows full well that on the eve of battle it's a canny bit of group therapy.

There is one serious final decision to be made. Ray will be between the posts tomorrow. Do we go with three outfield players on the bench? No. Given his still troublesome shoulder we can't risk not having a back-up. Young Matthew Gregg will be on a bonus. If we win.

A week that seemed in passing to crawl by is abruptly climaxing in no time. Have we done all we can? We reconvince ourselves we have and end the festivities by 11.45. Tonight it will be early to bed for a good night's sleep.

Dream on. Or, rather, not.

'LOOKING GOOD, TORQUAY'

Saturday 17 August

After all the huffing and puffing, actual and figurative, here it comes. Today's game is no friendly. First of 46, it's the real thing. I wake alive to the date and its significance and with a flutter in my stomach. Come 5pm all the shall-I shan't-I, should-we would-we, 4–4–2, 3–5–2 and take away the number you first thought of, will have crystallised into a starkly simple scoreline. It'll be plus or minus. Them or us. Or a boring draw. And none of it will really mean a thing. Except it will.

The flutter is pleasurable. A familiar old acquaintance. I know I'll be able to convert this nervy, heightened awareness into enhanced concentration and action when the first whistle blows.

At breakfast I learn that Kevin has been up since dawn's earliest light. To quieten his own galloping nervousness he's already taken a long stroll through the neighbouring woods. It hasn't helped him much. Nor will anything else. It's so much harder for him today than for me. He's the 'boss' – the first man in the firing line when the flak starts flying. And he's not playing today. Because I am, I've got the outlet, the diversion therapy. Kevin is fated to stand on the touchline attempting to direct events on the run in what will seem a desperately ineffectual exercise of authority. I, on the other hand, will have the illusion, at least, of exerting an influence on the game. I'll be caught up in its whoosh-thunk-thud detail. Football resembles Life in many respects: perhaps the most significant is the false impression they both impart that if you're running around like a blue-arsed fly you're accomplishing something.

Today's opponents are Lincoln. As I drive in I yet again regret this. Lincoln are a John Beck team. A skilful creative midfielder, John transmuted from Jekyll to Hyde on becoming a manager. Notoriously, all of his sides play a physical and a long-ball game that makes Wimbledon at their directest look like Pele's Brazilians. My regret isn't that we don't know what to expect but that, if Lincoln impose their style on the afternoon, we're not likely to learn too much about our own potential. And there's method in his one-track mindedness. For a team wanting to play to feet but not yet bedded in, the long ball, face it, can be bloody difficult to deal with ...

In the bright sunshine of this first League Saturday the ground looks as spick and span as a fresh coat of paint. It's the first unused page of a school exercise book. A wonderful future waits to be developed. Or, as I remember a second later, a myriad of blots and crossings out. Jesus, it's hot!

Bodies appear. Bags are put down on the changing room bench. The loud lads are louder, the quiet ones quieter. I must, I tell myself, do my best to focus this collective jangle of nerves ...

With that in mind, to boost morale, Hodgie takes the squad through a fairly formal set of stretching and warm-up exercises outside. Plainmoor will be about half-full come kick-off. Not bad at the height of summer for the team that won five out of 46 last year. Hey! Don't dwell on that ball!

When we're reassembled in the changing room, an example of Torquay United being one of football's poorer relations throws a spanner into our build-up. I stand to deliver my 'once more into the breach' Agincourt speech. Eat your heart out, Mr Fiennes! But we don't have a clock in the changing room and I've peaked too soon. The equivalent of 'God for Torquay, Garry and St Kev!' climaxes in … anti-climax. Hell! Have we peaked too soon? The long expected buzzer goes at last.

'All the best, everyone.'

Perversely time now goes to fast-forward. The corridor, the cheers, the grass, the whistle. What are we going to do? The best, let us hope, we can…

For the first 15 minutes it's a woebegone best. Lincoln launch straight into their aerial bombardment – long spiralling balls corkscrew out to either wing; Olympic distanced throws rain down around the penalty spot. Our own formation capitulates. I find myself alone in the centre circle, odd man out in a 9–1 line-up. So much for all that agonizing over systems!

But the long-ball game requires accuracy too. Lincoln haven't been at it enough for precision. Too many of those corkscrews to the corner flag skid out for throws or goal-kicks to us. And, tight together, our back three deal comfortably with such crosses and throws as do get into our box. Ray Newland isn't asked to make a save. We're starting to get some possession. About half-way through the first half we get a free kick just outside the Lincoln penalty area. It's down the inside right channel: the ideal position for Stuart Pearce to step up to and smash in a curler. Our left-foot marvel is Steve McCall. He stands over the ball as Lincoln pack their goal-line to fend off his strike. Over-pack. Macca calmly rolls a square ball across an area incredibly denuded of markers. From around the penalty spot unchallenged Jon Gittens drives in a screamer.

'One-nil, one nil!' the Gulls' fans sing and so does my heart.

The goal gives us confidence and still more shape. Up to the interval. Despite the half-time chat ('Let's have more of the same'), the resumption sees Lincoln increasingly muscling us on to the back foot. Up front I'm having to live off scraps far too much, but I roll out a number of nice square balls and pushes forward into space.

Then – shit! – Lincoln at last get it right. Right to left, left to right – the ball criss-crosses our goal-mouth. A knock down on the far post to a forward coming through and – bang! – they've equalised with a well-worked goal. My spirits privately sink. The second goal of a match is so often more significant than the first. Twenty minutes left. They're going to shade it now.

But they don't. We're at least as fit and, good on everyone, we don't buckle. We keep our shape. I see the draw approaching. Hodgie and I exchange glances. With 10 minutes left I go off to be replaced by Rodney Jack. His fresh legs up front should safeguard our point.

Before long they promise to do more. The best one-two of the game sees Macca putting the ball inside their right back for Rodney to race in one on one against their keeper. The angle's not too narrow. Hell! Using power instead of guile Rodney has smashed the ball straight against a man making a brave, blocking save. Oh, well … 90 minutes up. I'd have settled for a draw before kick-off. Hey! The ball has squirted to Rodney on the edge of their area. Centrally. For a second he has a clear left-footed shot on. But, jinking, pulling the ball sideways on to his right peg, he blows the chance. Now, belatedly, he shoots. The ball has no sooner left his boot than it strikes that of the defender closing him down. It's the merest of deflections. And the ultimate. The ball flies in a beautiful, beautiful shallow curve into the top right corner. The keeper, with every professional justification, hasn't even bothered to move.

Jack's the lad! Screaming, yelling, I'm up with Hodgie, with three sides of the ground applauding what has to be the winner. Yes! We're doing our nuts again as the whistle sounds. A win! A win! Torquay have won! We'd hardly dared to hope we would but we have. And of course it means a thing!

The red and white end of the ground is silent. Already the Lincoln faithful are turning their exiting backs on what will soon be a sickening memory to be suppressed as often as possible. But everywhere else it's as if we'd won the Cup.

The changing room is in euphoric uproar. The quiet ones are loud and the loud ones are ear splitting. We can do it! We can win! As of Monday we all have it to do again but, all the time now, at the back of our minds will be the sense that it's not a case of mission impossible. A psychological barrier has been breached.

Later, the three amigos but only two, alas, of their wives sit in the garden of a fine pub-restaurant hidden away in the depths of a maze of Devon lanes. A stream runs nearby; twilight gently falls; life is tranquil and good.

'You know,' Steve McCall says suddenly, 'it's not true what they say about playing in Division Three.'

We look at him.

'That it's easier, I mean. Slower paced. The crap ball you get, all the mistakes – you have to work harder all the time to make something out of nothing.'

It's a typically canny remark. Life's suddenly a mite less tranquil. The stream's gurgling is suddenly sardonic. Monday, it's saying, you've got it all to do again.

Monday 19 August

Euphoria still lingers in the smiles, the bright eyes of Plainmoor's skeleton-crew admin staff when I arrive this morning but future realities soon relegate it to the memory banks. For a start, the fax is chattering away. Torquay's pick-up spy ring has delivered some Grade A intelligence. Slippery between my fingers the fax sheets carry excellent information on the strengths and weaknesses, the strategies and set-pieces of Bristol City, Scunthorpe and Northampton. I read and try to inwardly digest. How to put this knowledge to best use …

What we won't be doing is sitting the squad down before a video of upcoming opponents in action and, fingers on the 'pause' button, slavishly taking them through every drawn-out minute of the game's 90. This could be attributable to our not having a video-recorder and monitor at Plainmoor. But even if we had, we wouldn't. Hodgie and I agreed at the outset that we wouldn't anchor our pre-match planning to balls-achingly detailed group analysis of what Exeter or Wigan or Katy did last week. There's the players' attention spans to protect. More significant still is the underlying psychological attitude. We don't want our lads on the mental back-foot thinking 'what are they going to do to us now?' all the time. We want them thinking positively. 'This is what we're going to do to them!' The coaching staff's response to the plays that forthcoming opponents threaten will be to sum them up in bullet points. No blinding with nit-picking science. That way we'll make big savings on time, inroads into squad enthusiasm and the electricity bill.

Tactics. Shape. Strategy. Most of my own Saturday night winner's fever had cooled in the cold, light of unromantic Sunday morning analysis. A last-gasp strike, more lucky than not, the difference, we'd been fortunate to take all three points. Our shortcomings made a long list. We'd not had anything like enough forward momentum. Players had passed the ball and not gone on for the return. They'd not made themselves available or run to draw defenders. The centre of the defence had looked solid but on the rare occasions we'd risked breaking out, we'd given the ball away far too cheaply. We'd fallen back on 'hit and hope' balls allowing Lincoln to impose their rhythm on the game for far too long. Hmmn! Plenty of remedial work to start tackling there. Urgent work. We had another game tomorrow. Bristol City in the Coca-Cola Cup. A side a whole division above us and light years different in style from Beck's aerial bombardiers.

Whereby hung a necessary but far from enjoyable task. 'Never change a winning side' the *Invincible Soccer Manual* doubtless states. But rules are made to be broken. Tomorrow's game would be all about trying to pass our way to taking maximum advantage of the home draw first leg. With that in mind it made sense to try further exploiting the promise of the exciting, if enigmatic, Rodney Jack by starting him against Bristol City. Man to be sacrificed would be Mark Hawthorne.

To a player living on only a short-term contract it must have seemed a judgement as stark as the ambience of the empty changing room in which we talked. To Mark's eternal credit, he accepted it professionally. His grimace was minimal and his outraged protest non-existent. This augurs well for his long-term career. Meanwhile, he was in the same bus as the rest of us. It was time for another magical mystery tour of Torquay council's cabbage patches. Climax of today's follies was a 30-minute practice match to acclimatise everyone to the 3–4–3 system we'll be aggressively deploying tomorrow. Today it looked great.

Tuesday 20 August

Three in the afternoon and an eerily deserted ground. This is easily a personal record. I've arrived for a match I'm involved in four and three-quarter hours before the kick-off. But I'm not just here with my gear. As well as Bristol City there's another mountain to climb. Paperwork.

As witness beleaguered Steve McCall. I enter the office to discover him hard at the pen-pushing his responsibilities as youth team manager require. He's been at it for a good half day. In terms of concentrated mind-set it's far from ideal to be asking him to down pen and mere hours later push passes not paper around.

A deal of writer's cramp later, I turned to drafting my pre-match briefing notes. Chief of these was to delegate specific tasks to specific players at set pieces – free kicks or corners – for or against. As for coaching philosophy, I'll cut the cackle here. No less to the point will be the breakdown of the strengths and styles of each Bristol player. Typical would be 'X: Will try to play but is niggly with it. Watch it. He'll be looking for free kicks. Y: Slow on turn; iffy when run at. Z: struggles on back pass.

And no excuse for it going in one ear and out the other. Having drawn such lightning sketches in information sheets, I saw to several being prominently displayed around the changing room.

Time on my hands now. I wandered over to the Lodge.

Owned by the club, set into a corner of the ground, The Lodge is TUFC's equivalent of a college hall of residence. It's home (of sorts) to a high percentage of our youngsters and the occasional itinerant more senior pro – Paul Baker for instance, on one of his fleeting visits. It's a distinct aid, I'm sure, to group morale among the youngsters – and it was so now to an oldster in search of some wisecracking distraction, a piece of toast and another cuppa.

Far too ridiculously hard on the heels, it seems, of the last game, show time again. After the elation of last Saturday the mood in the changing room seems quiet – 'too quiet, number one, I don't like it.' Sensing we're too laid back ('This is only the Coca-Cola. It's the League that counts'), I try to tighten the 'up for it' screw a turn or two. It doesn't work. Our being so relaxed is reflected in our play – our non-play – as Bristol City weave pretty patterns on the resuscitated and well up to snuff Plainmoor surface. The 'change the winning team' tactical switch doesn't come into play any more than the left to feed on scraps forward. Then a morsel of considerable substance. Our defence punts an 'anywhere will do' ball blindly up field. It clears a hesitant Alan McCleary to put me clean through on goal. Now the hesitation is all mine. Chip him? No, it's on my wrong foot! Shoot? Shit, he's closed me down too quickly! Round him, then! Round him! I've got to take it on round – *thunk!* Having chosen the right option I hit the turf hard. Prone alongside me is keeper Stuart Naylor who, having blatantly brought me down, now sports a face as red as the card he expects the ref to flourish. But few these days believe Nelson through on an open goal betokens a sure-fire score. Yellow's the colour. But Paul Baker's neatly tucked away penalty goes far to maintaining Stuart's rosy glow.

The half-time whistle. We'd have settled for a 1–0 lead at this stage before the start but it's come in left-handed fashion. During the break I combine patting the defense on the back for their cohesiveness with appeals for better passes forward. They reward me within 30 seconds of the resumption.

A solid challenge leads to possession and then a channel ball, a perfect left-foot cross from the left-foot forward and – yes! – Paul Baker executing a credible impersonation of Nat Lofthouse in burying the header.

'Two-nil! Two-nil!' the Torquay faithful complacently sing. It's in the bag, lads.

Oh yes? Bringing the so often false impression that the job is done, two up is always a dangerous lead, as a crisply taken goal from Shaun Goater now reminds us. Shock horror! 2–1. No complacency now on either terrace or pitch. In fact, galvanised Gulls rather than revitalised Robins are ruling the roost. This time with the run of play, Bakes had notched himself a 13-minute hat trick.

Just when you thought it safe to go back into your shell … Just when you thought it was safe. I clip the ball away and a well-timed late tackle has me on the ground. Sprawled alongside is Bristol City skipper Martin Kuhl.

'Who the hell d'you think you are writing things like that about me in your book?' he says.

Skipper and, it seems, literary critic.

His hand pushes into my face. Kuhl push gives way to Nelson shove. The referee thrusts in between us and, quite properly, tells us to grow up. Good boys again, we nod. He lets it go at that.

Sadly, Kuhl's actions tonight spoke louder than my words. As City refuse to cave in, he leads by example. Now they make two substitutions. On come Paul Agostino and Scott Partridge. To instant telling effect. Astute ones. Each player scores. 3–3. Before we've quite regained our balance the final whistle sounds and with three away goals surrendered, it'll be the north face of the Eiger for us at Ashton Gate.

Conditioned to home defeats, witnesses to a six-goal see-saw, the crowd went home semi-satisfied. In the changing room the head coach voiced his disappointment. And his assistant blew his indignant top. We'd looked a gift horse in the mouth, I stormed. Two goals up when we hadn't deserved to be! Who were we to pass up charity? If extravagant gifts were to come our way again they must be accepted with no thought of reciprocation. Winning was a habit you had to work at acquiring.

Wednesday 21 August

Work at last over I allocated myself some R&R in the English Riviera Centre's jacuzzi. But as I lay easing last night's tensions out of my muscles I found myself engulfed in guilt. Way back east in Essex Carole and the kids would be straining sinew and nerve as they packed to move out of 'our' rented house. I could hear the oft-repeated lament. 'He's never where he's needed.'

A Highland accent doesn't make it any the more soothing.

Thursday 22 August

Grapevine day. As requested, former Southend team-mate Derek Spence called to give his opinion on Scott Darton. We added the input to the judgements already on his file – feedback from Sam Allardyce (former manager), Gary Megson (current manager), Jock Morrison (former team-mate) and Fred O'Donoghue (Blackpool chief scout). The notes constitute essentially a thumbs-up verdict. But it's academic. Blackpool are asking for a nominal transfer fee. It's not the name of our game. Back to the drawing –

'*Brring, brring …*'

Now it's brain-picking in reverse. The caller is Lou Macari, now managing Stoke but steering Swindon when I was there. Our industrial relations, boss to player, had never been the best but, as Lou now sought to quiz me on a couple of former Charlton team-mates, I had a pleasing sense this iffy past was buried. I did my best to mark his card and in return he was quick to say he'd keep his eyes open on Torquay's behalf.

Friday 23 August

In British football the watershed rule of thumb to away games is a four-hour coach trip. Up to that time span you'll journey on the day of the game. Faced with a longer trip you'll travel the day before and overnight in a hotel reasonably convenient to the venue.

This is the background for a small victory today for professionalism. It doesn't take a doctorate in pure mathematics to appreciate that, with accommodation, devoting two days to an away game saddles a club with a far bigger bill than there and back in a day logistics. Away games are no negligible financial commitment for the minnows of the Nationwide. At Plainmoor in recent times financial pressure has seen that four-hour rule being stretched out to five … six … seven and rising.

You can see the chairman's point of view. Last season Torquay United managed just one away win. What's the point, the bank manager could argue, of staying in an overnight hotel when your clowns are 99 per cent certain to lose? The obverse side of the coin may be that the team's horrendous 'on the road' record derived from spending many horrendous hours on the road. A dawn's light 5.30 rendezvous followed by a six- or seven-hour metabolism-murdering Saturday coach ride is a less than ideal prelude to rolling out a feast of footballing finesse.

Tomorrow we've got Scunthorpe, geographically nearer Ajax than Torquay.

But today we've already got a result. His arm a touch twisted, his spirits warmed by our (bright-ish) start to the season, the chairman has coughed up for the over-night. As I looked out the coach window this bank holiday morning, at the snail's pace bumper to bumper motorway traffic, it seemed a sensible decision . Even more so by the time we'd arrived at our Leeds hotel. Seven and a half hours of confinement had our entire party creaking and groaning as they made their stiff-limbed descent from the coach. But we soon took their minds off that.

'Training in 15 minutes, lads!'

Saturday 24 August

We kept our first hotel team briefing brief and to the merciful point. The gist was that any team beating us this season will know they've been in a game. If we can match the commitment and endeavour of our first two games nobody can look on us as a soft-touch, three point banker. Enough said, lads.

This was highly relevant today. All of us were aware that last season Scunthorpe rolled over Torquay at Plainmoor to the grisly tune of 8–1 – a death march for the immediately sacked manager in question. Further piquancy: his initial successor, Mick Buxton, lasted just three days before opting for, yes, Scunthorpe. And here as we got freshly down from the coach at Glanford Park was Mick, his hand out and a ready invitation to join him for a post-match drink on his lips. That's where the hospitality ended for a while. Mick's sides are usually solid, robust and organised. Scunthorpe are no exception. We, on our side, matched them, overall, defensively. But shortcomings in our attacking play are recurring with dispiriting frequency. In particular, given time to play, several of our lads panic and give the ball away.

One mistake was always likely to decide things. It did. Midway through the second half a lapse in concentration gave the Scunthorpe attack the space it had previously been denied. They exploited it to the full. 0–1. A sucker punch of a goal.

Signals and numbers held up high on the touchline. I took my place alongside Kevin in the dug-out. A fresh striker on. But for a striker? For the moment I had neither energy nor heart to question the policy. Instead, big Alex Watson was sent forward to salvage the point we were undoubtedly worth. Justice, alas, was not done.

Hodgie and I did pick up points of a kind, however. As, suiting the bevvy to the mood, I drank bitter in Mick's office, he was no less generous in dispensing various distillations drawn from his long, seen it all, lifetime in football. Not a hint of condescension. A 'teach-in' for which two rookies were all ears and very grateful.

A losing team on a long ride home are not the most inspiriting of companions. The consolation was that, with much the same team, we were six goals better off than on our last encounter with Scunthorpe.

Sunday 25 August

The mood at breakfast *chez les Hodges* was in distinct contrast this morning to last week. No sweet smell of success. Instead the sour taste of defeat coated our Sugar Frosties. Inquest time.

Yes, all in all, we were solid. But our game seemed shot through, hamstrung by caution. Our players seemed inhibited – unwilling to risk the 10 per cent more inventiveness that was all it would take to turn over moderate opposition. But what to do? What to change? Personnel? Formation? Careers? Back to the drawing board.

Or rather the A4 sheets. As I paced, Hodgie scrawled. Hieroglyphics spewed from the tip of his pen. 3–5–2, 3–4–3, 4–4–2. Christmas trees. Diamond patterns. At one blast from the past stage even a 2–3–5 W-formation was mooted.

The only common factor in these systems was the absence of G Nelson up front. It's becoming a problem knowing where I should play. Running myself silly though I have been, with only token service from behind I've seen little of the ball. Virtually nothing of good ball. It's been hard to get into and influence the game. Maybe in midfield far less of it will frustratingly pass me by. Wing-back even?

One step at a time. No wholesale dismantling. Tomorrow we'd see if our existing wing-backs could play 20 or 30 yards further forward.

Monday 26 August

A nice lie in for all the bankers this morning. It's a holiday. All work and no play for the he-men, though. We've got serious coaching to get through. Tomorrow we're away against fancied-to-do-well Northampton Town.

We kicked off the session with some shadow play. Against no opposition our first team looked remarkably proficient.

Opposition (in this case disgruntled non-playing squad members and eager to learn youth trainees) on the field, our patterns still, overall, held up well. Good to see, considering some were variants. As per our post-Scunthorpe analysis we've encouraged the wing-backs to gamble more, to push the immediate man-marker back towards his own goal. We instructed every player finding time and space to regard knocking the simple ball as the best option. By session's end there was rewarding evidence the message had finally got through.

Encouraged, the teacher approached the Head.

'Getting there, Kev.'

'Yeah. I was pleased with that, Nelse.'

There was a smile of sorts on his face but it wasn't reaching his eyes. Turmoil was stamped right across his forehead. A basic fact of coaching life hit the teacher between his own eyes. You can't do it and play at the same time. In adopting a pedagogical rather than student role I had shot myself in the foot. Which since, by the nature of job description, the 11 hadn't included me, didn't really matter.

'Maybe it would make life simpler if I sat tomorrow out,' I said.

Part of me knew this was a token suggestion. Hodgie would respond there was no question of this: the team needed my experience, my drive, my non-stop running, my –

'I think that would be for the best,' Kevin said. 'It'll help you to take a step back and see it from the side with me.'

So there you had it. Dropped after three games. Not yet September even. A flying start to my Torquay career. Thank Christ I've started to wear two hats.

Tuesday 27 August

At least I've only lost my place. Andy King has been suspended (and just what does that mean, Mansfield Town?) after only two league games. It's just 10 days into the season and three managers have already collected their red cards. Few crumbs of comfort there! Disconsolately I have to acknowledge that the honeymoon period I had been getting such a bang out of – so to speak – was over. A clear-the-air session with my landlord is well in order.

Despite living cheek-by-jowl with Hodgie these past five weeks, I'm far from clear how he rates me as a player. If he's less than impressed I'd rather be told. It needs to be out in the open. But communication on this touchy yet nevertheless vital issue has been non-existent ... I set out to instigate it.

We talked. The air *was* cleared. Our relationship is the better for the frank exchange. And there are two bottom lines. My playing ability will be vital to Torquay's 1996/97 campaign. At Northampton tonight, I'll be on the bench.

Sound decision, Kevin. My replacement, Rodney Jack, shot us into an almost instant lead and his breathtaking all-round display was less that of a player on song than the St Vincent's Choral Society thundering out a reggae version of *The Messiah*. He had the Cobblers' fans audibly hooked by his enthralling performance right to the finish. Almost the finish. Victim of one lunging tackle too many at the back end of the match, Rodders was stretchered off to home-crowd applause as generous as loud.

This loss of our main man went a long way towards snapping the lead in our pencil. A game we'd dominated began to ebb away. We still made several juicy chances but, failing to convert any, our 1–0 lead began to look increasingly vulnerable. Overprotective we retreated deeper and deeper. The set-piece equaliser five minutes from time came with an air of inevitability.

A creditable draw, a pleasing result, most seemed to think. I couldn't but see it as two points dropped.

Wednesday 28 August

Who's that sleeping in my bed? Ah, I remember, my wife Carole, way down West again but, despite my tip-toeing best endeavours, malevolently cursing as my 3 am return from Northampton breaks into her golden slumber. Only four hours later, our car heading towards the lettings agent and the keys to our Chudleigh home, I was still full of sleep – but void of sweetness and light – myself.

A day off. Oh, yes? After the moving experience of man-handling two lorry loads of fully laden tea chests across the new threshold I couldn't wait for the morrow and the return it would bring me to the soft option of the day job.

Friday 30 August

A Friday and hence a full plenary session of the yellow jersey Bench Assizes (Western Circuit), Chief Justice Nelson presiding. On the docket a host of malefactors, each one fearful he would draw down sentencing as the week's sacrificial lamb.

'Order! Order!' Thus I began.

'May it please the court.'

Graciously I invited the advocacy of silver-tongued Ian Hathaway.

'I would draw the court's attention to 7.49 on the evening of Tuesday the 27th of August at the Sixfield Stadium,' he began.

'Very well … '

'This, m'lud, was the occasion of one Rodney Jack stealing … '

'Er which way round is his name to be understood, Mr Hathaway?'

'Even as stated, m'lud – Jack is the family name.'

'Most confusing. Very well. Proceed.'

'This was the occasion of Mr Jack nicking our only goal.'

'Indeed.'

'At this juncture the warbling of a mobile phone was heard by those cheering on the bench.'

'The bench, Mr Hathaway? But I am on the bench.'

'Not the bench, m'lud but the … er, bench. You were on that one too.'

'So I was. Proceed.'

'As, indeed, m'lud, in my own capacity of sub was I. It was I, you may recall, who turned to you saying – and I quote – 'It's the chairman for you, Nelse.'

'I'm not sure I do recall. I'm not as young as I seem to remember once being.'

'I assure you, m'lud, that such an exchange did take place.'

'Yes … And I must warn you, Mr Hathaway, that if you continue this line of argument it may prove highly prejudicial to your future playing career.'

'Be that as it may, m'lud, I feel bound to draw to the court's attention that it was at this precise moment that, eyes still on the game, you reached across and took from me one mature and fully ripened banana, to wit, Exhibit A.'

As judges frequently are, I was in a pickle. I'd bought the stitch-up as totally as I'd bought Stan Collymore's dummy. Worse for present purposes, I'd clean forgotten the incident.

'Please come to the point, Mr Hathaway.'

As if I bloody well didn't know what it was already.

'I submit, m'lud that this trial is a chicane. Er, charade. That you have forfeited your right to preside and that as regards the jersey you are this week's top banana and should be just as yellow.'

Laughter in court. Hoist by my own petard. Sentencing was a formality. I cranked up the laughter level by going through the motions of protesting ('And you can piss off back to your granny's cottage for a start, Hathaway!') but soon there was nothing for it but to doff wig and black cap and don not only the jersey but also matching yellow shorts and socks. A week's stealthy build-up! The plan had been brilliantly thought out and carried through. If they could only execute their other set pieces so slickly!

A tonic moment. I could still lose my worries in precious moments like these where I belonged and didn't stand outside. Moreover, it was a sovereign distraction from what was waiting later in the day. While the still wise-cracking squad made off for a training session, I headed off alone in a different direction and a very different mood.

My destination was Plymouth. During those heady Home Park days of '86 my kit sponsor had been Monica Richards. Ten years later I was making the sad journey to attend her funeral. It had only been 10 days since I'd seen her last, though. For the past four years she had been waging a tenacious rearguard action against the cancer which now, in her 74th year, had at last taken her. That final time of meeting, she had obviously been in a great deal of pain but, as we shared memories of that special promotion a lightening-fast decade ago, her eyes had sparkled and her grin had been as infectious as ever. As she had wished, she had died at home surrounded by her devoted family.

As she had also wished, this evening, the dignified service over, Richard, her husband, had attended Argyle's home match. This decision had shocked nobody. Together they had watched countless Plymouth games, travelling thousands of miles. What better therapy could he have found?

Monica and Richard were never rich. Nevertheless, in sponsoring many players over the years, they had gladly diverted no little of their hard-earned income to Argyle. A beneficiary myself, I took it hard that at the funeral of this best sort of supporter, there was no official club representative. A little too much to ask for, I suppose.

Tonight Plymouth beat Preston 2–1. Poignantly it put them top of the league. For Richard, perhaps, a first little toe-hold on the climb away from grief. A result appreciated, just possibly, by a supporter off pilgrimaging on her longest away trip yet.

Saturday 31 August

The operative word for today is 'local'. For me there's the luxury of a friendly neighbourhood drive. After the rally-stage commuting to 'home' games of my past five years, 20 minutes away seems like a stone's throw. For the South Devon fans the word to attach to 'local' is 'derby'. We've got Exeter today.

The fixture has come perhaps a mite early in the season for passion to be running at fever pitch, and the 'derby' factor probably means more to fans than players. For Torquay United the priority is consolidating our rehabilitation of a force-to-be-reckoned-with, solid-at-home record. Nevertheless, as three o'clock nears, I am delighted to hear that today's gate will come in at 4,000-plus. This is the sort of figure that through sustained success born of attractive play we would aim to make our norm. To be going on with, though, this will do nicely, thank you.

Mind you, I happen to know it's a figure artificially swollen. Scouts are in from Man United, Spurs, Newcastle, Forest, Wimbledon, Southampton, Bristol City and York. All the greats. They're here to check out the man of the moment, Hot Rod. I find this presence in numbers significant in three ways.

The first is simply how quickly the jungle drums can succeed in sending out the word. Just five games into the season and the tribal scouts are lining up. This is part and parcel of my second observation. Players are commodities. If you hear there's a chance of getting in on the ground floor of some gilt-edged stock, go for it. Perhaps he'll do 30 goals for you before the season is out. Perhaps you can buy at £200,000 and sell on at £2 million. Quick! Get a bid in before the stock has been snapped up!

My third thought is that the highly touted commodity is in the shop window because the past its sell-by date merchandise is not. Once again

I'm assigned to the bench – assigned by a schizoid conversation between wise old Nelse and eager young beaver Garry Nelson.

Nelse: Son, hard decision but I'm dropping you for Saturday. We'll put you on the bench.

Garry: Boss – you've got to be joking! When I came on on Tuesday I really did the business.

Nelse: Plenty of time, son. No call to rush you. You'll thank me for this decision 10 years from now.

But it's the right decision. The game is only 74 seconds young when local (adopted) hero, Rodney Jack, gets windward of the Exeter defence not only to score with all the aplomb of his great-great-uncle, David (the white sheep of the family), but also to transmit his assurance to the rest of the side. Playing with genuine poise we dominated for the first half hour in our best performance yet. Everyone looked hungry and sharp. We were getting forward in numbers. All this against a side containing players of the experience of Brian Gayle, Mark Chamberlain, and Noel Blake.

For player-manager Peter Fox it was a reversal of fortune. Two years ago Exeter finished the season propping up the Football League. As with us this time around, only the inferior standard of the Conference winner's ground kept Exeter up. Enter canny Mr Fox. Last year he steered Exeter to mid-table respectability and, better, anonymity. Now he was again doing his best to redress a no-win situation. Peter had justified choosing himself as keeper with several fine saves from Paul Baker pile-drivers. Here he came again. As Paul pulled the trigger Peter anticipated well. Too well. Scuffing the ball, other than getting the direction right Bakes made a complete pig's breakfast of the shot. It bobbled stupidly forward ... and on into the goal. The quickly down Fox had jumped right over the lazy ball. It was a striking example of Fate robbing Peter to pay Paul.

Half-time brought the team a standing ovation and me a sense of the crowd thinking 'This is different, this is good.' The changing room briefing was correspondingly simple. Take yourselves seriously: 2–0 up halfway through at Plainmoor is a three-point situation. No sitting back to concede the initiative. Keep the scruff of the game's neck where you've got it – in your own hands.

I did get on. And possibly significantly. Shortly after the resumption Richard Hancox had to come off with a nasty eye injury. I took over his wing-back role. Within moments I found myself nicking the ball away from an Exeter forward and, still in our penalty area, dribbling it past two more. On the left peg now … The 65-yard pass I proceeded to float into Rodney Jack's stride has, in all modesty, to be described as Hoddlesque. 'Who's he?' I could hear all those scouts wondering aloud. An up and down wing-back in my old age? It's a thought.

Two-nil it stayed. What we had we held. Afterwards there was a smashing, *grown up* feeling in the changing room.

Sunday 1 September

A day significant only for my off-duty complacency and England's stuttering 3–0 World Cup qualifying win over Moldova, their first under mint-new coach, the appointed in indecent and confusing haste Glenn Hoddle.

Monday 2 September

Two wins in the bag already! It's a Monday with a difference for the grinning Gulls this morning. The coaches made no effort to stop the non-stop repartee. Laughter, as an index of collective confidence, is essential to any team's success. For Torquay it's a fair indication we're emerging from the Dark Ages. Finding life less merry and bright, though, is Paul Adcock. He's halfway through his two-month extended trial period now and a 'trial' is what it's proving to be in every sense. He's been hit by a high-profile crisis of confidence that is threatening to wipe out the good impression he created throughout all his unselfish, high-quality pre-season work. It's his finishing that's proving his current undoing. His visible tensing up during finishing practices has him missing easy chances far too frequently. We've all been there and had our wildly struck or underhit bloopers met by a barrage of put-downs. Just ask Gareth Southgate.

In Paul's case all cracks from team-mates have now ceased. Knowing what he's going through they're commendably sympathetic but this silence, far from being golden, is a further inhibiting problem. It shrieks ear-splitting volumes.

Well acquainted with striker's drought myself, I arranged for an extra-time session – Paul, the keepers, me – in an effort to get him to relax. Short term it works a treat. Adders revels in this opportunity for unobserved action. But he's looking ultimately at doing the business out on the park.

With the days of his trial period ticking away fast, his long-term prospects aren't looking the greatest.

In much the same position – where he plays and in type of contract – is young Ellis Laight. Much of his failure to progress, though, it has to be said, may well be due to lack of opportunity. Torquay don't operate a team in any formal reserve league. We can't afford to. The consequence is a lot of thumb-twiddling disenchantment for our younger and fringe of first-team lads, who are being denied the chance to sharpen their talents and strut their stuff. The most challenging showcase we can hope to drum up is the occasional friendly when – or rather if – a worthy enough opponent can be found. It leaves a lot to be desired. One possible solution is the loan-out option, in which regard Weymouth have asked us if we will let Ellis join them in the Dr Martens League for a month. To my way of thinking this would seem ideal for him to put an edge on his training-ground techniques in the fire of proper games. But Ellis feels otherwise. On the grounds of wishing to stay in the Plainmoor picture he rejects the approach out of hand. I don't know … It's a decision that many a soccer likely lad has had and will have to make. Sometimes you have to take a pace back if you want to advance two. Perhaps he's just mad about my training sessions. Even so he may be letting an unthought-through snap decision put his long-term future with Torquay on the line.

Tuesday 3 September

Wonderful to relate we've a clean bill of health. Partly it indicates we're lucky. Partly it indicates we've the second leg of our Coca-Cola tie tonight. No one wants to miss out on the (slim) chance of returning from Bristol a local hero. Such ambitions apart, Ashton Gate is worth going to see these days. All-seater at last, it can claim to be the best stadium in the lower divisions. The playing surface is now quite superb. An even £100,000 has been ploughed into nourishing it, and the return on this outlay was evident in the extra spring in our step as we ran out. City's men, by contrast, looked guarded. One win from four league starts has put Joe Jordan's team under early pressure. An aggregate defeat at our hands would hardly lighten the load on the big man's shoulders.

He needn't have worried. The fizz bubbled out of the Coca-Cola for us the moment the whistle went. Flat, unable to add to the Jordanian pressure, we settled again for the quieter life of sitting deep. Inevitably our passing and our forward play suffered. City's superior skill level earned them a safe enough passage into the next round. 0–1 on the night. 3–4 overall. The scoreline was evidence that the contest had been close. That, I couldn't help but think, had been the trouble.

If we'd really carried the fight to City tonight we might – *might* – have nicked the decisive goal and the win. But I suspect too many of the Torquay team were thinking, 'Everyone can see we've run them close: there's no disgrace in losing now.' Not altogether true. I couldn't help but point out that twice we'd held a two-goal advantage. A pro side should be able to defend this. And tonight … there were already some indications we would find winning away from home this season every bit as difficult as last.

Thursday 5 September

EOB (every other business) to start the day. I initiate the first item by putting through a call to Graham Turner at Hereford. The masonic brotherhood of coaching etiquette book enables me to quiz him about Cambridge United, with whom his side have just drawn 1–1, but I'm not sure I'm any the wiser. My intelligence had been that Cambridge favour playing 4–3–3. Graham tells me that up at Edgar Street they've switched to 3–5–2. Getting in shape for us, I begin to wonder …

The door opens. In walks Rodney Jack. In his hand is a letter inviting him to join the squad from which the St Vincent and the Grenadines team will be picked to play Mexico in their World Cup clash next week. He'll need to fly out next Sunday. Since the group are playing a telescoped series of virtually back-to-back home and away fixtures, he'll be away four weeks. A tough break for us. And one that even if we wanted to (we don't: we wouldn't dream of denying him the honour and the thrill) we couldn't do anything about. FIFA have ruled that country takes precedence over club and end of story.

Jack is very much the lad today. Kevin is soon talking not to his namesake but to Newcastle number two, Terry McDermott. Newcastle liked what they saw on Saturday and are asking to have Rodney up with them training for a week. Again we won't stand in the way of his burgeoning career. (And, after all, the drop in training standards up there will give him a chance to recharge his batteries.) But this shows signs of becoming another situation we can't win. Yes, if Newcastle continue to be impressed, we might make a rather good bob or two out of selling him on. But his going would punch a big hole, I readily concede now, in the quality of what we'd be left able to field. Alternatively – something fans rarely stop to consider – there's the possibility he may not click up at St James' Park. Their subs' bench doesn't exactly lack for able bodies, after all. In that case, given the immediacy of the soccer grapevine ('Yeah, Newcastle had him up there but didn't reckon him') our commodity risks being instantly devalued. *Should* we want to sell him. Which we don't. But might. If.

From a probably rising star to a player with only one foot on the ladder. I seek out Paul Adcock to tell him that Dorchester have been on to us saying that they'd like to take him on loan. Paul says he'll think it over.

Done all that. Time for another magical mystery tour in search of a training ground. Not today though. The mini-bus is grounded. Its gearbox is in even worse shape than Torquay United FCs. Our alternative has to be the Plainmoor pitch. The groundsman isn't at all keen on us muscling onto his patch but a combination of grovelling, plea bargaining and calls to the chairman gain us an arm-twisted foothold. And very pleasant to coach on too.

And revealing. A by-product of the temporary arrangement is to remind me how a first-class surface quickly identifies those who can pass accurately and have the composure to make themselves that vital extra moment during a 'keep ball' session. It also quickly shows up those who are not prepared to work hard. Unfortunately this morning, in spite of (or because of) a day off yesterday, too many were still in play-school mode. Was it a case of 'didn't want it' or 'couldn't hack it' I asked myself as I mentally revised several report cards downwards. It was an attitude that after a rest day went beyond disappointing. At one stage in the eight-a-side 'keep ball' on a confined playing area our side strung together 23 passes. Criminal might be the better adjective. I wouldn't expect AC Milan to be able to do that. As people strolled through the session all the things we'd been working on – organisation, talking to each other, showing inside – went out the window. I was not best pleased.

Friday 6 September

The wheels on the bus continue not to go round and round but as the team is not broken, Hodgie is not trying to fix it. He's going with the same starting XI again. While it's essentially a case of letting well enough alone, we did take wing-back Richard Hancox aside for a quiet word, burden of which was that he should be more adventurous in getting forward and linking up. This is ironic. In past seasons Richard has consistently been played in his preferred role of out and out striker. If he now seems inhibited out on the park, it may well be due to a problem not entirely of his own making but which (since we're pretty much obliged to play him *somewhere*, so thin is our squad in first-team experience) Hodgie and I have certainly inherited. Richard, as it happens, is the chairman's son-in-law. At the end of last season, there were many supporters who felt that his retention on the Torquay books was at the expense of better players – and due solely to the most obvious reason. The too obvious reason, perhaps. I'm in no position to judge. I do, though, strongly suspect that feeling obliged to silence his critics through performance, Richard is actually trying too hard. He's clutching up. It could be a case of less effort achieving enhanced form. All may yet be well that ends well.

All does not end well today, however. Training has taken Ray Newland's continuously dodgy shoulder the far side of the 'chance it' divide. Rhys Wilmot is still far from fully fit but is the lesser handicap. He'll play at Cambridge.

Tomorrow in mind we ease through a gentle 5-a-side session but I'm pained to see one or two participants are still phoning their application in.

A call came in today from released Arsenal midfielder Tim Griggs. We went after this 19-year-old weeks ago but he didn't (want to) know about Torquay. Now he says he's interested. Either his career has stalled dramatically or he now thinks we're doing something right. He'll be joining us for two weeks. Watch this space.

Saturday 7 September

Away to Cambridge. A relative luxury not to be boarding the coach until 8.20 am but a distinct disappointment to find that the card school (euchre, by the way, is the 'in' game for Torquay studs) will be minus its head boy for the five-hour trip.

Chairman Mike Bateson has already proffered apologies for his absence. It's all down to the new little bit of fluff in his life. His love affair with the Gulls has been temporarily superseded by the arrival on the scene of a newly hatched hyacinth macaw chick. This is no Monty Python breed of parrot. Rarer than a Catholic Rangers supporter it's so valuable it makes your average Maltese falcon look like chicken feed, Sydney. Quite literally, endangered species though we could end up ourselves, it's worth more than the entire Torquay squad.

The Abbey Stadium at last. I grab a quick chat with David Preece, pumped up from just having signed a three-year deal as Cambridge's player-coach. Like meeting like. We were both on the same FA full license coaching course. David and I being the latest, a high proportion of that class of '92 are now gainfully employed throughout the Football League.

A firm handshake, our 'all the best' wishes, and then the worst of enemies for the next two hours as the afternoon again spun into 'fast forward'. Here were the completed team-sheets being exchanged and, no, it wasn't clear which formation Cambridge were going for. Change of Nelson plan. Preferring to don my information officer hat and concentrate on drawing up contingency plans, I skipped the usual warm-up. (Yelling from the subs' bench would do that for me, anyhow.) When the players clattered back in 15 minutes before the 'off' I made the following battle-stations speech: 'I don't want you even to consider them. If we're on our game, we've got more than enough to beat Cambridge.' Stirring stuff. But it didn't do the trick. It failed to rouse the snoozers from their first-half slumbers.

What followed was the worst 45 minutes the new Torquay regime had been forced to endure. It wasn't just the treacherous long grass Cambridge stick you with. A questionable off-side decision from an assistant-referee (sic) more eagle-pated than sighted gave Scott McGleish the chance to saunter away from a flat-footed back line. Then, climaxing a woeful series of personal defensive blunders, Jon Gittens dillied and dallied on a ball he had time enough to exercise four options on. He chose the fifth – a gentle prod into the stride of my again clear-through former Charlton team-mate. Two-nil at half-time. Scott had accepted both gifts with commendable efficiency, but it was plain that exposed one-on-one, Rhys Wilmot's restricted mobility simply didn't allow him to make sufficiently match-quick responses.

No more Mr Nice Guy time. Head Coach Hodges tore strips off the team as a whole. My fire was more concentrated. I aimed my vitriol exclusively in the direction of the man who, give or take one or two eccentricities, had hitherto put in a series of outstanding league performances. Today, I told Jon Gittens he wasn't at it, as we say in football. His performance today was all of a piece with the way he'd strolled through the last two days of training and had arrived late to meet the coach. Being strolling players was not what it was about.

Unhappy to be singled out, Jon denied my specific charges. The confrontation was in danger of degenerating into a toe-to-toe slanging or even (Azumah, my brother, where are you when I need you?) slugging match. But all the while part of my mind was conscious that the half-time clock was ticking. The potentially invaluable opportunity to analyse, rethink, remotivate and resurrect was leaking away. Some deep breathing, then. A word from Hodgie. The volcano was plugged.

Ten minutes into the second half I was given first-hand scope to translate big mouth theory into playing practice. The old double substitution whammy. Mitchell and Hancox off. Nelson and Hathaway on. And to the very real point. At last we succeeded in changing the pattern of the game.

With nothing to lose, we upped our momentum. We were prepared to risk leaving our men to press forward. With 20 minutes to go Ian Hathaway held the ball up nicely as he sensed me making a run outside him down the left wing. He released the ball into my stride with perfect timing and I was able to penetrate deep before crossing to the far post. Paul Baker rose to the opportunity and in his celebrated Mark Hateley impersonation headed back across and over the keeper. It was a move lifted straight from the coaching video. Light at the end of a tunnel that suddenly didn't seem so long. At last, with Cambridge living up to my dismissive pre-match assessment the match had the shape I'd predicted. But 'at last' came too late. The whistle went with us still a goal down and leaving the field euchred. Knowing what we *could* have done if we'd got it right from the off, the bad taste from the half-time row still in my mouth, I left the field feeling as sick as a hyacinth macaw.

It was a feeling soon put into perspective. Word came through that the injury David Preece had suffered was no less than a broken leg. Disappointed I might be, disabled or unemployed I wasn't.

Wishing David as speedy a revival as I wished Torquay I took to the road in a hired car with Rodney Jack. He was St Vincent-bound via Gatwick. Next Wednesday he'll be running out against Mexico.

'Going to add to your international goals total?' I asked him.

He smiled in happy resignation and shook his head.

'I played against them in the Azteca Stadium,' he said. 'They beat us 7–0. It'll be like chasing shadows.'

Tuesday 10 September

Another match day. A 7.45 kick-off against Cardiff City. Not, however, a day of leisure by way of preparation. Hodgie and I call the players in for an unexpected morning session aimed as much at concentrating minds as sharpening reflexes.

First, though, some alterations to the starting line-up are made. A quartet of players are successively summoned to the manager's office as the revolving door of selection works its whirligig 'in' and 'out' changes.

First in is Paul Mitchell, an 'out'. He's clearly disappointed to be dropped and has fair reason to be. He's not done a lot wrong. His failing has rather been not quite doing enough. He needs, we repeat to him, to do more for the team going forward. He's got a Lorimer-power shot in his armoury, we remind him. Why this reluctance to launch missiles?

The next head on the block is our other defender backwards in coming forwards, left wing-back Richard Hancox. He's showing no sign of pulling out of that crisis in confidence which has already led to several lacklustre performances. The key factor here continues to be the hammering he's been getting week on week, home and away, from a section of our fans, pillorying him for being the chairman's son-in-law. He's cruelly vulnerable to that charge of nepotism. Each Saturday has brought its variation on the theme of, 'You're rubbish, Hancox! You're only in the team for one reason!' Significantly, as Kevin delivers the news that we're asking him to step down, Richard conveys an impression of being relieved rather than put out.

The door continues to revolve and now it is showing us its pleasant aspect as it ushers in Jamie Ndah and Scott Stamps to learn that, for the first time this season they are both in the evening's starting line-up. Their long, far from patient wait is over. It's time to convert all their words of promise into action. Their grins and the spring in their steps as they leave our shoe-box promise they've every intention of giving this opportunity their best shot.

Now to training. An enjoyable money-raising piggy-in-the-middle was backed up by short, sharp team-spirit-raising sprints. Time now to announce the side formally. But picking the perfect moment to step forward is Jon Gittens.

'I'd just like to say while everyone's here,' he says, 'that I was well out of order last Saturday. Sorry. Down to me. But it won't happen again.' A handsomely civilised, thoroughly grown-up gesture on his part, the apology earned him a spontaneous round of applause. Just the response Hodgie and I had been hoping for, it signalled the return of harmony to our little band of brothers. As we wrapped up I had a good sense of our all being focused on the evening to come.

As, given Cardiff's dynamic duo of Steve White and Carl Dale, Big Jon will need to be. As independent strikers the two notched up over 60 goals last season. How well they operate in tandem this year is yet to be seen since Mr Dale's diary shows he's been out injured until today. Steve White, though, has four goals from just his last two outings. That's doubly ominous given our goalkeeper crisis.

The long-running nightmare we've been unable to shake off since the pre-season sunk to an all-time low three days ago. It was simply unfair on Rhys to ask him to go out and do a job while still essentially on the walking wounded list. But our hands had been figuratively forced by Ray Newland's consistently below par shoulder being further wrenched physically. It's still far from 100 per cent but it's less painful, more free than Saturday. Ray gets the nod tonight but once again it's a clear-cut case of opting for the lesser of two invalids. My inclusion is clearer-cut still. I'm in for Rodney Jack, away in the World Cup sunshine.

In the 90-minute event all 11 Torquay players produced an all we could have asked for performance. Virtue found its due reward. Jon Gittens let his feet continue to do his talking and as a preface to a night's impressive defending got forward early on to score in a goal-mouth scramble. Jamie Ndah marked his seasonal debut with a sweetly struck and, at two minutes into first half injury time, even more sweetly timed second goal that clinched his Man of the Match award.

A tight, professional performance in the second half allowed Cardiff few chances. When the ref called time it was our third successive home win. The two-match losing sequence had been nipped in the bud. Sixth in the table. If the play-off places were decided early in September ... Dream on. But the L-plated coaching staff did allow themselves to exchange satisfied grins.

Halfway down the second drink in the boardroom that same evening, a measure of dissatisfaction was being voiced. Not with the performance but at the gate. The crowd of 2,000 was half the attendance for the Exeter game. Cause for genuine concern when you've a 100 per cent home record in the league. OK, Tuesday night isn't Saturday afternoon. The box was showing Newcastle's UEFA Cup game live. As relevant a cause is probably that we've another home game this weekend. The feelgood factor isn't too evident in the West Country any more than in the North, South and East. Picking and choosing games you'll spend good money on is a feature of Devonian support as much as Lancastrian or Anglian.

Wednesday 11 September

I woke up this morning and then didn't. Suspended in that half-sleeping, half-awake limbo I was dozily aware of my brain trying to access the contact number for the Stannah Lift Co. Meanwhile my body was telling me that it might have been only 73 minutes out there last night but it seemed much longer. Like 35 years. As I'm deeply, seriously tired, it was telling me, let me lie back and enjoy it. I rolled over and up on to my feet just in time to beat the count of ten. Ten o'clock. A day off, after all. Oh, yes? Carole has already dressed for an excursion and the kill. Today marks our 13th wedding anniversary. Unlucky for some bank balances. A spending spree the length and breadth of Exeter's shops was about to make severe inroads into certain Torquay reserves. I love shopping. I love it about as much as I love bleep-tests, 12-minute runs and hill-climbs.

Rejuvenating therapy of a sort came courtesy of a session on the couch later that evening. The couch opposite the television. Juventus versus Man U. In denying them so much as a strike on goal worthy of the name, the Turin internationals humbled the Manchester internationals to the extent of making them look like apprentices. Juventus reopened that old wounding question. Is 'English' soccer anywhere near matching the best of European again?

There was a new question to answer too. Which idiot PR man caused Cantona to hype the match in a TV trailer by preening in front of camera and pursing his lips like a born again 'you are awful!' Dick Emery pout that Man U are 'the best'. They plainly aren't. A rejuvenating experience indeed.

Friday 13 September

Tony Adams has 'come out' with the admission he is a clinical alcoholic – a statement which all of the media have leapt on with yells of undisguised mercenary glee.

Burden of the commentary being implied about Adams is that he is weak-willed and stupid. I don't think he's either. His action is both brave and sensible.

Alcoholism for the flat-out victim, let us not forget, is a physiological rather than a mental problem. It's about matter rather than mind – your own body's chemical predilection for addiction. Your body might be a temple but when they were handing out the genes you copped a bunch riddling the edifice with, so to speak, wet rot.

If we take a sideways glance across North London to Adams' obvious opposite number, Gary Mabbutt, we find a player with another inherited chemical imbalance. Famously, Gary is a diabetic. For years everyone has applauded the way in which, taking sensible remedial action, he has refused to allow his in-built disability prevent him from playing the game at the highest level. He's been an inspirational role model to thousands of lesser diabetic sportsmen.

Adams, though, 'ho! ho! ho!', is a lush, a juicer, an alky. Bollocks. It's the same difference. An *inherent* problem. One now out in the open – which is a huge step towards addressing it. Without pausing for thought everyone can reel off a list of glittering footballing talents – Greaves, Best, Cooke; you could select a World Cup-winning side drawn from their ranks – whose careers were impaired and curtailed by booze. One of the best players in the sides I played for literally drank himself to death while still a registered player. Untold hundreds, thousands, of run of the mill pros who have woken up on that inescapable day to the soul-curdling certain realisation that they aren't going any further up the ladder have spent the rest of their abbreviated lives chasing consolation down bottle after bottle after bottle.

At super-star or corner-pub level there's always a hanger-on willing to buy his moment of, as he pathetically thinks, reflected glory by standing the player another drink. And on the player's side the biggest problem of all, of course, is that no less pathetically going through the motions of pretending everything is just fine, he denies there's any problem there in the first place.

In publicly staking out the personal area that he has to defend, Tony Adams, it seems to me, has pre-empted these sad scenarios. What kind of reflected glory will now shine upon the 'good mate' leading Tony into *Scribes* and asking him what he fancies? Let's hope that in displaying as much class off the field as on it he comes to serve as a role model too.

Saturday 14 September

All right for some. 'Some' being the end of season holiday-makers delighted to be basking in temperatures more suitable for the French than the English Riviera. No Cote d'Azur hedonism for us today but, rather, the Plainmoor sweatbox. Ninety minutes-plus added on time of shirt-soaking toil.

So it proved. As you might expect from a side managed by former

Goodison Great, Kevin Ratcliffe, Chester constituted stern opposition. Well organised around a strongly challenging defence but, thankfully, sterile in attack, they ground out a gritty no-score draw that severed some percentage points off of our hitherto 100 per cent home record.

Not to grieve unduly, though. After five games we're still unbeaten at Plainmoor. It won't last but so far we're still reasonably 'up'. We could point to our own strength in defence and the midfield looking out for each other. Less positive was the continuing inconsistency today of several of our Young Turks, one of whom, Scott Stamps, was now summoned by Hodgie to explain his high-profile tantrum on being substituted. Such a reaction, the triumph of ego over professionalism, is, of course, common-place in today's game. But who am I to cast the first stone? Recalling several such personal responses to seeing the Charlton number 10 card being held aloft, I kept a diplomatic silence and a wry smile. I could afford one. Today was my best game of the season. And, notwithstanding the sauna conditions, I'd lasted the full 90.

Monday 16 September

A slight let up in the pace. No mid-week game for the first time this season. We decide to give our regulars a recharge the batteries day off. It's a chance for several to catch up on far-flung family life. It's Newcastle for Paul Baker, of course, but Liverpool for Ray Newland, Winchester for Jon Gittens and Bournemouth for Paul Mitchell. All can be forgiven for seeing Plainmoor games as playing away.

Once it was mandatory that any player signing for a club should live within 35 miles of its training ground. While searching for the latest in his succession of 'Dunroamins' he might well find temporary shelter in one of the club's own properties. Indeed, in those short-term days of penny-wise Thatcherite boom, one considerable inducement to a change of clubs was the nice little earner of a mark-up you could make putting your current des res on the market. In the negative equity '90s, though, when getting rid of your house might be a nightmare, long distance commuting became – don't I know it! – an integral part of football.

Which brings us back to Paul Baker. His limpet-like adhesion to the North-East is looking like a canny non-move. His consistent appearance on the scoresheet has engendered interest in Geordieland that wasn't there in the close season. This is confirmed by the chairman abruptly calling Hodgie and me in to inform us of renewed Hartlepool interest in Paul.

We can't win this one whatever happens. Bakes is enjoying an all-time high popularity rating with the fans. His departure will leave us the long-term villains of the piece and, indeed, accommodating his wish to find a club on his own doorstep seems certain now to compromise any chance of marked Torquay success. But here's a new twist. The Birdman of La Manga now seems set on exacting a transfer fee for Paul that will cover the signing on fee the club punted his way in the close season. All right. This will probably delay Bakes' departure. But. How will it affect his so far total commitment? One forward-looking (and critic-silencing) move will be to sign a well up to snuff replacement. A contingency list of target men (in both senses) is a priority. But so is a cool consideration of the Cash In/Cash Out balance. This casts a sharper light still on two of the forwards we now go out to work with.

Ellis Laight and Paul Adcock have only a month to run on their short-term contracts. With rumours rumbling of our looking to sign another striker, their anxiety levels are liable to go off the scale. They realise that Paul Baker's exit will almost certainly mean *finis* to their own Torquay careers. Funds for a striker firing on most of his cylinders will have to be found from somewhere.

Tuesday 17 September

Regathering of the Torquay clan revitalised and raring to go – until its members discover that the main item on the morning agenda is running. A six-minute run, 18 power runs, 200 stomachs, thrust runs and a set of doggies is all we ask of our little lads. Save for one or two bleats they respond with terrific attitude.

Leading by example as ever is skipper Alex Watson. It doesn't escape our notice. Afterwards, we call him into the office to express our thanks. If our finances were on a more sound footing, we'd be opening discussion about a contract extension. Instead we offer Alex another day off. It's the best we can do.

Contracts. Money. Contacts. The spider web of club to club base-touching continues to spin its endlessly different identical patterns. Hartlepool have stepped up their interest in Paul Baker. He has our permission to talk terms with Keith Houchen. That's page one. No agreement and no deal. Even so ... I speak to Oxford coach Malcolm Crosby to discover whether Mark Druce will play for the Reserves at Wimbledon tomorrow. 'Yes,' is the answer. I at once line up Pete Evans, more and more our south coast scout to examine the merchandise. Meanwhile, responding to a fax, Kevin speaks to Luton's Lennie Lawrence about 6ft 3in forward John Taylor. Coincidentally, John is a good friend of my former Charlton room-mate Phil Chapple. Why, I haven't spoken to Phil in – ooh, it must be days. High time I called him to congratulate him on his recent high match ratings. And more Addick connections. Charlton's elegant left back of the '80s, Mark Reid, is living back in Scotland. Gosh, look. He's not far from Airdrie where Steve Cooper, Hodgie's and my mutual Plymouth team-mate, is now plying his trade.

'Oh, by the way, Mark … '

So it goes, the old pals' act, the soccer grapevine.

Wednesday 18 September

A variation on my responsibilities theme. The afternoon found me driving to Bridport in Dorset where our 'unofficial' reserve team had a friendly against the Screwfix Direct Western League side. Although a much needed focal point for collective concentration and hence a morale rediscovering exercise, the game itself, a 6–0 victory, saw the second strings scarcely break sweat. Two goals apiece for Messrs Laight and Adcock proved that, at this level, they are both strikers to be reckoned with.

Thursday 19 September

The world turned gently upside down. Today there's a reward for the hard-working 'disenchanteds' – a day off. Training will consist of the starting XI for next Saturday playing an Organisation and Methods practice match against Steve McCall's kids. Happily lining up for the bibs was recently returned Paul Baker, the Hartlepool venture put temporarily on hold. His contribution to the session was exemplary. It only served to highlight the body blow his loss would be.

Sadly – it's never a fun job for long – a loss of a kind had to be recorded later in the day, as Hodgie and I informed Timmy Griggs, recently of Arsenal, that we would not be offering him a contract. He's 19. His face is still unlined. Except when it has disappointment etched right across it.

When I offered to talk to a couple of Conference clubs on his behalf, his disbelieving face fell even further. That was part-time stuff: he was a full-time footballer. You and about 400 other recently let go players, I felt like saying. I didn't, though. That he is 19 isn't much his fault either. Two incoming faxes, by contrast, name players who definitely would improve our squad – Ian Ormondroyd of Bradford City and Reading's Stuart Lovell. Both gave me moments of heart-thumping excitement. Then we discarded them from the reckoning. The wages of both men – whether bought or borrowed – would render us blue. As well as deeply in the red.

Saturday 21 September

'That's where we used to train, Kev … I spent four years at college there … See that estate? Just round the corner's where we used to live … ' As the coach progressed through Worthing I was winning friends and influencing people fast. Well, influencing people, anyway. My guided tour culminated in the team bus pulling up on Marine Drive. A few quick bursts of 'The old home town looks the say-hame' as I stepped down from the bus. And there we all were taking a stroll along the prom, prom, prom. The preparations for our match against Brighton are far more relaxed and, let's be candid, considerably more professional than those preceding our stuttering little promenade at Cambridge.

When we reached the Goldstone I was shocked to discover my former field of dreams is a shambles. A tip. It's run down and dingy on three sides and on the fourth derelict. Significantly there's not an advertising board in sight. The prospect is of playing in a coffin. The changing rooms and loos are worse to a possible health hazard extent. It's clear no money has been spent on basic maintenance: that this really is going to be the last season of soccer on this site. Things are past the point of no return in every sense. Where Brighton will go on to play nobody knows. Or, at any rate is saying. But there are thousands of Seagull fans who care passionately about their club's future. Vocal complaint, pitch invasions, road blocking, sit-ins and end of match demos have been regular features of recent home games. To no avail. No information has been vouchsafed. The crisis lurches from chronic to worse. Cruelly my job today is to assist in ensuring that, following their club's first home defeat of the season, the Albion fans will again be demonstrating.

In the fifth minute of the game I had the chance to plant the first nail in that coffin. Perhaps I was still weak-kneed from the warmth of the reception I'd received from the home supporters on running out. But I now proceeded to demonstrate that I'd failed to bring back with me the finishing ability that had formerly had them cheering in the past. I was put fortuitously through one on one against the keeper. Ah, here comes my 150th goal at last. What better arena to witness it than the Goldstone. A crisp ... shit! With reactions far quicker than mine second choice keeper Mark Ormerod had raced from goal to block what was less crisp chip than droopy dim sum. In a split second what would prove to be my sole chance of the game was gone.

Disappointment of a more general nature enveloped me on the final whistle. The 2–2 result marked an excellent first-half Torquay performance that we should have capitalised on to the extent of possessing a clear two-goal lead. We went in 2–1 up, true, but we'd gifted them their goal and hit the woodwork twice. In the second half we hit the bar again and missed a penalty. That (Paul Baker!) miss denied us our first away win of the season.

The result didn't seem the primary concern of many Seagull fans. Taking the trouble to give their former striker a wonderful send off first, they proceeded to don combat gear and prepared for another bout of trench warfare. Adopting battle stations is one thing. Having the clout to win the war is quite another. Looking in from outside I'd predict that the good guys are already fighting a lost cause.

Monday 23 September

The Paul Baker saga is giving every indication of building to its big finish. Six goals in 10 games has acted like a course of hormone replacement therapy on our veteran striker's career prospects. How those drums are beating! How his fee is rising! How his current coaching staff are revising upwards their laid-back pre-season response to his wish to relocate.

Shall he stay or shall he go? It's not the beating of drums this morning but the ring of a crack of working day phone call. It's from recently installed Rochdale manager Graham Barrow who's keen to establish the up-to-the-minute state of play. It's a friendly but brief conversation. The update that Mike Bateson is now looking for a £20,000 transfer fee soon reminds Graham of the phone bill Rochdale are running up.

The call leaves Hodgie and I looking at each other. There's no way of informing Paul of this latest nibble because he's training 350 miles away. But it does set us off on another spiral of reviewing the situation. We didn't – still don't – want to stand in the way of Paul getting back among his friends in the North. But pre-season, our planning perspectives made fuzzy by fantasies and under-our-noses detail alike, we hadn't reckoned on Paul making such a difference. His goals have been our means of transferring possession into points. They've given us early-day hopes of a play-off spot. And, crucially, nobody else on staff begins to look like filling his target-man boots. Let him go now and we're likely to lose not only our strike force but also our place in the top half of the table. And not even get a parking lot as compensation.

Finally, though, it's the chairman's decision. We know where he's coming from. A 20 grand lump sum safely gathered in and Paul's not insignificant salary pruned from the wages bill will look like a considerable result in the club's bank balance. In terms of future points, we could well be short-changed.

Tuesday 24 September

Tuesday of a match-free week can only mean one thing – lung-busting, heart-thumping running. Hodgie and I try to put sugar round the pill by devising exercises that involve the comfort aid of a football. But our attempt fails to quell audible speculation as to the orthodoxy of our respective births.

It's not only the squad that runs and runs. Immediately on return from training the two allegedly fatherless coaches found themselves co-opted into an impromptu meeting in the chairman's office. The Spotland phone bill can't be that big. In the face of a confirmed £20,000 quote Rochdale are maintaining a guarded interest in Paul Baker. An *immediate* deal, however, isn't that likely.

Hodgie and I seize on this. We're staring at three tough games on the trot. We express our hope that we can keep Paul for these. Mike felt this potentially played it too long; that to ask for such a moratorium would jeopardise this or any other deal and that one way or another the action could well hot up before the week's end.

Wednesday 25 September

Tonight, as Old Trafford's 50,000 roared their heroes on, I was also involved in a clash of two sides embodying the best the game has to offer ... in Devon. In front of 700.

Torquay v Exeter in the Devon Professional Bowl lived up to all that the roaring ... well, chatting ... 700 might have expected. It ended a goalless draw.

Thursday 26 September

Cost-counting exercises this morning. Last night's clash has landed us with four injuries, two of which, Paul Mitchell's and Rhys Wilmot's, are throwing dark shadows forward over Saturday.

Two further injuries tie in unhappily with the Paul Baker saga. Rodney Jack, our other (very different) goal threat has returned from his Caribbean World Cup games with a suspected stress fracture to his right foot. St Vincent and the Grenadines did most commendably well to go down to Mexico only 0–3 and then hold Jamaica to a 1–1 draw. But there's a cost to count for Rodney too. His chance in a million opportunity to go up to Newcastle and dazzle is momentarily on hold and his involvement in our own next few vital games appears highly problematic.

Paul Adcock didn't get a game last night. A foot injury sidelined him. Conjoined to his recent crisis of confidence and the probability that to replace Bakes we'll have to shave the wages bill still further, this is seriously bad timing.

Friday 27 September

Working its week-to-week miracle cures, Time has again averted the threatened injury crisis. Paul Mitchell's recovery will not affect tomorrow's starting line-up – he's on the bench. The (surgically) stitched-up Rhys Wilmot's availability, though, is of consequence. He and Ray Newland are like two figures on a weather clock, in and out in strict alternation. Ray's injuries now outweigh Rhys'. He's picked up a nagging groin injury.

With one or two other lads fending off minor knocks we kept today's session light and concise. By midday most of the squad were homeward bound.

Not Paul Baker, though. Kevin had asked him to stay on so as to apprise him of Rochdale's interest. In that ideal world some little way on beyond Plainmoor, both of us would rather have kept this news to ourselves over the weekend. Thus Paul would have stayed focused on Saturday. A worse scenario, though, was that he should learn of this latest feeler from another source.

Our instinct to play it straight was justified at once. Within minutes of our telling him, the office phone was conveying the firmed-up news that

Rochdale would stump up the fee. They would like him up there to negotiate personal terms on Monday.

With alarming alacrity it's all coming together. We've got Paul for top-drawer Carlisle tomorrow but before we visit table-topping Fulham on Tuesday, he'll be gone.

Saturday 28 September

All the way from Cumbria to Devon. Not with love in mind, though, but conquest. From all reports Carlisle are a well-drilled outfit blessed with talent and extremely dangerous at corners and free-kicks. So it proved. Riding their luck in the first half Carlisle went on in the second to deploy their tight organisation in stifling our less and less frequent, more and more desperate forays forward. Winning ever increasing possession they turned the screw on us and with it the tide. With just 10 minutes left they were given (rather than won) a corner. A perfect delivery curled directly on to the head of an utterly unmarked David Reeves. One-nil to the visitors when overall justice would say they should just be equalising. Such lines of argument were superfluous two minutes later when they worked a second classy goal.

We got one back, a Paul Baker prod in a last-gasp goalmouth scramble. While it no doubt added to his CV, it was beside the point for the side as a whole. After a draw at home, a defeat. 'Fortress Plainmoor' was yesterday's fantasy and we were down to 11th in the table.

All the same, given my long-range forecast that Mervyn Day's side is the one that will top Division Three come May, I was not too disappointed. Ahead on points for a long time we'd given them one hell of a fight.

I was, however, severely disappointed in one respect.

After nine league games I've yet to score. Actions, after all, speak louder than words. Much sooner than later someone is going to ask me when I intend leading by example.

Two tough away games next week. Fulham and Barnet. With no Paul Baker (probably) no Rodney Jack (certainly), and my own goal drought, I foresee a torridly significant seven days.

Monday 30 September

'Don't look back.' This is the sound advice every athletics coach tells his middle-distance protégé as they plot their last bend tactics.

A cardinal rule. One I've just broken.

We've now got 12 points. In a bunched league we're comfortably mid-table. We must have a big edge already over last year's chopping block Gulls. To boost my morale I begin the day looking up Torquay's record over the first six games of last season. Wrong move, Nelse.

It was as near as dammit identical to the current read-out. At the end of September '95 Torquay were mid-table with 10 points. It was as they moved into October that they really hit a rich vein of form. Well, consistent anyway. They lost eight games in a row.

Gulp. I feel a current of ice-water threading its way through my veins. There's no reason history shouldn't repeat itself. Well before the final bend the rest of the pack will come surging past ... Yes there is! Snap out of it! There's going to be every reason! That was then and this is now and we're going to do our best.

With this in mind Kevin and I led a pre-training, low-key discussion designed to avoid making a crisis out of a hiccough. The thoroughly plausible thesis was that, on reflection, last Saturday hadn't been that bad. We'd pushed arguably the best side in the division all the way; we had matched their work rate; we had certainly matched their creativity. Through our commitment to intelligent teamwork we could beat the best of the rest. Only believe.

Absent, of course, from this counselling was Paul Baker – off in brother Tom's Tardis to Spotland to dot the i's and cross the t's in the personal terms Rochdale are offering. He'll be negotiating on the front foot. As interested in the outcome as Hodgie and I, we now learn, is Mick Buxton at Scunthorpe. But one thing's for sure. There's less chance of Bakes staying at Torquay then of the Gulls winning this year's Coca-Cola.

And now we have another striking problem. Jamie Ndah enters the managerial cubicle to confirm that hamstring and thigh niggles compel him to sit out the Craven Cottage two-step. It's rearranging the deck-chairs time. We structure our practice session around this less than titanic game plan. Ellis Laight – four weeks remaining on his contract – will partner the assistant coach up front. Ian Hathaway is set to make his first starting line-up appearance in the midfield. Then another twist in the tale. Forget *Dr Who*, it's *Mr Where*. An afternoon call announces that Paul Baker has played too hard to get for Rochdale's liking. The Tardis will be materialising on the banks of the Thames tomorrow.

Tuesday 1 October

A not exactly ecstatic birthday for Carole. Breakfast in bed over and done with, she was deprived of my presence for the rest of the day – and night. A hastily arranged scouting mission taking in two Avon Insurance Combination games will keep me up in the Smoke tonight. I promise to do everything possible to make it up to her later in the week.

'Just a present will do, love,' she makes a caustic point of letting me know.

The lightest of training – some gentle stretches, a few cursory sprints – precedes our pre-travel pasta. Then it's all aboard and, as far as possible, close the mind to the joys of the open road. Missing the experience is the chairman. A batch of just-hatched open eggs at the La Manga Fledgling Maternity Ward has Matron Mike working round the clock in Intensive Care.

What he lost on the roundabouts we gained on the tow-path. A fastish run brought the coach to Putney ahead of schedule and we seized the chance to take the squad on a gentle, bonding stroll in the warm evening along the south bank of the Thames to see where the famous Touring Theatre Cricket team rendezvous. The river was at flood tide. The seasonal surge was spilling up over the embankment.

There was no hint of Thames mud about the Craven Cottage pitch but after 45 minutes of non-play we had floundered to new depths. Hit and hope balls were failing to keep our game afloat whereas Fulham, hitting measured passes through and over our midfield to the wings were breaching our defence at will. We were fortunate to go in at half-time only one goal down – a stunning volleyed strike from Rob Scott. The interval was occasion for a lot of verbal sandbagging in the Torquay changing room.

As the second half kicked off, the Thames tide was turning. So it was in our affairs as well. Upping our stroke-rate we played further up the field, pressing Fulham and closing them down. We got the ball on the floor and working harder off it, playing to feet, looked like another team as we produced our best football of the young season. All the same, as the tide ebbed, time was running out too.

Then a reward. Spurred on by several hundred vociferous Torquay fans – good on you, London Branch – Lee Barrow launched a mortar-bomb throw into the penalty box. Alex Watson saw his flick on blocked. But he had drawn two defenders and as the ball dropped it was to a

Torquay striker who swivelled through 180 degrees to smack an unstoppable shot into the top corner. As impersonations of Jurgen Klinsmann go, that wasn't half bad, the assistant coach thought. Then I was swamped by no fewer than six delirious team-mates.

'One-fifty! That's your 150th!' Paul Baker was screaming.

It was in my book. But, thanks to a Press Association's representative deciding from his perch high in the Roker Park stand some years ago that my strike had been so drastically deflected by Terry Butcher as to constitute an own goal, the bible of the *Rothmans Football Yearbook* pegged me at 148.

Who's counting? Two minutes later shrugging off the tiring 20-something defender down the wide left channel I had only the keeper to beat. Wait for it! Hard and low across him! Thus have I preached at every shooting session. NOW! ... Damn! Hard and low it was. On target ... not quite. No cheers now. Hodgie gave his sub-striker the nod to strip off. Better Laight than 'never going to get it right again' Nelse.

The finishing line was in sight as we won another throw. Lee Barrow again chanced his arm. Fulham cleared but only to an alert Steve McCall. From close to the corner flag he hooked the ball back into the box immediately. Unmarked on the far post was Nelson on 149 not out. Torquay, if not England, expected as I weighed the options. Header? The ball was begging to be attacked. No! I've always been hit and miss in the air – especially on left-wing crosses. Wait. Let it drop. NOW! ... Perfectly timed, the volley was a peach. So was Mark Walton's instinctive save. Only ... the ball was spinning from his outstretched hand. In motion that doesn't come any slower it bounced, rolled, crawled over the line. *Thunk!* A defender had booted it clear. Agony! ... And ecstasy! Happy birthday Carole! The defender's clearance had come inches too late to convince the hawk-eyed ref that the ball had not crossed the line – 150 in the book *whoever* is counting!

One further run into the channel was a run too far now. My legs were shot and so upwards shot the number 8 card. The last five minutes were exquisite torture but finally the merciful whistle blew on Torquay's first ever win at Craven Cottage. We had shown we could fight back and could beat the current best of the rest. Was it a watershed result? How many other tides had turned tonight? Whatever, the return ride westwards would now be on unbridled euphoria. Not, though, for the two human coaches.

Wednesday 2 October

No five-star luxury for the talent-spotting two. Our overnight billet is the Blackheath home of an erstwhile Valley Party candidate. A firm believer in re-incarnation, he says he'll take a rain check on the return favour until the Charlton-Torquay cup final rolls around.

A busy day in prospect offered us the early blessing of a slow start. Kick-off for the first match we would be clocking at Plough Lane was 1400 hours. Before getting down to business in SW19 we could while away a few sightseeing, socialising hours in SE7 and SE9.

First stop the born-again Valley, still bright and shiny, holding up well. Hodgie couldn't but let out an envious sigh or two at the relative grandeur of the real estate but the warm welcome of the office staff soon took the edge away. At the New Eltham training ground, however, his sense of being a 'have not' was far less easily deflected. Five perfectly surfaced training pitches. Practice balls surplus to all conceivable requirements. Two poor relations couldn't help but make odious comparison with their own country cousin set-up.

'Could be worse. They could be in the Premiership,' Hodgie tried to cheer himself up with.

It was easier for me. A series of 'All right, Nelse's?' massaged my ego very nicely, thank you lads. I couldn't avoid a slight qualm of conscience, however. Would I have been so keen to make this speedy return down memory lane if it hadn't been on the back of a fine away win and a pair of goals attributed to Nelson in the morning papers? It wasn't a problem long. Fate knows how to portion out its consequences.

'77th and 83rd minute,' Curbs said. 'If you'd still been with us, I'd have had you off hours before then.'

There's many a true word … It seemed a good moment to leave Curbs trying to pick up Charlton's broken early season pieces. As we left something clocked home in my mind. My loyalty had changed. I was driving down the same twisting service road I'd travelled at last season's end. But this time there was no sadness. Charlton were an old flame. The love of my life was now Torquay.

And an abiding hate, the South Circular. At the wheel of our 'loan' car (physio Damien's Peugeot 406) I had ample time to reacquaint myself with the route's inadequacy as we ground out the yardage across to Wimbledon and an unofficial minnow managers' convention. Crystal Palace v Brighton in the Avon Insurance Combination League Cup on the pitch. In the stand, shoulder to shoulder, Micky Adams and Alan Cork of Fulham ('Thanks for the comps, Micky. Oh, and the points!'), Pat Holland of Orient and persons unknown to me from four other London clubs.

The two very young sides set out to play a smooth, flowing, passing game. And succeeded. Quick to catch my eye were Palace's two strikers, Jason Harris and Leon McKenzie. Strong, quick, combining well, they pulled Brighton's young defenders apart. We pulled out our ballpoints and added their names to our 'could do a job' list along with those of two other prospects. Pens flashed and clicked to left and right of us. All that was lacking was some flamenco guitar.

On 70 minutes I got the curly finger. Time to go home, said Hodgie. Well, to Yate, actually, for the highly charged evening Cup encounter between the stiffs of Bristol Rovers and Swansea. Soon it was the Magic Roundabout with a vengeance – the traffic-clogged, variable speed-controlled M25.

But, making perfect time, I was ahead of the game. Here approaching fast was Junction 18 of the M4, our off-ramp. And there, glowing bright, was the flashing red battery light. Don't panic! Don't panic! Coolness personified I glided up the slip road and gently applied the brakes. With that all visual hell broke loose. The dashboard lit up like a pinball machine with the word STOP heavily featured in flashing neon.

Don't panic! Don't panic! This wasn't the optimum spot to break down. Better that chevroned area between exits. I headed for it – the car stalled. OK. Nothing behind. I turned the ignition key back on. At once we heard the banshee wail of a slipping fan-belt. It was the audio back-up to the clouds of dense smoke billowing out from the bonnet.

We panicked. Showing our quickest reactions of the week Hodgie and I baled out like Gordon Banks saving from Pele, as we dived full length into the damp roadside grass. Prostrately protecting prostates and other adjacent organs we waited for the big bang. It never came. We'd got our sums wrong. Not looking each other in the eye, like perpetrators of a two-man own goal, we picked ourselves up and approached the still smouldering saloon. From the ensuing 10-minute search for the bonnet release catch, a casual observer might now have deduced that our combined knowledge of auto-mechanics was less than comprehensive. A casual eavesdropper might have deduced from our opinions of Mr Davey's choice of vehicle and M Peugeot's conception of what constituted the drive of your life that our joint command of English idiom was total. Hodgie struck out to a local lay-by to find a phone and thereby a very nice man. So to speak.

We crossed our respective thresholds well into the small hours.

We never did get to Yate.

Thursday 3 October

A new face in the changing room. Scott Darton, now on the periphery of Gary Megson's Blackpool plans had joined us. Initially his stay will be a short one. If he impresses sufficiently, he'll become one of our five permitted loan-signings.

He couldn't have picked a better first day. Having clearly enjoyed a great trip home – no comment! – and an even better Wednesday night out, the whole squad were in top form. Our piss-taking, put-downing chat pinballed around at *Cheers* or *Drop the Dead Donkey* level. A few short months ago it had been all division and despair. Today, at least, the togetherness was complete. In the shower later somebody was singing 'Things can only get better … '

Ah. Wrong move. A grinning fate was about to administer a much profounder comeuppance than a Curbs' wisecrack.

Carole handed me the phone as I came through the door.

'Kevin,' she said.

'Yeah, hello … ?'

'We've lost Bakes.'

'He called their bluff, then. They upped their offer.'

'No. Not to Rochdale. He's gone to Scunthorpe.'

'Ah. Why the hell couldn't it have waited until Sunday?'

'I know. We'd have had him for Barnet.'

'And a whole week to look for someone else.'

'Yeah.'

Friday 4 October

A day to bring a smile to the chops of every BT fat cat. Work concentrated on two focal points. The search for a striker. The telephone.

First call of the countless was to David Jones, once a fellow alumnus of the Class of '92 Coaching Course and now manager of potent Stockport County. He has a lad in his locker we'd dearly love to net.

'Richard Landon,' I said, the niceties done, 'any chance of getting him on loan?'

Item one: Rotherham have recently made Stockport a cash offer for the not so obscure object of our desire. Item two: pending a full-bore sale David preferred keeping his man on hand as cover.

Hmmn. Maybe I should take a leaf out of the Rotherham book and make a pitch for Bristol City's Scott Partridge or David Seal. Transfer or loan, both are available … No. Not for us. Neither have the basic height. No point in targeting either as a target man. My next call is to Stoke City and in the absence of Super Lou to assistant Chic Bates. My quarry now was Keith Scott, sold on by Lou to Norwich but now out of favour at Carrow Road.

'He'll do you a job.'

Not totally conclusive. Across from me Hodgie seeks more detail to the profile with yet another call to Gary Megson.

'He'll certainly do you a job at that level,' was the ex-Norwich manager's steely-eyed reply.

'OK. We need to look at him,' Hodgie says to me. 'Where's Norwich's next reserve game?'

A brief game of hunt the fixtures through the scrap paper and fax sheets.

'Next week. Home to Arsenal.'

More time on the blower. Phil Chapple's dad looks after the ball-boys for the Canaries' reserve games. Now he can kill two birds with one stone. Mark Barham, moreover, will be more than happy to submit a shrewd second opinion.

Meanwhile it's make-do time, largely with a miraculously mended Jamie Ndah. He tells us he's fully fit and raring to go. We say 'fine' and tell him he's in for Saturday. We also tell him he needs to be up for it. He needs to perform.

One player still unable to is Paul Adcock. His foot injury is lingering on. But his contract is running out. Given Torquay's shoestring budget he's become too much of a fringe benefit. We have to tell him we won't be keeping him on.

Trying to let him down gently, Kevin suggests he gets some games under his belt at Dorchester or Bath. In the meantime, while no longer contracted to (i.e. paid by) Torquay, he's welcome to report in daily for training.

Easily the lowest point of a very up and down week. Hardworking, honest, a dedicated footballer, Adders is a smashing lad. And unlucky. It's a series of niggly injuries and, when he did play, a few costly missed 'not by much' chances that condemn him to pick up his boots and walk. A bigger club could afford to carry him until fitness, confidence and form return. Among the small fry the difference between success and failure is in some ways even finer than higher up the leagues. It's a typical 'back stage' soccer scenario – a fact that's absolutely no comfort to Paul.

Saturday 5 October

Return to the Smoke, Part II. Barnet at Underhill. Our early one o'clock arrival is in itself a mini-result. It gives me the chance to renew auld acquaintance with several blasts from the past. First the 'Silver Fox' himself, Alan Pardew, plying his trade these days as a classy lower-level libero. On the subject of barnets, Alan no longer bothers to try fooling the U-21 selectors by dying his silver locks. 'Hello' next to Linvoy Primus, a young, superbly athletic centre-half released by Charlton with a casualness bordering on criminality. These days his outstanding performances on Barnet's slope is attracting him considerable attention from the higher ones. Unlucky for some. For me. Today I'll get a first-hand impression of how far he's improved since our Happy Valley days. Three proves an Old Boy charm when personified by Lee Harrison, my goalkeeping coach Stateside this past summer. I won't have the privilege of sticking one past him (or otherwise!) today. Like a goodly number of capable keepers, the chief cross he has to handle these days is being a number 2. Word is that Barnet's hot shot-stopper Maik Taylor is turning in rave review performances.

Reunion proved to be today's sub-plot. I ran out to a *déjà ecouté* chorus of '*Oh Garry, Garry … Garry, Garry, Garry Nelson!*' I instinctively waved to the away end before I clocked that wedged in among the Torquay blue and yellow was a phalanx of red Charlton shirts. Stuck with another fixture-less weekend a score or so of Valley faithful had decided to go slumming down memory lane. Much appreciated, lads.

I wish I had a travelling fan club every week. Gratitude, nostalgia … whatever it was I came off 90 playing minutes later feeling I'd really earned my corn. Rolling back the years (Hodgie's ambivalent programme compliment!) I turned in a performance that even I could accept as measuring up. It was one of those rare days when I felt less like a journeyman and more like a game runner.

But there was a game saver at work too. Justifying his billing Maik Taylor robbed me of the winning goal with his finger tips. He did as much to thwart splendid strikes from Charlie Oatway, Jamie Ndah, Jon Gittens and Ian Hathaway. Thanks to his brilliance our excellent all-round, territorially dominant performance was rewarded with only a single point. Nevertheless, with our unbeaten away record now stretching to three games, I sense a small corner is being turned. And so, it seems, do our supporters. As I shook hands with Maik Taylor I could discern a distinct if muffled burst of *'The Gulls are going up!'* Hmmn ... There's still a lot of football to be played yet, Brian. No-one wants to tempt fate. On the other hand, if you don't dare to dream ...

Tuesday 8 October

After a day's rest and recuperation the rescue mission, the search for our '20 goal, cost-nothing' striker, resumes. No sooner was I into my training kit than it was finger-warming exercises. The first combination of key pad digits gave me a clear line through to Mel Machin's operations room at Bournemouth.

This week's main target, Keith Scott, had an eight-game run at Dean Court last season and I was seeking feedback on his performance. The ungrudgingly given assessment was that at Torquay's relatively modest level he could, yes, do a job for us. It's beginning to sound like the standard party line. Hmmn... Our scouts get the go signal to stake Scott out tomorrow night at Carrow Road. Simultaneously in place will be our East Midlands agent. Barry Fry has just sought to stiffen the resolve in his stiffs by terrifying them. He's airwaved a fax announcing they're all up for sale. Well ... he's only done 12 deals this past fortnight. It could be just a cunning plan, though, to ensure a capacity crowd at London Road.

I doubt if there'll be one at Clevedon tomorrow. But Hodgie and I will be there – as will Scott Partridge and David Seal. A call to Joe Jordan has confirmed they'll both be on the auction block tomorrow. Scouting is certainly one way of seeing the world. The small world.

Later comes news it's hard to know how best to react to. One player we now know we won't be signing is Carlisle's match winner David Reeves. He's moving to Preston. For £300,000. That's just under a third of a million more than we've got to spend. My first response is to sigh and go back to thumbing the pages of our increasingly loose-leafed *Rothmans Football Yearbook*. Then, though, I put myself in Mervyn Day's probable shoes. We've lost Bakes. He's losing an even more potent striker. Are Carlisle shooting themselves in the foot with an even bigger calibre shell than Torquay? It'll be interesting watching their immediate form.

Our own reserves' game this week was tonight. Against Taunton Town. It represented the last throw of the dice for Paul Adcock and one of his diminishing last few for Ellis Laight. A glittering display might yet set their feet back on the path to glory, glory. Sadly, the 1–0 win was memorable only for the celebratory dance of 17-year-old Leon Hapgood following his sweetly struck fifth minute goal. The rest was absolutely average.

Scott Darton's contribution was polished enough. He has an exquisite left foot. But the hard truth is that he doesn't give us any more than we already have. The best offer we can make, we tell him, is to monitor his progress over the next couple of months.

Wednesday 9 October

A rest day. For the reserves to get over last night's stresses and strains. For the privileged first-teamers the chance to get over the shocks to the system of their first formal 'social' evening, held last night.

'What a life!' I hear people saying. 'What a bunch of skiving, free-wheeling, don't know they're born playboys! Just look at them! A couple of hours a day training and an hour and a half's work Saturdays. It's taking money under false pretences!'

To all such foaming at the mouth I'm bound to say it's not that simple. I won't call for the defense such witnesses as the eight-hour coach trips there and back, the eight-year (on average) career spans and – then what? Cripple-kneed middle-age? All of this might be thought to deserve occasional compensation. Let's just keep the argument short term and pragmatic.

All professional athletes need to tread a careful path between sustaining optimum fitness and becoming burnt-out physical wrecks. Too many sportsmen and women leave their best performances on the training track or ground, the practice ring, courts or nets. Just recall how many world class performers appeared in the Atlanta Olympic's arena strapped up before they'd been so much as called to their marks. Think back to how many broke down while competing.

There, mark you, were competitors with the luxury of needing to build for just one specific occasion. Intense mental pressure betrayed some, at least, into the most simplistic of fallacies (the one shared by so many thousands of mediocre executives): 'The harder I train, the better I'll be. If I train the hardest, I'll be the best.'

Any class trainer or trainee knows there's more to it than that. Rest is a key element in maintaining equilibrium as tissues rebuild, minds relax. For English soccer players faced with 50-plus match schedules in a contact sport, rest, sanctioned rest, is as essentially positive as positively essential.

On a lower level of calculation it can also be said that soccer managers find the rest day a highly motivational tool. It can be a reward-cum-bribe for a good performance. It can be a punishment (the day off denied) when players let themselves down. No punitive measures have so far been called for at Torquay. On the other hand, we've been comparatively generous with our days off. Always the question of balance. But in the sense that every manager and coach wants his players to be willing to die for him, I'd say we seem to be getting it about right. We seem to have motivated a side that at the end of last season had all the commitment of an MP expected to pay his own way in Harrods.

Instead I saved my gripes for Peterborough. They've put a tag of £150,000 on Sean Farrell. Worth every penny according to our scout's glowing assessment. This being so clearly the case, however, there's no way that even a manager who chops and changes real players as if they were Panini cards would let him out to us for a month. Barry Fry knows that Torquay could never stretch to a cash deal, signing-on fee included, come D-day.

One down, two to go. Bristol City Reserves v Oxford United Reserves. Animal magic time as it's eyes down to clock City's 9 and 10, Messrs Seal and Partridge. David Seal notched two goals but in my book lacked sufficient appetite for the game. Scott Partridge's classy, hard-working performance was in evident contrast.

Unusually for two scouts in regulation uniform Hodgie and I went the full distance. Kevin wanted a quick word with *de facto* counterpart Joe Jordan.

'How much for Scottie Partridge?'

'I'd have to speak to my directors, Kevin. But it won't be a lot.'

'OK ... Could you get back to me tomorrow?'

'Sure.'

Back home to a still warm video tape and a player we won't be bothering to pursue. England 2, Poland 1. Carrying on where he left off in Euro '96 Alan Shearer added two more classy finishes to his England collection. That was the difference. Outplayed between the penalty areas, our brave lads were distinctly lucky to take all three points from a more polished Polish side that was technically better by some way.

A novel question in an England context comes to mind. Are we actually over-doing the build-up routine? Our international squad now seems to have buckets of time to prepare collectively. They spend hour upon hour on the training ground working at tactics, free kicks. But the performance is still below par. Chief obvious difference is the superior manner in which most of our serious opposition pass the ball under pressure. Still, 2–1, Des. Never mind the quality, feel the result.

Thursday 10 October

Drove to work today with that 'up' feeling of anticipation we can sometimes get. I could sense a heady day of wheeling and dealing. Of something decisive being accomplished. It still lingered as Kevin and I set out to re-rearrange the deckchairs on our master-plan.

Brring – brring.

The chairman. He was just calling to appraise us of the surprise packet among his many morning mail missives. Strictly speaking there should have been no need. Transfer requests are supposed to be submitted in duplicate. Technically Hodgie should have been able to join Mike Bateson for a bout of synchronised swearing as he opened his own letter. The chairman's letter, though, had been hand-delivered. Instead of Postman Pat it had been wing-back Scott apparently lacking the postage. Soon, possibly, we'll all be short of Stamps.

A shock. Hastily we called a meeting to put the obvious question to Scott.

'Why?'

'Personal problems back home.'

A fair enough answer. One we wouldn't dream of gainsaying or ignoring. Family pressures can so often be pole position laws unto themselves. All the same, whether coming through the mail or personally delivered, the request's timing was unquestionably too early in the day. Although capable of some very tasty moments, Stampsie will have to play with a great deal more consistency to earn a move. Request politely denied. Dutch uncle fashion, however, we let him know that should the family problems continue to impact on him adversely then, for everyone's benefit, we'd think sympathetically about circulating his availability throughout the League.

Short term this seemed to remove much of the heavy and, I'm sure, genuine weight from his slender shoulders. Thanking us, he left Hodgie and me two on one with the chairman. Kevin quickly brought us up to collective speed.

'We all agree that Scott Partridge would be a great addition to the playing staff. Joe Jordan wants a fee but if we can recoup some of that by selling Ian Hathaway to Exeter, we'd like to bring him in.'

'I'll phone Peter Fox to see what he feels about that,' Mike Bateson said. 'Sean Farrell's a definite 'no, no'. They want 100 grand. But the Bury chairman's been on about Phil Stant.'

'We'd only want him for a month,' Hodgie says.

'I'll see what their chairman thinks. Let's speak again after training.'

Off we went – working seriously hard *en route* at switching brains into eye-on-the-ball focus. All these possible scenarios might be buzzing about in our squad-strengthening minds but a bird in the hand – we mustn't let them endanger what we already had. Back to the basics and proper preparation for Saturday's game. Beginning with a shock-to-the-system running session – 'that'll balance up your extra rest day!' – we modulated into a practice match.

As I reeled off their names the players came forward for their bibs. Red for the superstars, white for the also-rans. In my mind we'd be fielding the same team against Hereford as drew at Barnet. I'd completely forgotten the fact that previous ever-present Steve McCall was injured last Saturday. On automatic pilot I handed his temporary replacement Mark Hawthorne a bib whiter than the driven cross.

It's nice to know you're wanted. Mark, he of the hopping-mad body language and steam-venting ears was less than enchanted by my gigantic *faux pas*. I was nowhere near fast enough upgrading him. When he did finally don Steve's red bib, Mark clearly felt that he and everyone else had been told of his precarious access to on-going first-team glory in the worst possible way. What a ricket for me of all people to drop! How often have I been in the identical position? Non-position. I knew exactly what he was feeling but that didn't lessen his discomfort any more than mine. Garry Nelson ace man-manager! He might have the red bib but I was the one with the red face.

On our return to Plainmoor it was clear that Mark's Saturday midfield berth was secure. We wouldn't need to make room for new talent.

Joe Jordan was unavailable and the price on Scott Partridge's head still therefore an unknown. The Bury chairman was similarly incommunicado. One call that had been returned was from Mark Barham rave-reviewing Norwich's Keith Scott. His goal against Arsenal's second strings had been the cherry on the top of a good all-round performance. I was reaching for the Carrow Road number while still saying goodbye to Mark. In vain. John Faulkner, Mike Walker's number two, told me that the natives had been no less impressed. Keith Scott was a yellow bird no longer licensed to spread his wings.

On the drive home, that sunny morning sense of positive anticipation seemed light years away. This evening's moorland gloom was far more appropriate.

Friday 11 October

Those stage-managed gab-fests, the annual political party conferences are about to erupt at various of England's coastal towns. Why should Torquay be left out? Hodgie and I decided on a conventional approach to today. We began with a fringe meeting on the Ian Hathaway issue.

Ian was told of Exeter's interest yesterday. What we now asked was whether, after sleeping on it, he wanted to cross the floor or stay loyal to the blue and yellow. He said that one look at Exeter's standing in the Division Three polls had convinced him that he was better off where he was – particularly as he was now no longer a side-bencher but a regular fixture in the Torquay team of all talents.

We now went into main session with that very team. Rally the faithful time. New attitude, new Torquay. We laboured the importance of the next two home games. It would all prove to have been pointless putting in so much effort getting things right on the road if we followed up with displays in front of our own fans so disappointing as to leave us ... pointless.

Conferences always OD on audio visual aid crap. We were more functional. A simple handwritten information sheet this time reminded the squad of our own collective strengths. We'd got as far by virtue of work-rate, togetherness, defending well as a team, maintaining a good yet flexible shape, hitting our stride from the first whistle. Above all we'd built an excellent team spirit. What we now needed in addition was still more belief and self-confidence. Given that, we could go back to our constituencies and prepare for promotion.

Not quite a 13-minute (orchestrated) standing ovation. But again, a visible heads up atmosphere. Conference now passed a resolution delegating the leadership to inform the chairman that an extra £3 million to punt around the transfer market wouldn't go amiss either. The leadership was constrained to point out the chairman wasn't party to any foreign investments.

And if we had that sort of money, would we be? Faustino Asprilla, who cost Newcastle not only £6 million but also arguably the Premiership title, has gone walkabout on his way back from Columbia to the frozen banks of the Tyne. Tomas Brolin has declared that he prefers retirement to ongoing durance vile at Elland Road. Andrea Silenzi looks set to slip silently out of the City Ground's side door *en route* to Venezia of Serie B.

Three examples drawn from the long list balancing the Ravanelli, Bjornebye, Bilic success stories. There's always an element of Russian roulette every time you buy a Kanchelskis or a Kulkov. On hearing of the latest highly priced, excessively salaried overseas 'acquisition' I always ask myself how many young UK professionals have been consigned to the scrap-heap to subsidise the deal.

Saturday 12 October

'Dad! Dad! Wake up!'

'Huh … ?'

'Can you put Sky Sports on?!'

Saturday morning becomes prime time courtesy of an international talent contest. Man U v Liverpool. Fifty-six thousand paying customers were but a drop in the ocean to the countless viewers based at home and delighted at this excuse for foregoing the weekly visit to Homebase.

Fully awake, I was soon finding the electronic spectacle rivetingly motivating. The quality on show was breathtaking at times. Precise one-touch passing despite the intensest of close-quarter marking had me drooling. 1–0 to the Red Devils. Manchester United were the better cracksmen – just – when it came to prising open a defence with a through ball.

After the morning's warm-up bout, the main event – Torquay v Hereford. But first I had to get Chris to school. He was rendezvousing there to catch the school bus. Along with 40 of his class mates he was a guest for the day of Plainmoor's Football in the Community programme.

The shrieking cherubs had scarcely put backside to seat before they had a goal to savour. So much for pre-match resolutions to defend tightly and start brightly. A minute gone and Dad's army were a goal down. Signed *just this week* (lucky for some) my ex-Argyle team-mate Nicky Law had Big Bertha'd a throw into our penalty area that, to the neglect of their duties, sent most of our defenders scrambling for chicken-hearted cover. Nineteen minutes later and Chris' proxy celebrity status and street-cred stood at zero. In a freeze frame moment of acute hesitation his father's belated strike foozled away a gilt-edged chance to equalise. The visiting keeper's reactions were far keener.

We were three minutes into first half injury time before I could breathe a little easier. Alex Watson's finely executed sharp-shot – that's the way to do it! – at last brought the Chudleigh Primary Scholars to their feet.

The woeful second half was, alas, no object lesson for youngsters. The morning's televised master-class was civilisations away as Torquay and Hereford both fell into the non-rhythm of huff and puff, blow by blow football. One landmark, though, did shine through this wasteland. We did manage a classic goal. Astute McCall pass to Nelson; a lightning turn and whipped in cross to a Stevie Winter leaping like a salmon to pick an unreachable spot for his unstoppable header. A 22-carat goal worthy of winning better games than today's but just the gem you'd want to treasure as your first ever League goal.

Our fifth win of the season and it takes us up to the dizzy heights of fifth in the table. Never mind the quality ...

The prize for Man of the Match was a bottle of scotch.

'What a great choice,' I whispered to the chairman as I collected it. 'Scotch I mean. Not so sure about the player. I don't think the sponsors are the best of judges.'

'Cheeky git,' he said at once. 'The sponsors pulled out yesterday. I was the one who picked you.'

'Fancy a drink?' I heard myself saying.

A second exchange in the bar pleased me more. I was approached by a supporter long (suffering) in possession of a season ticket.

'You're getting there,' he said. ' Last year if we'd gone a goal down in the first minute we'd have folded.'

I muttered something suitably modest but a warm glow lit up the spot he'd hit. Running the bastards into the ground, giving them days off, gagging about with Micky Mouse yellow jerseys ... Balance. Somewhere in there we might be in danger of getting it right.

Monday 14 October

Fifth in the table. The Division Three table. We're still among the English game's poor relation also-rans – a status of which, exposed to the autumn's first serious cold and rain on a South Devon headland, we are now feelingly reminded. Our one-off training kit is still all we're stood up in. We've no club issue wet tops; no leg-covering bottoms. It's freeze your butt off time. And likely to be for many another day given the drenching nature of West Country winters. It's also false economy time. If as the result of a pull sustained during cryogenic training conditions we lose one key man for just one game, the money begrudged for protective kit will be money ill-saved. We could, of course, bring along our own. That, though, will have us mustering on parade in the guise of the raggedest-arsed army since Woodstock. Not a recommended recipe for fostering group morale

The only immediate remedy for the chill circumstances is a progressively more taxing warm-up. That's a crowd pleaser too! I take the curse off it to some extent by joining the ranks and working as hard as anyone. This politically motivated involvement, though, only points up another negative. I'm not feeling my best. I'm tired in general and there's a distinct niggle in my foot. Before the day is out I lay me down for a physio session from Damien Davey now firing on all cylinders again after the fitting of a new alternator to his 406.

This isn't a case of the boss pampering himself. We've got Doncaster tomorrow and are struggling to field a side who all have first-team experience. Jamie Ndah – durability is not the word that springs to mind on mention of the name – is a definite non-starter. Rodney Jack is fit to play – sort of. We'll have to risk him. A left-handed benefit of his returning to us from the Caribbean with a foot injury is that we were able to tell St Vincent last week he was not fit enough to rejoin their squad – already unable to qualify for the next World Cup qualifying stage – without crossing our fingers.

Tuesday 15 October

D-Day. D for Doncaster. The Chinese whispers are that they're low on confidence of late – particularly after the *pas de deux* 90 minutes before a Saturday kick-off which saw Sammy Chung elbowed aside to make way for Kerry Dixon. We need the three points from a home game but I don't think I'm projecting my own misgivings onto the squad in privately sensing that our collective battery is close to being flat. The gleam in our eye is in danger of fading away. Perhaps it's adjusting our sights from big to diminutive striker that we're finding so draining.

On the night we carried on from where we'd left off on Saturday. In two respects. Our performance, to put it flatteringly, was dire. Once again we won thanks to a second Stevie Wonder – sorry, Winter – goal. Having discovered the way and acquired the taste, long may he nurture the habit.

With 20 minutes still to go I acquired something I could better do without – a personal concern to go with my coach's worry over our lacklustre form. Nobody's fault but I came out of a challenge, a brush of bodies with a distinct tug and persistent low-level pain in a groin muscle. I've had it before and it usually costs me at least one missed game.

Doncaster showed a spirit and determination that viewed a day or two hence will considerably encourage their new supremo. Immediately, though, our genuinely sympathetic pats on the back and 'well played, you deserved better' compliments will have offered no comfort for Kerry and his crestfallen players on the pointless trek back to Yorkshire.

Wednesday 16 October

Woke up this morning staring two sets of statistics in the face. They respectively grinned and grimaced at me like the masks that traditionally represent the theatre.

The comic one was, alas, the more superficial. The figures now show that after 13 games Torquay have already managed more wins this season than they registered last year from 46. So far, let's cautiously say, so relatively good.

More serious and, alas, threatening to be more permanent too, are the home gates statistics. The trend is clearly downwards. Yesterday wasn't a dark and stormy night but it was wet and windy. Only 1,800 souls were hardy enough to venture forth to Plainmoor. That's 200 down on last Saturday's unsatisfactory gate.

Of course we're looking at a mid-week match here. People come home from work (those who have it) tired and to find other demands on their time – homework, Guides, baby-sitting, whatever. But also demanding their mid-week attention is TV's blanket coverage of top soccer. For mid-week matches, its main victim, it's become a wet blanket indeed. Given the choice between a 'live' game and a real-life game, potential spectators in their thousands are taking the easy option of voting with their index finger on the remote. You would have thought that overcrowded as the commercially driven fixture list has become, the Football League and the FA could have liaised with each other and their European counterparts to offset the humble Division Two and Three fixtures to some extent from those of the big-boy clashes.

Not that I'm sure this would help too much. Access to blanket television soccer pre-supposes a Sky hook-up. That, at Torquay rates, works out at roughly the price of three turnstile admissions a month. I can see why, worn out after a hard working day at office, factory or job centre, many of our would-be spectators go not only for the less labour intensive but also the pre-paid option.

Thursday 17 October

Just two items on today's Torquay agenda. First we've only got 10 players with first-team experience likely to be fit for Saturday. Definitely missing will be G Nelson. As I'd predicted the groin strain is still too sore for me to move freely. Second: we've got Wigan away on Saturday. The two factors don't dovetail happily. Currently disputing the leadership of our division with Fulham, Wigan have a 100 per cent home record. Springfield Park these days is a very tough fortress to storm. Further, if any side is, Wigan are the aristocrats of the division. Surprisingly their chairman, David Whelan, is an ex-pro player (with Blackburn). Even more surprisingly, given that previous, he's a multi-millionaire. Rumour has it that his personal holding in his sports goods empire is worth better than £300 million. A smidgen of this has rubbed off on the Latics who have not only a canny manager in ex-Norwich stalwart John Deehan but a very competent and experienced nucleus to their side in such 'names' as Wayne Biggins and Gavin Johnson. As further salt in our own wounds is their acquisition of Doncaster's clearly upwardly mobile striker, Graeme Jones, in the close season – a snip, spies say, at £150,000.

Then again … we've got 10 men.

Unable to exercise much more than my dialling pinkie, I work on trying to redress the balance via another round of manager's blind-date. Forest's Stephen Guinan is said to be not only 6ft 1 but also skilful with it. Word is that he can possibly be prised loose from Frank Clark's clutches for a loan period. Steve McCall checks talent coordinates with John McGovern, who, until sacked by Rotherham was after him, and

David Phillips who has played with him. Both endorse the rumours positively. On Forest's form, though, can Frank Clark afford any generosity?

Currently flying, albeit two divisions lower, are Brentford. Their Joe Omigie is also tipped as able to make a fist of things up front. Figuratively speaking. The chairman follows up on this one. All he learns is that when a lad is rated, possession is nine-tenths of the loan. Omigie figures in David Webb's plans.

Friday 18 October

My groin strain is still giving me faint but persistent grief. Maybe I'll make tomorrow's bench. Maybe. Training today will be brief and to the pre-match point but if short, sharp. No way I'm taking part. I'll leave it to an ultra-late fitness test up in Wigan before making a final decision on whether to try eking out our human resources. Today the most positive thing I can do is to brief those players on how they'll be deployed at Springfield Park. We're going with Ellis Laight up front as a lone ranger. In a sense his role will be to keep both Wigan's central defenders occupied. Tucked in behind him will be Rodney Jack and Ian Hathaway. Licensed to roam, their mission is to come forward and through whenever opportunity, please God, presents itself. High balls to the back stick are out. If we're going to have any chance tomorrow it's got to be on the ground and to feet. At worst into open channel space.

Saturday 19 October

An overnight in Lancashire might have made a vital difference today. Certainly our 8.30 am departure by coach was a miscalculation. We hadn't built the density of Saturday morning traffic into the travel equation. I had plenty of opportunity to go over the subtler tactical implications of our modified formation as we sat jammed in the vicinity of the notorious Thelwall Viaduct.

By 2 pm two things were now crystal clear. I had no chance of undergoing an 11th hour fitness test at 1.30 pm. When in doubt, don't. I wouldn't be involved today. More ominously, still, we had no chance of making it to Springfield Park before the 2.15 pm deadline for the handing in of the team sheet. But not to panic. The invention of the mobile phone had been made with us in mind.

Alex Watson had gone up ahead of us to spend the night with relatives. He was consequently pacing the away dressing room in nervous solitary splendour when our SOS got through to him. Ever reliable, he meticulously pencilled all the right names into all the right places and then sprinted to the ref's room.

The coach got to the ground at 2.25 pm – less than an ideal touch down for a three o'clock kick-off. Did it cost us? You never know, do you, with football. What is certain is that rushing through their changing room rituals the team went out all unbalanced in a muck sweat and delivered a brilliant performance.

We not only stood toe to toe with Wigan in commitment but also matched them brain cell to brain cell. It was quality stuff. Twice Graeme Jones, the £150,000 signing, struck with well taken goals. Each time, however, not buckling, we battled and outwitted our way back with no less impressive strikes from Rodney Jack and Ellis Laight. The clock was ticking down. We'd earned, it seemed, a valuable point against the odds. Their 100 per cent home record was on the point of being surrendered. Then Wigan were awarded a dodgy (honest!) free kick. It was pumped high into our box. We headed it clear. Back it came to the far post. Upwardly mobile and unchallenged as he completed his hat-trick and took his personal tally for the season to 12 was that man again, Graeme Jones. In the 89th minute. For agonising seconds everything was bedlam – and despair. I couldn't believe it but I'd known all along it would happen. I took my head out of my hands. There not 30 feet from our silent, numbed dug-out cavorted John Deehan, naturally quite delirious with joy and punching the air in triumph. In the midst of his ecstasy he caught my eye. His arms relaxed, spread into a shrug and his look, old pro to old pro, said it all: 'Sorry mate, you didn't deserve that.'

As the coach bore on down the motorway, I was at private pains to point out to Mike Bateson that the difference on the day had been Wigan's possessing a £150,000 finisher up front.

'I thought you were supposed to be ours,' he came back with right away.

Quick, I thought, but his arithmetic's way out.

Sunday 20 October

Melt-down threat to the National grid again. Newcastle v Man U. The Geordies' drubbing in the Charity Shield still an open wound, Keegan's last season tirade against Ferguson's style still a living memory, revenge, pride, intent to dominate the Premiership were circling hostilely around before today's kick-off.

In the event it was to become a day of joy for Manchester United's legion of non-supporters. Avoiding all their usual banana skins – perhaps Mark Lawrenson had hoovered them away – Newcastle got everything right. Wave upon wave of their Cavalier surges set Ferguson's New Model Roundheads back on their heels. Few sides can have played as well as United in losing so heavily. Ginola looked as much at home again on grass as on a catwalk. Robert Lee was prodigious in weaving together all the potentially loose ends of individual Magpie flair. And while Philippe Albert's goal will not prove to be the best of the season, it will certainly be the wittiest.

The Reds had conceded five goals without reply. All of their haloes had slipped but one of their number had elbowed his right into touch. Shackled into anonymity by the same Albert, Eric Cantona increasingly opted for a 'No more Mr Nice Guy' role as the going got tougher. He was lucky not to see more red than was increasingly misting his eyes over. One tackle went unnoticed by the possibly unsighted referee but was as gross as it was evident to the millions of other viewers. More of a give-away still was the sly chop at his Belgian gaoler. It was calculatedly surreptitious – a professional foul of the most cheap-skate order. Grace under pressure comes easy when there is no pressure. Now that it was unrelenting, Manchester's Frenchman could only muster petulance.

A great fall. You have to wonder whether Newcastle today severed the spinal cord of United's confidence. If they have, then, in one respect at least, it is an ill-timed pity. After Wednesday's excellent performance in beating Fenerbahce 2–0 away, United promised to have come of European age. Perhaps so much flattered, they now feel themselves deceived. As will others. Going to school tomorrow tens of thousands of long-range, fair weather United supporters will discover their shrill 10-year-old's complacency shattered to fragments. That can't be bad for grassroots football in this country. The Torquay Club Shop may even sell a couple of shirts this week.

Monday 21 October

Video nasty day. Not in the Old Trafford boardroom but at Plainmoor. I play through Wigan's last-gasp winner over and over again. Repetition doesn't ease the pain. Nor is it any consolation, happy though I am for him, that we face training without Rodney Jack. He's flown north to join in the Tyneside carnival. He's sure of one result already. Whatever its outcome, he won't spend his trial week washing his own kit.

Tuesday 22 October

Video nasty: the sequel. I convene a meeting made up of the back five and Rhys Wilmot. The purpose isn't to yell a lot and apportion blame. In that last minute Saturday horror two of our central defenders went for the same ball while the third, arm aloft, stepped up to put Wigan offside and then found himself a Pied Piper with no-one in tow. No wonder Graeme Jones was unmarked. The object of today's trial is to prevent any similar gifting of a goal rendering meaningless all the skill and effort we put into the other 89 minutes of the game. One training ground exercise will be mandatory this week. We'll be working on the defenders pushing out in a line – establishing to what point they advance, whose responsibility it is to give the 'get out!' call. It's fundamental. We may play out of our skins going forward but 19 times out of 20 conceding three goals is to guarantee defeat.

On a much broader front, if certain papers are to be believed, a different sort of defensive line is being organised. If I were to believe some of the more outrageous press coverage, I should be grabbing the nearest placard and marching off to picket the Lytham St Annes offices of – *hiss! boo!* – the Football League.

Not necessary. Not yet, anyway. To date there is no unresolvable industrial dispute between said League and the body representing on the park players, the Professional Footballers Association. All that has so far transpired is the declaration of the result of a referendum conducted among its members by the PFA. The question wasn't whether players were in favour of across the board strike action (i.e. ceasing to play Division One, Two and Three football) but merely, modestly, were they in favour of pulling the plug on *live television coverage* of Nationwide League games. The returned ballot papers gave the PFA's astute secretary, Gordon Taylor, a 90 per cent 'yes' response.

What is at issue is, as always, money. Renegotiated broadcasting rights have recently led to Sky TV making a hugely enhanced multi-million pound contribution to Football League revenues. In turn, the PFA feels it has every right to expect that a reasonable percentage of this windfall be passed on to contribute to the well-being of those who actually make up the game.

The PFA is not only literally a benevolent organisation but a farsighted one as well. Membership costs players approximately a quid a week. In return they gain – and they're largely youngsters, remember, many of them only tokenly schooled – subsidised educational courses, vocational training and (possible source of grievance to Football League boardrooms) contractual advice. Like many another union the PFA offers a channel to competitively priced pension schemes, insurance cover of all kinds and financial services. More than his former clubs, more than the fans, the PFA has helped many a forgotten player keep the wolf from the door in later life. But as more and more pros take advantage of its range of benefits its running costs continue to rise.

The PFA's concept of a 'modest percentage' of the Nationwide/Sky TV money is 10 per cent. In the age of Eric Hall, Cedric Brown and Rupert Murdoch this is incontrovertibly just.

Not everyone connected to soccer thinks so. The Football League and boardrooms generally argue that the players and their association receive 'ample' incomes already: why should they be allocated more? I can't help but think that such a viewpoint is argued because the PFA claim coincides with many clubs' obsession of grabbing more and more from the pot so they can turn right around and spend, spend, spend it on over-valued and over-paid superstars.

This is only round one. Today the Football League. Tomorrow the Premiership. As TV deals promise (i.e. threaten) to grow even larger – a European Super-League: what prime-time viewing that will make for Ford, Levi's and Pepsi! – the PFA will be forced to fight their corner over and over again.

For the moment the corner is safe. Almost certainly as a result of the players' solidarity the two camps seem to have reached a mutually satisfactory settlement. A bigger crumb from the League's table will keep PFA players on the tube.

For which relief much thanks. I very much fear that any long-running dispute will ultimately grievously impact on those the PFA is working hardest to serve – its members.

At Torquay as throughout the lower leagues money from whatever source is always gratefully received. The firm conviction that the divvy-up of Sky TV money is disproportionately weighted in favour of those who need it least and waste it most does not detract from the value of such monies as the minnows do receive. In the day-to-day battle for financial survival every pound counts.

This is highlighted for me at every home game by that disturbing (given that we're doing so much better than a year ago) fall in Plainmoor gates. We've already had to engage in some squad trimming, I foresee more. Right now a fifth of our players are on nothing more secure and confidence-aiding than month to month contracts. They watch the attendance figures too. That their career prospects are under constant, renewable threat is no recipe for long-term success.

It's virtually a vicious circle. What money we can get is welcome. More would be nice. But overwhelmingly the major source of the money is television. Overwhelmingly it is television's live coverage of the game that accounts for our dwindling crowds. If we are to have the one, then, sadly, it seems we may have to do without the other. Perhaps, after all, we should turn the cameras off while we're still able to produce a few home-grown talents.

Wednesday 23 October

Having strutted their stuff on paper, trialists from the length and breadth of the country and ranging from ages 16–26 made their way to Plainmoor this week. From Scotland, from London, from wherever, 70 wannabe's travelled not only in hope but also, be it well understood, at their own expense. They were purchasing the chance to strut their stuff on our pitch, to set out their wannabe stalls under the shrewd eye of Steve McCall. Three trial games were played.

If many had come, few were chosen. The overall standard was not so much depressing as awful. The vast majority utterly failed to live up to the five-star publicity of their own CVs. When at close of play Macca consulted with his assistants it was decreed that, for the purposes of closer inspection, just three of the hopefuls should be offered a week-long trial in the company of our first-team squad. Still at their own expense, you realise. Since the prospect of cut-backs in that self-same squad is a growing possibility, the chances of any of these Johnny-come-latelies ever scrawling their signatures across a blue Football League contract seems remote to the point of impossible. But equally, given our own poverty, we can't afford not to nurture our own dream that we might, just might, turn up an uncut diamond.

And the unmagnificent 67? We always recommend purchase of a return ticket. They will have used it to transport themselves and their newly acquired small deaths of the heart back to the same wherever. On that long drawn-out haul they will have stared out not at the landscape but the grey downer of anonymous reality. The rain that swept down on the Riviera as they left will have washed away the last of their dreams. We weren't even able to bung them a few readies to take back to the day job. You have to feel for them. Some will come to derive great pleasure from the beautiful game as they play in the local park on Sunday. But many won't. Blinded by the prospect of glory they won't have the inner resource to bounce back. When you've been steamrollered by Newcastle five-nil, football can be tough at the top. It's a bloody sight tougher at the bottom.

Whither we may be returning if we can't conjure up that do-the-business striker. We may have plenty of nothing but it's time for another shopping expedition – this time down the Ninian Park mall. Via the impressive second Severn Crossing (I was impressed that it saved us a gallon of petrol) we arrive in the land of perpetual throat-clearing to see Cardiff City's stiffs take on Southampton.

The view from the bridge was better than from the stand. Cardiff won a dreadful game 1–0. As for our star-trekking – although we did note the name of Danny Wallace lookalike Frankie Bennett – we will have to boldly go on looking for our man in still remoter galaxies.

Friday 25 October

Less than doom but certainly gloom to begin the working day. Forest's Stephen Guinan won't be coming to Torquay: certainly not in time for tomorrow's game against Swansea and probably not for the foreseeable future. Well, put the kettle on. Things can only get ...worse. As they immediately do. A rap at the door is followed by Jon Gittens entering and minimising the office elbow-room. His manner is utterly civilised but the message borders on the bare-knuckle.

His joining Torquay has all been a mistake. He's unhappy here. The club lacks proper ambition. On his new, much reduced Torquay salary he can't keep his family in the style to which they've become accustomed. He'd like, pretty please, to go on the transfer list.

It was all but a knock-out blow. Gamely Hodgie staggered to his conversational feet somewhere about the count of eight. No ambition! We were in a play-off position, he said (making no mention of players let go and fruitless expeditions to replace them), and looking to climb higher. Nobody had played a bigger role on the field in getting us where we'd got to than Jon. I was sitting there wondering whether Jon had been tapped and knowing that Hodgie was wondering too and knowing that Jon knew that we both knew that he knew we were wondering. He never dropped the slightest hint that he'd been approached.

'I've made a mistake,' he repeated.

There was something else too. Something he didn't care to voice was most definitely troubling him, I was sure. But… what …?

This *could be* a 'call my bluff' poker game whose hidden agenda was to raise the stake Jon holds in the club; to increase his wages. Any such upgrading would require the drawing up of a new contract, and a new contract automatically has to be couched in terms of an extra year's tenure. *That* would take Jon up past the age of 35, the career stage at which pro soccer players qualify for a pension. Hmmn …

As so often in cases like this, a short-term compromise was agreed. There would be a 'sleep on it' period of two weeks. Then, since we wouldn't wish to stand in the way of a disgruntled player we would allow his name to be circulated.

He was not the only player to feel less than gruntled this morning. Fines for having been booked figured prominently on today's agenda. At the going rate of 10 per cent of basic wage they were levied for verbal or body-language dissent and for being cautioned. The chairman had already notified Ian Hathaway, Scott Stamps and Charlie Oatway that, subject to appeal, their pay packets would be easier to pick up this week.

Only Stampsie waived the right to protest. The Fines Committee of Wilmot (PFA rep), Watson (captain), Gittens (senior pro), Hawthorne (representing the young pros), Hodges, Nelson, McCall and Bateson sat in serious judgment that lasted a good half-hour.

The findings were that Oatway's fine would be suspended but that, guilty of peevishly kicking the ball away, Ian Hathaway must suffer the full rigour of the law.

As playing staff clocked out for the day the coaches sat down with the chairman. At last an upbeat topic surfaced. Mike Bateson told us he'd been in discussion with Newcastle about Rodney Jack. They had made an initial offer of around £250,000 which long-term add-ons could eventually increase significantly. He, though, was in no rush to accept; further, there were work permit complications. D of E officials would expect Rodney to feature in at least 75 per cent of Newcastle's first-team games – clearly impossible to guarantee in the context of a team that had just thrashed Man U and a sport that had just seen Tony Coton crippled out for at least the rest of the season. Immediate upshot was that Rodney would be flying back to the sticks to play against Swansea tomorrow.

Another striker briefly on the simultaneous move is Andy Saville, goal-scoring architect of Preston's promotion push last season but now out of first-team favour. A Gary Peters fax had today circulated his availability and, clutching at it along with his other straws, Hodgie now phoned Deepdale to explore loan-transfer possibilities. It didn't measure up. Mr Saville didn't feel cut out for life at Torquay. A £100,000 permanent move to conveniently adjacent, well-heeled Wigan had been tailored and suited both player and boss far better.

It all made perfect sense but, hopes momentarily dashed yet again, I couldn't but help feeling a bit brought down.

Saturday 26 October

Swansea at home and a restored to full fitness Nelson an automatic first-team choice. Not so fast my all-knowing friend. Head coach Hodges has a different game-plane to the obvious 'Well done, Ellis, but you're back on the bench.'

I cite this decision to make me a substitute today not as evidence of a shock-horror Hodges-Nelson disagreement (of which there have been gratifyingly few) but as an insight as to how you inevitably have to develop a more objective viewpoint if you wish to take yourself seriously/be taken seriously as a coach.

Ellis is 20. In a fortnight he comes to the end of his four-month contract. Last week, given the opportunity of first-team action, he grabbed it with both feet. A cool finish capped good overall play. Taking the longer view, to drop him now might be counter-productive to his form and morale. We'll start today with me sitting this one out.

Swansea have a player-manager too: Jan Molby, the Danish Scouser and rather more of a force to be reckoned with than the Essex Evertonian. He dominates our match reports. Stop him and you stop Swansea.

At Charlton this premise would have triggered countless training ground hours of anti-Molby preparation. At Torquay, however, as I've indicated, we don't go in for this reactive force-feeding. In the belief that our lads should be grown up enough to take on board what they need, we simply spell out the key aspects of individual opponents' styles and methods. Which gives us the last laugh today. Molby is sitting this one out too. *His* tweaked groin has not responded to treatment in time.

After 30 minutes the bench acquires another wall-flower. Our loose cannon has clattered one too many to the deck. Two bookable offences, the second just minutes after the first, earn Jon Gittens a sending off.

One hour left to battle through with just 10 men. But the latter-day character of the side shines through brighter than ever. There is no surrender as, comfortably reverting to a flat back four, the defence copes magnificently. They not only resist but also provide sufficient sense of security for the midfield three to take calculated risks on forward runs. On one, Ian Hathaway and Charlie Oatway extend their increasingly good training ground understanding to fashion an excellent opening goal – Charlie's first ever in the League.

Our Rodders required assistance from nobody as, our defence still rock steady, the game entered its last couple of minutes. His searing pace taking him beyond the Welsh back line he guaranteed us our sixth home win of the season by applying the coolest of finishes.

The final whistle was greeted by a loud cheer from the encouragingly 'up' gate of 2,700. Then one still louder broke from their throats. Manchester United had gone down 3–6 at the Dell.

Monday 28 October

Gale force winds to start our new week and underline that we have no indoor training facility. Cones in the air, gentlemen. Twenty-five token minutes was all it took before Hodgie's whistle down the wind called a halt to the farce.

Back at the office I rang up the curtain on a sequel production by ringing up the Oxford back room. I wanted to discover the whereabouts of Mark Druce. After a month of knocking in goals for Rotherham with monotonous regularity he was now conspicuous by his end-of-loan-period absence.

'Signed permanently for 50 grand,' came the terse curtain line to the one-act play.

Another one bites the dust. As, it seems, will our interest in Wrexham's Steve Watkin, scorer of the winner in their famous 2–1 triumph over Arsenal. Kevin Reeves (once himself object of £1 million transfers) confirmed that Steve is now surplus to Brian Flynn's requirements but that he would only be sub-let to a club able to pay the full transfer asking price (OIRO £100,000) at the end of the loan.

Now it was me doing the biting. I all but champed my ballpoint in two as I learned that Fred Davies, also at Ninian Park mid-week, had wasted no time in spiriting Southampton's Frankie Bennett away to Shrewsbury. I sat back in my chair and thought a great thought: if you're going fishing it helps having a hook on the end of your line. It helps even more to have some bait.

Tuesday 29 October

To Field Mill home of Mansfield and, at 30, the league's youngest manager, Steve Parkin. During his short tenancy Mansfield's results have improved and Hodgie and I are emphasizing that under no circumstances should tonight's opposition be taken for granted.

We began with a first. All three Torquay coaches were on the touch-line as the game kicked off. We witnessed a lively opening 10 minutes climaxed by Ian Hathaway's Zola-esque free-kick (although I accuse the goalkeeper!) curling directly into the top left corner. His first of the season. There was no balancing luck for veteran Brian Kilcline. His stunning drive from 30 yards beat everyone … but not the post.

The Stags' luck continued to be out for the rest of the half but their neat, purposeful play, their lively foraging forward had the three touch-line stooges fearing the worst. At half-time we urgently called for the increased tempo that would pre-empt such raiding but we returned to our seats to find we had been wasting our breath. Seven minutes into the second half Mansfield equalised.

Upbeat notes continued to issue from the away section. (Sheffield Wednesday's famous band doing a Tuesday moonlight for our supporters may yet be our only loan signing of the season.) But the evidence before our eyes continued to convince us that Parkin's players were the more likely lads.

'Strip off, Nelse. We need an old head out there.'

'Not so much of the old, Kev.'

After 10 minutes of sustained non-contact with the ball I was as brassed off as the band. It seemed that my experience was completely irrelevant to proceedings. As much so as any skills I might still possess. Then came my moment. I latched on to a Jon Gittens through ball and, two young defenders whipper-snappering at my heels, bore down on goal. NOW! From the edge of the box I stroked the perfect side-foot shot low and hard to the right of the advancing keeper. 'Goal!' I instinctively claimed, knowing I'd got it just right. 'Past it, old git!' I'm sure I heard from the crowd. From nowhere Ian Bowling had shot out an improbably long arm to collar the ball.

I was still morbidly replaying the strike over in my mind when I picked up a pass wide some 40 yards out. Cutting inside with a shimmy and a shake I nutmegged a defender and jinked around him. Once more I found myself bearing down on goal. As Killer Kilcline closed – NOW! I unleashed something not totally characteristic of my game – a genuine pile-driving screamer. The ball flew into the bulging top left corner of the goal to leave a motionless Ian Bowling green with diminishing disbelief.

There was nothing geriatric about my sprint towards the rocking and rolling Torquay fans in the far corner of the ground. The ensuing five-minute long recovery period that then proved necessary, however, was somewhat evidence I have not altogether escaped the ageing process.

Two-one at the final whistle. Our second away win! The Gulls are still soaring upwards.

Wednesday 30 October

Being a football manager or coach is a bifocal occupation. Your attention is constantly split between right in front of you detail and longer range, sometime-never considerations. Whatever the stage of the season there's always going to be foreground flak. So-and-so's routine niggle isn't responding to routine treatment; the first-team regular's ruffled feathers; the promising prospect's inexplicable loss of confidence ... Some little local difficulties can be sorted at once by a tactful word here, a raised eyebrow there. Inevitably, though, just as many bleed on. If so-and-so doesn't respond to treatment, we'll have to no option other than to blood whosehisface, a raw teenager not ready for first-team duty. It'll be unfair on him (the likely blow to his confidence could knock him back months) and unfair on the rest of the side (group morale could plummet). But then the whole squad is two to three solid players short of a six-pack. We need to buy in some competent pros. There's no way we can do that unless we sell (which by definition depletes us further) or triple our gates. That, of course, is an impossible dream but maybe we ought to bear down more professionally in the way we market ourselves in the greater Torbay area ... Of course, if we could sign three stalwarts and win consistently we would increase gates. The transfer outlay would start to come back. Gates would certainly go up if we homed in on promotion. If by a miracle we did go up, though, we'd struggle with this squad. We'd need to invest. So, in 'ifs' and 'buts', your switch-back thinking goes.

The successive scenarios of wishful thinking and paranoia – no, hang about, paranoia is *irrational* fear – spiral further and further on out. It's not surprising that the temptation speedily becomes to keep your head down, concentrating on day to day fire-fighting – sprains, late arrivals, dodgy kit. But you can't. If you've got any ambition for your club, you've got to compel yourself to think long term. And it's always easier to pull your head out of the sand when you're on a bit of a roll, as we are now.

We're disputing fifth/sixth place in the league. We're in the play-off frame, albeit after just 16 games. 'This is Mission Control commencing docking. Looking good, Torquay.'

I wonder. Our squad is so thin. I have a nasty, if private, suspicion that we're flattering to deceive. A succession of midfielders and wing-backs have come through to nick the winning goal for us in recent games and so mask the inadequacy of our up-front fire-power. But I don't count on the miracle being sustained. Our defence now looks drilled and skilled enough to keep us mid-table and we've learned to defend from the front in any case. But we badly need a striker capable of grabbing a goal every other game, a consistent midfield ball-winner ... hell, I'd better check on Jamie Ndah's niggle...

Thursday 31 October

Courtesy of the of course disinterested press an unacceptable face of English soccer has stared out at us this week. Bruised, literally battered, it belongs to Mrs Sheryl Gascoigne and is the handiwork of her husband Paul. It is a striking as well as stricken image. It has evoked other unacceptable features of our national game and, yes, nation.

Rwanda? Forget it. Which MP hasn't been bought by a pressure group? Who cares? The one question preoccupying the land of hope and glory's tiny tabloid mind this week is whether, after giving his bride of a few formal weeks a right seeing to (in the pugilistic sense) the man, Gascoigne, should be selected for – should be considered for selection for – the England squad.

For me the core question is: what sort of signal are Glenn Hoddle and the FA prepared to send to the English public at large and to world soccer. I myself don't believe that Gascoigne should be in the frame at all. His selection, I would argue, will send the wrong message to a society already veering far too dangerously towards the power of the fist and of what weapons can be held in that fist – 'If you'd just like to glance through our catalogue, sir.'

It's abundantly clear that millions disagree with me. Unable to conceive of any issue being more important than qualifying for the World Cup, they see his inclusion in the England XI as crucial and beyond argument. Besides being one of us – that Fivebellies, what a laugh! – he's our match-winning star and we can't begin to think of facing Georgia without him. Much more pertinently, let me concede, this is a view held by probably the majority of Gascoigne's international team-mates and peers – all players operating on a far higher level, of course, than I ever have or ever will achieve. They have first-hand experience of his skills on the ball and, in many cases, of his off-field kindnesses when the 'good guy' side of his Jekyll and Hyde nature has had the upper hand.

Nevertheless, I beg leave to submit a minority report. Gazza's talent, it seems to me, is not the issue here: and in this case his generosity on other occasions shouldn't be given the status of extenuating evidence. What is the issue – surely the only mark of a man that counts – is his behaviour.

In one intriguingly interesting way not only Gascoigne but also Hoddle are lucky still to have open options. Sheryl Gascoigne has chosen not to bring charges against her husband. Police involvement would have dramatically upped the ante-selection process.

It is police involvement elsewhere that has shown us another unacceptable face of soccer and English institutions. They were 'involved' at Hillsborough. My word they were. Now the Court of Appeal has found two to one in favour of those boys in blue who helped pick up the post-disaster corpses receiving coin of the realm compensation for the post-traumatic stress disorder they thereby incurred.

Well. Suffice to say I've played against Vinnie Jones. I never put in a post-match claim for compensation. I'd signed a contract. I thought it came with the territory.

POST-HONEYMOON DISTRESS

Friday 1 November

An outside overview of Torquay United FC today and one guaranteed to create a landmark day for Kevin Hodges. Our head coach has been named Division Three Manager of the Month. It surely earns him a *Guinness Book of Records* entry. He's only been at the job two and a half months.

Modesty personified – the award genuinely took him by surprise – Kevin spent the morning explaining that while he was the target man for the award, the credit had to be shared among all the Plainmoor players and staff. It was their across the board rejuvenation that had worked the small miracle of turning last year's whipping boys into this season's surprise packet.

No-one rushed forward to contradict this, it's true. But let's give main credit where main credit is due. Not a loud-mouthed, rule by fear, bully them into performing manager, Kevin has quickly shaped the team by to the point suggestion and throw-away encouragement. Within overall patterns, he's allowed each of the squad to play to his own strengths. He's been prepared to be sensibly flexible tactically: known how not to interfere downstream with a job he's previously delegated. The limelight isn't Kevin's cup of tea, but there are occasional times when you have to stand up and take a bow. Not least when you richly deserve the applause.

Which couldn't go on all day, alas. The party over, business as usual was resumed. Jamie Ndah, he of the recurring hamstring strain, was called in to the office for a home-truths session. The message was tersely to the point. Sort your leg out over the next couple of weeks or you may well need to sort out a new employer. At 25 and with a contract expiring in the summer, Jamie needs an injury-free run-in to the season's end starting right now. A consistent run of form wouldn't come amiss, either. He's got it all to do, as they say. And as we just told him.

Somebody else to get called in today was, yes, Paul Gascoigne. He's in the England squad for Georgia. I'm not totally surprised. All the same I'm blinking. Pretty though it is, Georgia is a country's, not a girl's, name.

As English supremo, Glenn Hoddle has no need to justify Gazza's selection publicly, but the past week's barrage of comment has put the English coach on the back foot ethically.

He's stonewalled with great finesse. Continuing Gazza's England career will offer him the best route possible to personal redemption; the game he loves will be his fast lane therapy. It's even almost plausible.

The born-again Christian rejoicing over the return of one lost sheep to the fold must make sure he doesn't close off all his selection options. If his good-shepherd-cum-social-worker policy is applied on a consistent basis, he may find himself having to drop Les Ferdinand so as to make room to partner Alan Shearer with Liam Gallagher.

Saturday 2 November

A trip to the Orient in hopes of a three-point takeaway – hopes raised by the knowledge that Barry Hearn has been snookered in his attempts to date to break in a new manager. Perhaps the O's will be lacking that hint of eastern promise today.

Two omens darkly argue otherwise, though. Managerless teams so often display a bloody-minded determination to stand the form book on its head. And – worse! – there is an age-old curse laid upon the Manager of the Month award. Time and time again winning it is prelude to a tail-spin.

Cue nightmare. Uninspired Torquay gifted toothless Orient a perfect 'freebie' with which to end their long goal drought. An 'It's yours … No! Mine! … Oh, shit! It's theirs!' mess-up of monumental proportions between Lee Barrow and Rhys Wilmot generated screams of blue murder in the half-time post mortem that followed, unfortunately, only two minutes later.

At least we still had the second 45 minutes to set things to rights. Improved considerably, we managed lots of play, lots of movement, but when the handful of opportunities were created had no-one of sufficient class on the day, myself included, to pot the white.

1–0. We only lost 1–0. And deserved bugger all else. Seriously annoyed by the loss of three not only important but, as he'd thought, accessible points, Hodgie maintained it had been our worst display of the season. Jon Gittens and Charlie Oatway apart, no-one was in any personal position to argue with him. The curse had struck. The still unopened Manager of the Month champagne was going to taste flat.

Monday 4 November

Via the wonders of the fax, Jon Gittens' transfer request was duly circulated today.

Tuesday 5 November

If this is Tuesday it must be run 'til you drop time. For the Torquay United FC first-team squad there was a variation on the seasonal rhyme.

Please to remember
The 5th of November,

Full laps, power runs and sprints ...

Their anarchist view as to the best way of celebrating the anniversary of the Jacobean terrorist bomb would undoubtedly be to bind both coaches to the largest available rocket, light the blue touch paper and retire immediately to the snooker hall. Not the order of the day. Chanted jibes of 'Build a bonfire, build a bonfire and stick the gaffer on top' did fill the air as we set off from Plainmoor on foot. Not another economy measure. The two miles of stretching, walking and jogging that brought us to the unappreciated view of Anstey's Cove had a warm-up purpose.

Next up was an hour's gruelling punishment – half laps x 3; full laps x 3; power runs x 12: four sets of 'doggies' (that's hell for leather to the first cone and back ... the second cone and back ... the third ...). Soon the latter day conspirators were thinking of nothing less than blowing up the manager's office. But not by the close of tortuous play.

Let the record show that throughout the session Messrs Hodges and Nelson matched their younger charges stride for stride. If you can't beat 'em, join 'em. The muttered jags fizzled out as the squad took on board that they weren't the only ones being put through their paces. Appreciation for the two old age pensioners making themselves their own severest task-masters was renewed.

One he-ancient, however, was still in the frame for imminent conversion to Joan of Arc status. Steve 'Harold' (as in Steptoe) McCall was flirting dangerously with the probability of ending up knee-deep in faggots. So to speak. His ongoing Achilles had caused Matron to give him a chit letting him off the morning's games. Clad in warm clothing as he wielded the stopwatch, Macca became a convenient focus for all our wrath. But his sardonic wit enabled him to take all abusive fireworks in his non-stride. Plus his class. That class as deployed across the park has earned him more respect from the Plainmoor playing staff, I would venture to say, than anyone else has collected this season. His motor might not be running today but all of us know that it has been engineered to his own BMW's standards.

Recently hoping to be allowed to continue to run and run are expiring contract holders Ellis Laight and Mark Hawthorne. Ourselves back at Plainmoor and pulses back to normal, Hodgie and I asked to see them both.

Ellis first. Once again it was time for some gloves-off realism as Kevin made very clear.

'One month ago you were a dead-cert for release,' he said. 'All right –

your goal at Wigan and performance here against Swansea have got you out of gaol. For the moment. We're prepared to give you another month and put the ball back in your court.'

Ellis failed to cartwheel about the room in joy. Crests don't fall much lower.

'I'll think it over,' he stalled with. It was, we all knew, a not unreasonable gesture towards retaining a smidgen of leverage and dignity. He'll re-sign, though, no question. He's no other irons in the fire.

A similar mini-scenario featured Mark Hawthorne. He's a four-square, sturdy midfielder and in training his 'can do' workmanlike qualities characterise him as the perfect squad member. When he's with the squad. When he's out socialising Mark is just as enthusiastic, I suspect. Wherever he is, it's his nature to go with the flow. The upshot of this cheery attitude is that he's a few pounds above his best playing weight and, for all his ground-covering work-rate on the park, his mental attitude to games is less sharply focused than I'd like to see it. Which is precisely why there is doubt in our minds now. The leagues are full of players who unfailingly do the business Monday to Friday but, when Saturday comes, play like Sean Bean. Mark isn't that bad. Given his first-team chances he has filled in adequately. But no better. He's never threatened to impose his authority upon the midfield area. 'More' is what he needs to do. Quite a lot more. Once again we offer him the grace of a month's extension and once again the dismay is very evident. The response will be the same.

Thursday 7 November

Another false dawn. My 300-mile drive-a-thon of yesterday routed to take in the reserve games of Cardiff against QPR and Bristol Rovers against Wimbledon yielded a clutch of new names. That of Jason Euell had both the chauffeur and his head coach barely able to prevent their excitement bursting forth from their scouting uniforms. Here in one package were pace, strength, skill and balance a ballerina would give her left leg to possess. These attributes were given tangible confirmation by two exquisitely taken goals which proclaimed that on a wet and windy night in Yate we were watching a rising star.

The day's first ASAP chore was to contact Wimbledon FC. Since I'd neglected to introduce myself as Senor Robson or Signor Lippi, Joe Kinnear was not contactable. This put an initial damper on our enthusiasm not totally lifted by the Don's youth team coach promising to relay our enquiry to soccer's current greatest living Irishman.

Next spot on the dial, Southend – as embodied by Theo Foley. His experienced eye has focused on the yet to be snapped/wrapped up talent of our Rodney Jack. Clearly should Newcastle not get him the Shrimpers have a far better chance of giving Rodders the 75 per cent first-team outing guarantee that the D of E illogically make the be all and end all of a work permit. However, to be going on with I could only explain that all negotiations as to which box Jack will end up in are temporarily suspended. We're all waiting on the lad's return from yet another round of World Cup Caribbean capers on 17 November. To be continued, we agreed.

For Rodney, the excitements of escape to St Vincent: for Torquay, the need for the intervention of St Jude.

When Damien Davey entered the office to declare that a complex problem with his hand will keep Stevie Winter out of Saturday's reckoning, recourse to the patron saint of lost causes seems as practical an option as is left to us. The news brings our injury list up to seven.

Seven non-combatants is something a Chelsea or a Villa can largely shrug off. For a Division Three squad, seven is anything but a lucky number. As he formally added Stevie's name to the non-runners list – the others are just out of shoulder surgery Ray Newland, the fragilely hamstrung Jamie Ndah, the foot-in-cast Paul Mitchell, the banned Jon Gittens, the World Cup-ing Rodney Jack, and the struggling to be fit for Saturday Ian Hathaway – Hodgie and I exchanged an anxious glance. It was not the best moment for Damien to forget his oath ever to give succour to the infirm.

'Christ, Kev,' he said, 'you'll have to get your own boots out.'

He got not a laugh but the frostiest of looks. Deservedly. His cold comfort remark hadn't been that calculated to thaw out the inches thick ice wrapped around the cockles of both our hearts.

We have reason to feel down. The squad is stretched to the limit and four weeks of phoning, scouting and searching have proved absolutely fruitless. They've yielded –

'Brring. Brring.'

'Hello.'

'Switchboard. Message here from Wimbledon. Euell have to keep on with the looking. Jason's not available.'

'Very droll. Right. Thanks.'

They've yielded zilch.

Friday 8 November

The shattered lowered leg is seemingly held together by no more than its encasing sock. No matter how many times you look at it, the grotesque, horrendous image never fails to shock. To sicken. Peter Schmeichel, hardman goalkeeper, required counselling to help him come to terms with what he'd seen in the flesh and bone. Today, seeing the picture again after an eight-month gap I found I couldn't eat my breakfast. David Busst's injury against Manchester United. What has occasioned the reprise reprinting of the once in a million still of the once in a million accident is yesterday's sad but inevitable announcement that David's playing career is over. Everyone having the slightest connection with the game will feel for him.

Nobody has ever suggested that the incident which saw him trapped between all out challenges from Dennis Irwin and Brian McClair was anything other than the as near as damn it ultimate sod's law accident. All the same, it's devoutly to be hoped that Manchester United won't be backwards about coming forwards to participate in a benefit match on behalf of the career in pieces Sky Blue.

But it's an ill wind that has no silver lining. The incident promises to be a jackpot day for the East Loamshire police force. Estimates hazard that 127 of their regular and auxiliary constabulary have submitted claims for compensation in respect of the mental stress that Busst's own PTSD experience (playing terminated *sine die*) has inflicted on them.

Sky Blue is not the lucky colour of the week. Also in apparently urgent need of psychological counselling is Steve Coppell. Thirty-three days into his Manchester City management role he has found that the stress and demands of the job are too great. He has resigned. Making the public announcement himself, he has done so with style and dignity, albeit looking mentally exhausted and physically drained. We don't know what skeleton-enclosing cupboards he was required to peer into but it seems sensible to say that soccer management is not for the unduly squeamish. Coppell seems to have decided that life is more important than football and to get out before having to be carried out.

Saturday 9 November

The footballing eyes of the nation – well those red-veined ones in possession of cable or dish hook-up – found themselves striving for earlier than usual focus today. England having flown east, the shift in time

142

zones found stay-at-home supporters viewing what Gladys Knight would doubtless describe as a midday terrain in Georgia. They witnessed no derailment. Although playing on a surface that made the Plainmoor pitch appear billiard-table flat, England delivered a thoroughly professional performance. Georgia, meanwhile, gave a thoroughly passable impersonation of Torquay – neat in the middle, guilty of occasional and catastrophic lapses in defence, toothless up front. Paul Gascoigne began the game for England and was there at the end. His performance received the most fulsome of praise from the coach responsible for both those circumstances. This has to be seen as the triumph of wishful thinking over objective evidence. Gascoigne was by some way the most ineffectual English participant.

Later that same day Torquay managed a creditably passable imitation of Georgia. Colchester adapted to the relative merits of the Plainmoor pitch that vital bit more slickly than the home side. 0–2 in Tblisi. 0–2 in Torquay. Football is a universal language. As Georgians and Devonians alike made the slouch-shouldered trudge home, their complaint would have been identical. Where the hell, Mikhail, are we ever going to find a quality striker?

Monday 11 November

For the minnows of the Football League the start of Cup Week count-down. The first round proper. Not for me a totally new experience. I've been here before. And on occasion got no further. Humiliating defeats at Harlow and Dagenham still occupy painfully disproportionate space in my memory bank. This year at Torquay the week's decision was to let our preparations get off to a calculatedly low-key start. We may have lost on Saturday but it had by no means been a bad performance. It will be counter-productive to come on like sore losers. The consequent coaching decision was to let them down lightly now with a 'get your heads up, everything's going to come good' day off.

Tuesday 12 November

It's poignant that Chelsea, the side supported by Prime Minister John Major and his yesterday's man sidekick, David 'Gissa comp, Batesy' Mellor, are now comfortably capable of fielding a Premiership side without a single Englishman in its ranks. Euro-sceptic Tory backbenchers are calling an emergency meeting of the 1922 Committee, following the London side's acquisition of the Parma international, Zola, who will thus join his compatriots Di Matteo and Vialli at the Bridge in, for those of you with black and white sets, an all Azzurri tricolour.

Zola reportedly cost £5 million. His salary will be commensurate and a further huge weekly/monthly outgoing for Chelsea to cover. If, that is, Gianfranco opts to stick around.

That's not an idle thought. The question of how long foreign superstars are prepared to tolerate English culture, cuisine, climate and fixture congestion is hugely relevant as Bryan Robson can confirm. Having invested hugely in Fjortoft, Juninho and Emerson, Robbo is currently seeing his long-term team-building reduced to house of cards shakiness through the destabilising behaviour of his South American imports.

Branco has already jumped ship. To keep him afloat he took, we are told, a £500,000 wad in his back pocket. Such a life-jacket would keep some 20 English youngsters afloat for a two-season period. But they would be neither instant solutions or box office. Branco clearly was both and deserves every penny of his severance pay for the commitment and loyalty he displayed in the course of his arduous Premiership treadmill career of no fewer than seven full appearances.

Now it's Emerson who is consulting the airline schedules. Initially the midfield maestro (rather akin to his boss in his combination of skill and aggression) won the hearts of a good many soccer enthusiasts beyond Teesside. Claiming that the chill wind from off the North Sea is particularly uncongenial to his little, homesick-for-Ipanema *esposa*, the midfielder has currently lost all his markers. At the end of an agreed holiday time-out he's gone walkabout. When Boro forked out £4.5 million they didn't appreciate they were getting two for the price of one. Not necessarily in this case a bargain. In an effort to bring him to heel the club has been forced to try instigating a FIFA-wide ban on their investment playing anywhere else. This will probably end by doing the trick but the whole episode serves to underline that there are some things money can't buy. Loyalty. Honour. Self-respect.

Or even solidarity. To complete a particularly unhappy week for the glum-looking Robson (there's something permanent, at least) Juninho's agent has picked the moment to suggest that his mercurial midget may find life in Spain or Italy more user-friendly to his Latin temperament. Despite Juninho's clear-cut contractual tie to Middlesbrough, discussions have already begun, it seems, with potential suitors. The commission, should a deal be consummated, will not be incompatible with the agent's temperament.

There are huge general dangers lurking on the fringes of such finagling. Few fans would argue that the multi-national make-up of today's Premiership has not been one of its biggest attractions. But the literal cost has been enormous. Money has gone out of the country. Money has not gone to lesser British clubs. In a manner directly reflecting the practice within British industry as a whole, training and development budgets have suffered. Whether the influx of superstars will raise standards permanently and *in depth* is a question that time alone will decide. But I know what answer my money's on. Some foreign imports have already proved ludicrously misjudged and ruinously expensive. Even the masterly players may prove eventually to have given our game a quick fix at the expense of a sustained healthy regimen. And certainly as the annual accounts of more and more clubs reveal just how much ram-raiding superstars have taken out of the game, British fans will increasingly question the long-term viability of glamour imports. The European Super League may recook all the accountants' books but even that is by no means a gilt-edged certainty. Meanwhile the Premiership may be on more of a course with bankruptcy than it cares to make known. South American superstars? Torquay is taking a firm stand. We're rejecting all approaches from Santos and River Plate.

Wednesday 13 November

Yesterday's ruminating on gilt-edged dross left an unpleasant taste in the mouth. But, calling back to mind my underlying love for the beautiful game, today has been a spirit renewing breath of fresh air. It's our youth team that I have to thank for it all.

Chance had provided them with a potential local derby dog-fight in the first round of the FA Youth Cup – an away tie just up the road against Exeter. Wrong. The stuff of blood and thunder it was not. Out-thinking, out-manoeuvring and in the later stages simply outclassing their opponents, Steve McCall's Torquay tots netted seven goals without conceding any. Forget Boca Juniors, these are Macca's – an eloquent testimony to the wealth of talent waiting in the Plainmoor wings and a timely reminder that punting big bucks in the (probable) direction of a Swiss bank account is not the only way to build for the future. Certainly three or four of tonight's team are destined to become regular first-team players sooner rather than later. It's an exciting prospect but, the pessimistic voice of caution whispers in my ear, one not to get too excited about in advance. In the 16 months of their YTS careers at Torquay these lads have already worked under three coaches. My chances of getting to work long-term with these uncut gems is at best, the numbers game suggests, even money.

Friday 15 November

Cup Fever is rampant on the English Riviera. Twenty-four hours before the kick off against Lennie Lawrence's upwardly mobile Luton the frenzy rivals the atmosphere of ... well, when I say frenzy there's a certain degree of expectant ...well ... er, put it this way: 'Is there anyone out there?' Deciding Mahomet on this occasion would go to the mountainous crowds of well-wishers, we organised a stroll along the sun-kissed Torquay seafront for our Wembley-bound warriors. We discovered even fewer traces of human presence than you'll come across these days at the Goldstone home end. But the expedition was not all loss. Peering out across the bay proud Cortez-fashion we scanned the distant horizon for a glimpse of the Canaries-bound QE2. Aboard her would be Chairman Mike and wife Sue. Unable to bear the tension of another (or even a first) epic Cup run coinciding with the stress of our imminent AGM, they had opted for a week-long autumnal cruise. Jumping out of the frying pan may not be all plain sailing, however. There's a depression forecast for the Bay of Biscay.

And probably for Plainmoor. Unbeaten in 13 league games Luton are likely to give us as stern a test as we've so far faced. Have we swotted enough for this exam, then? I think so. Hence today's emphasis on relaxing mind and muscles.

There's certainly an extra spring in my autumnal step. But that's the Cup itself. And if we get over the next two hurdles our balls will be in the hat along with those of the big boys. That could be my best chance to hear those devoutly to be wished lines: 'Everton will play ...Torquay United.'

Come on you Gulls! Give the old 'un a break tomorrow.

Saturday 16 November

Slept well, untroubled by eve of Cup nerves. Driving in to the ground I worked at keeping it that way. Yes, I've experienced my share of first round lows. But the past 19 seasons have also brought a fair share of glamour and glory. Goals against Leeds and Arsenal. An against all odds win at Blackburn. Cherished appearances at Old Trafford and Anfield. Who could tell? Today might be the start of something big.

Eventually. Initially it was the start of something irritating. The Torquay mascot for the day had turned up with absolutely filthy boots. Normally valeting services are not the province of player-coaches. But today's mascot was one Nelson C. It was Nelson G who was required to rediscover and employ his boot boy skills. Of course most fathers will do anything for their sons, even if the little sod has announced to the world in the Gulls' programme that his favourite player is Rodney Jack.

Show time. We run out to the cheers from a crowd whose size is important. These are the sort of numbers we should be pulling in all the time. See! With them behind us we hit top gear the moment the whistle goes. For the first 15–20 minutes we played quite splendidly – as well as we've managed all season. Ian Feuer in the Luton goal had to make three stunning saves to prevent us grabbing the psychological advantage with a lead that would have been no more than we deserved. My frustration mounted as our superiority went unrewarded. I knew it couldn't last. Five minutes from half-time Ceri Hughes produces unwelcome confirmation of my judgement. A corner. A neat bringing of the ball down on the edge of the area, a training ground strike. Goal.

On the resumption anxiety brought out the sloppiness in us. We gave the ball away too easily. Too stupidly. Our development of second ball situations went into slow motion. Luton grew in poise and control. Essentially a level of craft above us they killed the game off working the ball into corners, winning free kicks, denying us possession. For a while the Gulls had been gallant but over the 90 minutes Luton's (self) possession made them worthy winners.

For me there was to be injury added to wrong result. Five minutes from the end I tried to get my foot in on a hefty clearance. The interception was never really on. Getting there late, the best I could manage was to collect the imprint of two studs slap bang – and I do mean 'bang'! – on the site of many another old war wound, the middle of my left instep. I hobbled to the bench in pain that not even the announcement that the local paper had made me 'Man of the Match' could lighten. It wouldn't alter the scoreline. And I needed a bottle not of whisky but methadone.

There was to be a sour aftertaste to the day. In a decent suit, one elegant shoe and, on my swollen, now half-frozen, injured foot a flip-flop, I was in a McDonald's with Carole, Carly and Christopher. The family treat was to be the capper on Chris's mascot moment in the Plainmoor spotlight. Abruptly a bunch of Luton supporters were looming over our table in 'in your face' mode.

'*One-nil to the Luton Town,*' they sang with raucous unoriginality and mindless repetition.

'Have to say you deserved it, lads,' I said knowing that, their crow crowed, they'd proceed to withdraw. Wrong.

'*One-nil to the Luton Town.*'

I pointed out that having been there in person I was aware of the game's result. Like talking to … Luton supporters. The McDonald's staff all appeared to be about the same age as Carly. It would be unfair to involve them. It was we who moved – to the establishment's upstairs floor. Unbelievably the louts followed us up to renew their one-note serenade. Footsore or not, I now made my feelings unmistakably clear and, at overdue last, they staggered off to win more friends. With them, alas, had gone the buzz on the button to Christopher's day.

With supporters like that who needs enemies?

Sunday 17 November

Hopalong Nelson time. My foot's in ice. Rodney Jack would probably like to be up to his neck in ice right now. The result of his latest World Cup fixture has just come in. St Vincent 3 ('yes!') – Jamaica 11 (eleven!).

I spend the day hurting at either end. In the next round of the Cup Luton have drawn non-league opponents. We could probably have seen them off and then … almost certain defeat but maybe a transfer fee level share of the gate from a glamour tie. Meanwhile, salt in the financial sore, after a good win yesterday Exeter are drawn away to Plymouth. A second round money-spinner; both clubs should come away from the tie some 60 grand to the good. At our level that's two, maybe three players. Time to freshen up the ice. On my forehead.

Monday 18 November

A Wednesday game, so training today. No need to read the riot act over last Saturday; the flesh, at least, was willing. But soon Hodgie is obliged to halt today's ball skills and tactical session because the spirit is not.

'This isn't on,' he says. 'It's just not good enough.'

He's dead right. Standing on the touchline *hors de combat* and any real involvement, I'm less than amused by today's slack, piss-taking attitude to training. They can't think they've done enough already this season, I think; and then I find myself looking quickly around. Did I say that out loud? No. But maybe I should have.

Now I observe a strange but not unfamiliar phenomenon. Partly to underline his disgust, partly because they need it today, Hodgie sets the squad to some seriously heavy running exercises. It's cold, wet, horrible. They go into and complete the runs as if their lives depended on it. Where before it was all arsing about, now the commitment is total.

Why? Is it because the running is overwhelmingly a matter of dogged determination and they can get their minds round that whereas, requiring technique and intelligence, ball skills and positional play offer immediate scope for appearing a prat? There's a germ of truth here. If you're likely to embarrass yourself sooner rather than later why not head the egg-on-face moment off at the pass by goofing around. Your bad moment will then be camouflaged.

All bad things come to an end. We load up the van and set off. Up front the coaching staff sit discussing the down shift in our recent fortunes when ringing indication comes that something more tangible has shifted downwards at an even faster rate of knots. Ding, ding, ding went the cross-bars. A study in concentration at the wheel, Kevin had just circumnavigated yet another of the mini-roundabouts on our way back when, clanking metallically, our set of crossbars, so many stainless steel cabers, were cartwheeling in our wake and in the direction of several terrified Torquay motorists. Eyes closed, hands over them, we shudderingly awaited the inevitable end result of dropping so many clangers – the sound of British steel upon Osaka and Panmunjon metal. It never came. Brakes and tyres screaming in agonized protest, yes, but, like their owners' latterday attempts on conventional goals, the twisting torpedoes had failed to find a significant target.

Red-faced and ever so humble (litigation over damages could well have bankrupted the club), we retrieved our 24 ft kebab skewers and lashed them, securely this time, to the roof.

'Never happened before,' Kevin muttered.

'Yeah, well,' Matthew Wright, one of our youngsters, responded at once. 'First time I've loaded the van, innit.'

All eyes turned as one. All minds were synchronised in thinking of the yellow jersey. Misdirected cabers? We'd found the right tosser.

And not the right loan signing. Compound interest is still piling up on our morale overdraft. Back at base we found there'd been another rapid shift in the goalposts as evidenced by a message from Wrexham regarding Steve Watkin. The club had already given us a green light on approaching him. Here was his response.

'Sorry. Not interested.'

Tuesday 19 November

Hey, ho, the wind and the rain. They're everywhere today, sweeping in from the sea at near gale force strength. No cones or DIY goalposts for us today. We're indoors at the Acorn Leisure Centre going through the aerobic motions.

However intense our efforts the burn they generated will have been a lot less than our commercial representative, Cedric Munslow, has suffered. Having risen in the small hours there he was, still before Heathrow sunrise, clocking the passengers from the day's American Airlines flight from Miami as they emerged from Customs and Immigration. Out they came, pairs, individuals, groups. Then there were none. In particular no Rodney Jack, entire object of Cedric's pre-dawn motorway dash. Naïvely we had failed to anticipate the possibility of a seasonal tropical storm delaying our World Cup star from taking his place in the starting line-up at Hull. Naïvely we had failed to anticipate the possibility of him not feeling sufficiently impelled – 'Well, man, we do things differently out here' – to get home *somehow*. I'm not sure after a 1–5 thrashing from Mexico I would have either. But I would have telephoned to say I'd been delayed.

Now it's Cedric who phones. It's a double whammy. We'll have to fork out for his 24-hour overnight in London and, given the phenomenon of jet-lag, think in terms of 'including Rodney out' for tomorrow.

Grim news. I'm out with my painful instep. Macca's out with his Achilles. Behind closed doors Hodgie's head visibly drops. On the Nobo board the team reads: Wilmot/Usual Back Three/Then what?

There's more not so oblique grief. There are a lot of league matches scheduled for tonight. But the weather continues foul right across the country. One by one, as Ceefax updates us, the fixtures are shuffled into the limbo of postponement. We, of course, play tomorrow. The forecast is that the storms will blow themselves out overnight. Why us, oh Lord?

It doesn't get better. In the evening, team selection still as clear as mud, the three wise monkeys swing on down to Plymouth. We want to see what we think of Chesterfield's Gary Lund. See him we do. Shortly before kick-off he takes up his position just behind us in the directors' box.

Both on and off the field Plymouth are in a lot of turmoil. In the first regard Neil Warnock, despite spending other people's money like it was no object, has delivered his terms to Argyle's two remaining directors: make more funds available or I walk. It's an ultimatum that rather suggests a pre-selected destination should he stroll on.

Perhaps this uncertainty is the reason for Plymouth getting caned tonight.

Another manager has announced he's taking a wee walk today. El Tel is to become guru to the Australian World Cup squad. He says he looks upon his new post as 'a challenge'. I would too. Even with my family I'd have to pull out all the stops to get right through a £200,000 pa second income.

Wednesday 20 November

To Hull and back. And initially an arrival some two hours ahead of our ETA. What to do? We go to a hotel for tea and toast. The bill will probably deprive us of a pre-match overnight later in the season.

Hull are yet another outfit undergoing 'political' upheaval. Protest is in the Humberside air. The fans have stayed away in droves. When we run out it's to a paltry gate of 1,700.

The dissatisfaction can't be with the Boothferry Park pitch. Huge, it's in superb condition. It's always going to be one of the last in the League to succumb to postponement. Tonight its size is a major factor in showing up our limitations.

With a touch of desperation we've gone with an experimentalish tactical three up front: teenager Tony Bedeau, 20-year old Ellis Laight and the chairman's son-in-law, Richard Hancox, recalled from the Reserves and from wing-back to forward. Basic strategy is that two will always stay up, the third trailing back in defence down his flank and the midfielders drifting across to cover. Ah, the best laid plans ... Over-enthusiastic the upfront novices chase back far too unthinkingly. Frequently the Hull defence finds itself marking just a lone Torquay striker. When we repossess the ball the outlet options are minimal.

On the bench I try to yell corrective instructions. But the pitch is wide, the wind blustery and just along from me the Sheffield Wednesday Brass Band is blowing up a storm of its own. Their heart is in the right place but like our forwards their positioning isn't. As they go for it *fortissimo* I can hardly hear myself think let alone communicate with our pulled about lads.

Hull now proceed to have us on toast. They score once five minutes before half-time and again 10 minutes after the resumption. No amount of choruses of 'Pick Yourself Up' will be able to do anything about that. After the game we keep the team in the changing room for 30 minutes of a 'let's learn from our mistakes while they're fresh in our minds' teach-in. It was rooted in statistical reality. We've now suffered four successive defeats and gone for 372 minutes without scoring a goal.

Wednesday 21 November

Yesterday seamlessly blended into today in the course of the dozing journey back across England to the South West. It was four in the morning when we fetched up at the motel where we'd parked up. More harsh reality awaited us. We'd not anticipated the heavy frost that had reduced our various cars to iced clean clones.

And, in the case of Damien's 406, immobility. New alternator or not, the drive of his life, the car from hell, wouldn't turn over. Jump start. Push start. There was no more hint of ignition than among our forward line. By the time Damien has settled for a lift our bodies were as blue as our words.

I got home around 4.30. Thankfully I sank down towards a long, oblivion-conferring restorative sleep.

'Dad! Dad! How'd you do!? How'd you get on!?'

Seven-thirty. Rodney Jack's number one fan wants to know last night's score. Ah, children! The little … dears!

No chance of getting back to sleep. Rise and pretend to shine time. The rest of the first-team squad have the day off but I'm in the office by midday for some more of the eyes-down Plainmoor grind. And little for my comfort. Charlton's reserve game, the fax tells me, is off. My motorway-lagged brain cells aren't totally distraught about this but it means we can't speedily run the rule over Valley-discontent, Paul Sturgess, a strong experienced wing-back who could be invaluable at our level. Kevin, meanwhile, is on to Tony Pulis, Gillingham's manager. He asks him where he stands on loaning out Ian Chapman. 'Firm' is the one word bottom line.

Another grey day, then. If the light at the end of the Championship League tunnel is beginning to fade for Manchester United, 1–0 losers to Juventus last night, for Torquay United the shades of night are falling so fast that … Glory be! The phone has gone again and all at once, faint a glow though it may be emitting, there is a flicker of hope at the end of our tunnel that doesn't vanish as soon as glimpsed. Ipswich say they can see their way to loaning out Neil Gregory, a neat, compact striker with some Division One outings under his belt and an eye-catching record of seven goals in 10 loan outings for Scunthorpe. He'll be delighted to get in some first-team appearances with us. All is set fair to get the lad's autograph on the dotted line in time for Saturday's game against Hartlepool. That, though, presupposes we've got Chairman Mike's formal blessing. And he … he's still all at sea. His seven days of enjoying some of life's more luxurious ups and downs on the QE2 are not quite over.

Sometimes it's a small as well as a funny old world. Even as the race to make Neil Gregory legally ours for Saturday begins, the QE2 is forsaking the Western Approaches for the marginally calmer waters of Torbay. The liner does, of course, have a ship-to-shore link. But the rate is £5 a minute. BT say it's nice to talk, but Torquay say only when talk is cheap. We need to put Mike Bateson thoroughly in the Neil Gregory picture. The hook-up threatens to cost as much as will a loan-signing month of his services … What else to do?

So near and yet so far. Like hitting the bar. And then a small miracle occurs. The phone rings. It's Mike Bateson. He wants to let us know that, thanks to inclement weather, Torquay's Mr Football is coming home ahead of schedule. We reply that there's worse trouble on land but there might be an Ipswich solution. He responds like a good 'un. He gives us a green light and it's full steam ahead for Gregory. We zip back to Portman Road on the phone … and everything goes hard astern.

Neil Gregory, we learn, is injured.

In the evening TUFC's AGM is held. There's a deal of speechifying. Opinions, damned opinions and statistics. The bottom line is that last season the club, finishing 92nd out of 92, made a loss of £54,000 compared with a profit of £148,000 the year before. No-one volunteered to organise a sweepstake on the 1996/97 bottom line.

Friday 22 November

Lately the drive to Plainmoor has been getting longer, more sombre by the day. This morning when I arrive I see it has got to Hodgie. He's flipped. He's beaming. Totally irrational. What has this man got to smile about, I ask myself.

'It's Ipswich,' he explains. 'Total cock-up yesterday. Wires all crossed. Neil Gregory's injury turned out to be no more than a minor knock. He can come after all.'

Terrific! I grin too. But it's now Friday morning. A frantic paper-chase ensues to get our man registered as a loan signing by the noon deadline. If we achieve this Neil will be available for selection tomorrow. It's tight but, thanks to the fax, we make it. Instructions are issued. Neil Gregory's first day as a Torquay temp will be spent pretending that the train is taking the strain as he negotiates the eight-hour journey from Ipswich to Newton Abbot. He'll be involved tomorrow.

Somebody who won't is me. In the course of the morning I try one relatively uninhibited volley of a training ball. The pain cuts through me like a knife. Lengthways. This could be more than a bruising. I could be out for several games.

As could several others. Gregory and the restored Rodney Jack up front, then. For the first time in several games, we've got a thin range of options. Including de-selection. We call four players in to give it to them straight. First is Ian Hathaway. He's still not at his best fighting weight, we tell him. He needs to get his calorie intake down and his work-rate up.

Next on the block, as Sod's Law will have it, is a good mate of Ian, Richard Hancox. With Neil Gregory's arrival, Richard's claim on a regular first-team place is looking increasingly tenuous. And, certainly as regards the immediate future, he's not in the forefront of our plans.

Third candidate for the short-term chop is Jamie Ndah. His overall fitness – held back by specific injuries – is too suspect, we let him know. He's not sharp enough because he's not physically equipped enough. And, possibly, as well, because he's not whole-hearted enough. He knows what, inside and out, he needs to work on.

Last in is Ellis Laight. We tell him he's a bit unlucky. His being dropped is essentially a tactical decision. Tomorrow we intend going with a three man midfield of Mark Hawthorne, Charlie Oatway and Paul Mitchell that will be asked to bomb forward in constant support of the Jack-Gregory pairing up front. This being highly labour intensive, youngsters Tony Bedeau and Wayne Thomas have got the nod for the subs' bench. A lot as it may seem for us to ask of him, we urge him to be patient.

Bad news obviously for all of the quartet. But Ellis takes demotion the least well. I understand why. No way lacking in the commitment department, he knows he's a borderline thumbs down. That makes it all the harder to take. Further, he's still living hand to mouth on monthly renewals of his contract. I see his young face harden. He's about to give us a verbal volley. Then he remembers our advice. He opts for patience.

The truth is that I know how they all feel. As a player I've been there myself many times. Sometimes I've been dropped because of my form, sometimes through politics, sometimes because a manager has some hare-brained notion that Snooks, the squad's greatest living donkey, has got it all over Nelson for speed, control, finishing, whatever. I'll make one proud claim now. Such setbacks always made me resolve to battle back. But the other side of the coin – and the one face up as it was offered me – was that they always hurt me as a player.

When I accepted the Torquay job I knew that inevitably there would come times when I'd have to be part of dishing out bad news to downwardly mobile players. I hadn't realised then that I would find it just as unpleasant a process as being on the receiving end.

I find myself calling Alan Curbishley again. It must be the association of ideas. But I'm not about to whinge about being left out against Reading in 1995. I'm chasing up that other potential loan-signing, Paul Sturgess. There's good news and there's bad news. Charlton are quite prepared to loan him out. But, Curbs virtuously tells me that, coming back from injury, Sturge is still a goodish way off match fitness.

Training today is severely restricted by fierce rain. Gritting our teeth, though, we try to improve the non-shining hour by walking through a succession of 'Shadow Play' scenarios. This is where you must be in *this* situation. This is what you must do. These are your primary tasks. Later we back up this exercise with diagrams on the Nobo Board. More than has been the case before other games, I take the squad through a full run down of set pieces. Attacking. Defending. *This* is what you do. This is your job *here*.

This return to classroom basics stems from the feeling Hodgie and I have that we're close to needing to start again from our pre-season square one. With recent defeats an ominous negative factor has begun to prejudice our collective efforts. The enthusiasm that was so high to begin with and gave us our more than acceptable start has dipped dangerously close to zero. With it has gone self-belief. Worse – resignation – has flowed into the vacuum. 'We're giving it our best shot,' you can sense some players thinking. 'Losing by the odd goal's not that bad. Not on our wages.'

It's partly in an attempt to rekindle some 'go for it' commitment that I publicly recycle to the squad a saying of my former Plymouth manager, the wily and kind Dave Smith.

'Always remember,' he was fond of remarking, 'that 100 per cent of shots never taken are missed.'

I pause. Blank faces stare at me. They are waiting for the punch line.

That same evening my home phone rings with nicely judged irony. The caller is none other than Paul Baker. The man who, if we'd not sold him, if he'd grabbed goals for us as frequently as he's doing for his new club, Scunthorpe, would have earned us another six to eight points. We exchange news and pleasantries and then he comes to his point.

'Nelse – you remember at the start of the season you set the players targets?'

'Yes.'

'I had to score so many goals.'

'Yes.'

'Well, if you count in my Scunthorpe ones I've reached my target already. Am I still on for a pay-out?'

I laugh and tell him to piss off. He wishes me and Torquay all the best. I know he means it. It's nice of him to keep in touch. My foot stabs at me viciously. There must be some salt in the wound.

Saturday 23 November

Hartlepool, frankly, don't look to be up to much. With over half an hour gone there's no score but we're definitely getting the better of it. From the bench I sense the conviction is growing that the message we gave in the changing room – 'They're there for the taking' – wasn't just feelgood bullshit. We've got some enthusiasm back and there's an edge to it.

Then in the 39th minute, Jon Gittens comes striding forward carrying the ball out of defence. Somebody closes him down. They're side by side jostling, a shirt or two is pulled. Abruptly, clutching his head, the Hartlepool player crashes to the ground. From where I stand I can't quite make out what's happened. The referee has no doubts. His hand is already waving the red card. The decision hasn't gone our way. Jon sulks off as, in the worst traditions of the game, one or two other players square up to him and each other. Hodgie and I ignore Jon. Time for that later. He stalks up the tunnel some 60 minutes ahead of schedule. We set about switching Paul Mitchell to left back. Ten minutes to the half-time whistle and we're reduced to one man up front. Welcome to Plainmoor, Neil Gregory.

At half-time it's still 0–0. We try to pump up the 10 men. We tell them – and it's true – they're still in with a good shout.

The second half. Despite a disallowed Hartlepool goal we're still morally in the lead. Charlie Oatway and Mark Hawthorne are running themselves into the ground and glory alike in the midfield.

Time ticking on. Ten minutes to go. Fresh legs? Steve McCall is on the bench but he's all about guile not chasing-back pace. Debutant Gregory, though, looks close to out of it. Ploughing a lone furrow is a lot to ask from a man lacking match practice. We swap him for Tony Bedeau. Almost at once the lad is brought down in the penalty area. Spot kick? No. Well, I thought their goal might have been allowed. We'll call that quits.

The 10 are still looking for three points. We frequently attack. We win free kicks. But our set-piece, dead-ball delivery is bad beyond belief. It's as if we'd never talked these opportunities through yesterday. In goal, Hartlepool have a rookie who seems as short a keeper as I've ever seen between league sticks. But, as ever, size isn't important. The potential handicap goes untested and unpunished. Oh to be out there!

Injury time. We've salvaged a point, stopped up the loss haemorrhage. Or have we? A goal-kick, surely. But the ref has given a corner. This must be the game's last spasm. Over comes the cross. Up goes Hartlepool's Joe Allon. The challenge on him is half a light year late. He has a free, unimpeded header. He loops the ball over Rhys to the far post where Scott Stamps ... isn't. It was Stampsie who was nowhere near making the aerial challenge. If he'd held his ground – *'that's your job in this situation, your primary task'* – he'd have been able to clear the ball with his eyes shut.

Deep into injury time we've snatched defeat from 10-man moral victory. The players can hardly bring themselves to shake hands with the Hartlepool lads. It's not animosity. It's heart-sickness. In the tunnel four or so of our lot can hold in their feelings no longer. They turn on the ref and beat him about the ears with soccer's no-no 'C' word. 'Cheat! Cheat!' they yell.

They're still on about the disputed corner. Unfortunately for them I witness this. In the dressing room I go ballistic. Off the Richter scale.

It's not a question of whether the corner decision was a correct call, I storm: the point is that once it was given we should have been professionally capable of dealing with it. It should have been routine. Sharp prosecuting questions reveal Stampsie is not the lone villain of the piece. As we lined up to defend somebody panicked over the Pool having that extra man.

'Pick him up, Scott.' Stampsie, hearing, obeyed. And so fell between two stools. Given my initial flash he's lucky not to have been felled across one bench.

There's an interesting added dimension to my rage, I'm interested to note. It's genuine, but throughout part of my brain remains ice cool. You're doing it this way, it's saying to me, because shocking them into remembering is the best way to get the lesson across. The outburst, in fact, is totally divorced from performance art. When to emphasise my fury I lash out and kick something with my ailing foot, it's not the wall or a bench, but a calculatedly nice and soft kit-bag.

Time, now, I reason, to become Mr Nice Guy. I go round the room reminding the players of how well they battled for the other 92 minutes. If only they could have added precision to the mix when we had those set pieces ... 'All of you were up at *six* level, today,' I tell them. '*Seven* one or two of you. But when are we going to see the *eights* the *nines* that turn games, run them, win them?'

I know that upstairs the directors are waiting. I shower, dress and brace myself. Someone's got to do it. I go upstairs into the boardroom. The atmosphere is frigid – New Year's Day in Greenland. They're all sitting there like Eskimos around a water-hole waiting for a baby seal to surface.

'That new striker you brought in,' the chairman's wife says. 'He didn't show up too well.'

I think of Neil Gregory travelling all day yesterday to arrive late, sleep in a strange bed and play today with a bunch of total strangers reduced for two-thirds of the game to 10 men.

'I thought he did OK,' I say. Whatever my own overall feelings, part of my job is to shield our players from the criticism of others.

Sunday 24 November

You can't have yesterday back. Just get through this one. Read the papers (they rate Neil Gregory); make the tea; screw around with a mindless computer game; watch the greed spreading over everyone's face in *The Antiques Roadshow*.

You can't keep it up. Thoughts and issues breach your defences. Jon

Gittens. He cost us a win yesterday. With his record he'll be suspended for three weeks minimum. We'll need to fine him. Hell, worry about that tomorrow.

Monday 25 November

Hodgie and I had barely made it through the subterranean doors of the manager's office this morning when we were confronted by Richard Hancox. And I do mean confronted. The chairman's son-in-law was steaming.

Why had we dropped him!? We'd no right to drop him! We'd no right to drop him to make way for an unimpressive (his words rendered polite) loan-signing Neil Gregory. Our only attitude to training was piss-taking. We'd split the dressing room into factions. And so on.

I glanced across at Hodgie. He too, I could tell, was not unduly disturbed. Knowing the charges to be substantially untrue, neither of us felt unduly threatened.

For starters, it's an everyday fact of professional footballing life that every squad is split into two 'factions' – those who are basically In and those who are basically Out. (It's amazing how loyalty wavers, though, as a consequence of team changes.) More specifically, Hodgie and I had inherited a squad already somewhat, no, not divided, but tending to pull a little in different directions, along the lines of whether they belonged to 'The Class Of' this previous manager or that. I was confident that as newcomers wiping the old slate clean, Hodgie and I had somewhat blurred these divisions.

Piss-taking? Fact one: put-downs and mickey-takes are the common currency, the social cement that bonds players in the changing room and on the training ground. Training is *hard*. It goes better when there's a smile on the face. Play hard on the pitch. Play hard off it, if you like. Work hard all the time. When a reprimand is in order, then if a nod is as good as a wink, a piss-taking crack is almost always preferable to a full-bore bollocking. I was very confident that neither Hodgie or I had ever abused our position as 'gaffers' to turn squad members into stooges.

Confidence breeds restraint. Holding my peace I didn't launch into a fierce justification of my training-ground ways. No more did Hodgie. We could appreciate that Richard was coming from a further psychological distance than a weekend family discussion. Much more of an Out these past couple of seasons, he has found being the chairman's son-in-law an inevitable millstone. The allegation of nepotism has cost him a lot more than his fair share of stick – that: 'You're only in the side for one reason, Hancox' – from the Gulls' supporters. It would have been hugely to his advantage to have been on the books of a 'neutral' club and judged purely on his footballing merits.

Of which there are several. Left-footed, he's versatile, able to play in a number of positions. Perhaps that has been a long-term disadvantage making him a classic utility player – 'adequate in several positions, specialist in none'. His preference is to play up front. But from my time spent working with him I hadn't gained any sense that he was worthy of displacing our established forwards or, indeed, that we haven't been utilising him to his full capacity. His sudden (and, as I suspect, secondhand) criticism of Neil Gregory therefore touched me on a raw nerve. I didn't bite my tongue completely.

All the same, part of me admired him. As the tempest began to blow itself out, two things became clear. An unseemly row wouldn't do anything for anyone; and Richard, quite simply, had come in to call it a day. He was implementing the parachute clause in his contract. And doing so with a bang not a whimper. Very understandably his frustration and pride had prevented him going quietly. Fair enough – in his position I might well have done the same.

Hancox half-hour had begun as a bitter exchange. It ended with handshakes. Hodgie and I – very genuinely – wished Richard all the best as he left to pursue a business career outside football. Exactly what, he still wasn't sure, but at 28 with a family to support, he clearly feels that the chances of improving his lot in life don't lie amidst the, as he sees it, far from level playing-fields of Plainmoor.

He went without slamming the door. I stared at it. A quick montage of some of the more iffy bits of my career dimly screened itself at the back of my mind. In his position. Non-position. There but for the grace … And time for it yet.

Mercifully intervening, the phone rang. The chairman summoning us to his office. Sat before Mike Bateson was a visibly downcast Jon Gittens. He knew that his second sending off of the season, on top of his offence against West Ham, had to bring further disciplinary action and yet another hefty fine. But that was just the end result tip of the iceberg. Submerged from casual view was the root problem needing to be sorted.

The heart of the matter was the impossibility of Jon being able to travel back to his family every day and the consequent lonely, stir-crazy nights he was condemned to spend in his small Torquay flat. It was a rerun, in fact, of the Paul Baker (two more goals again on Saturday, dammit!) scenario. What was required was a workable solution that would satisfy all parties. Easier wished for than arranged. As a starter, though, the still transfer-listed Jon was given three days off during which, back home in Hampshire, he could clarify exactly what 'extra time' he needed with his family each week. It's our genuine, not to say self-interested, wish that when he returns he'll be focused enough to continue the outstanding work he has – most of the time – contributed on the field.

Less mortified, Jon left for home. He thereby left room for the chairman to swing an all but knock-out blow. Out of a cloudy grey sky he informed us that he was calling an extraordinary meeting of the Torquay FC board so as to tell his fellow directors of his intention to resign by the end of the season. Although rocked back, Hodgie and I were not quite knocked off our feet by what came across as less than a complete haymaker (until Mike can find someone to buy him out, his 'resignation' speech has to be regarded as a declaration of intent rather than hard fact) and had been more than a little telegraphed. Mike's enthusiasm has clearly waned from its pre-season high. Continual criticism, confrontation with fans, the alarming slump in gates and the sheer demands on his time which the hands-on role of MD exacts have clearly been taking an erosive toll. Then there's the parrots.

The past week must have crystallised his impressions. He had returned from a battery-charging week's cruise on the QE2 to be welcomed by the worst Saturday gate in the Football League, a loss in injury time and his daughter's husband deciding to call it a day as a pro player. And there was the capper. The AGM had made public news of a trading loss of £54,000 for the previous financial year.

Hodgie and I sucked in our breath, let it out again. I suppose we said something. We went off for training. It was a very low key affair.

Tuesday 26 November

A scouting mission with precise purpose. Swansea, our Saturday opponents, were replaying their first round Cup-tie with Bristol City. An excellent chance to do some constructive homework. Barely had I jotted down the 3–4–1–2 formation Swansea were adopting before an added question mark as to its efficacy became necessary. No more than 15 seconds had elapsed before their keeper Roger Freestone was retrieving the ball from his net. My notes went straight to the jugular. We might experience much joy, I scribbled, if we could put Swansea under intense pressure for the first 30 seconds ...

Wednesday 27 November

Well watered and fed by mid-west scout Chris Carter's hospitality we set off from Swindon this morning on the second leg of our three game Scoutathon. Our destination was that awe-inspiring San Siro of football, Park View Road, home of Welling United and as I know only too well to my cost, Charlton Athletic Reserves.

Pavlovian instinct had me heading for the bench but Hodgie discreetly took my elbow and with soothing words distracted me all the way to the comforts of a director's box seat at the back of the ground's only stand – a position some three rows in from the dug-outs. Our main attention was still focused on Charlton's recently listed left-back, Paul Sturgess. Kevin was hoping for eye-witness confirmation of all that I had built young 'Sturge' up to be. When, after 60 minutes of none too memorable involvement, Paul was substituted, Hodgie must have been questioning my judgement. In the lad's defence, it was his first game for five weeks (he was some way off full match fitness), he was being played out of position and the atrociously uneven pitch – Park View *is* like the San Siro in that respect – made life difficult for all the players. As of the moment, though, the young Robin has no likelihood of being metamorphosed into a Gull.

If we had the slightest chance of scraping together the cash, I'm sure Hodgie would have been there on the final whistle to sign Steve Brown. My former commuting companion of happy 'Gatwick Express' memory now finds himself out of favour at the Valley and is also listed. Head and shoulders above the rest today he must be worth every penny that canny Curbs is looking to realise on him. But in a quick post-match chat with Alan we never even asked the asking price. What would have been the point? We've not got the wherewithal. We've nobody to swap.

All we've got is an evening appointment with a game at Totton.

Southampton's training ground is off the beaten track but is well worth the where-the-hell-is-it visit. It boasts a perfect training ground surface . Green with envy, blue with cold, Kevin and I watched the likes of Rocastle, Newton, Sinclair and Phelan exploit the pitch to the full as they passed their way through the Saints' frozen stiffs. After an hour they were comfortably in control at 2–0 up.

Time to go home, said Zebedee. After 24 hours of nothing but football the now less than totally dynamic Torquay duo called it quits. Ice and fog were our travelling companions on the final leg home.

Thursday 28 November

Using the knowledge we had gleaned from our Ashton Gate spying mission we devoted training today to setting up a practice match, first team versus a 'rest' made up of reserves, youth team and all available physiotherapists. Object of the exercise was to accustom our players to the specially formulated tactical plan we intended deploying. We've got to do something, after all. A page one rule of sport is: change a losing game. We've lost five in a row without scoring once. Enough is enough.

Since we can't change the personnel, what we must vary are our tactics – specifically, our plans of attack. We're essentially sound in defence. Up front we are failing to create anything like enough chances for the practically starving forwards to feed on. Most glaringly, we need more crosses, high, low, far post, near post, into the box. Thus, first off, we will use the quicksilver but enigmatic Rodney Jack out wide with instructions to run the ball at the Swansea defenders. Balancing this we'll reintroduce Ian Hathaway on the left. This should make for a better balance and, we hope, the forging of a productive link between Ian and Scott Stamps. For the first time this season, we'll employ a flat back four. Jon Gittens will move to right back, with Lee Barrow partnering Alex Watson in the middle.

These plans communicated and rehearsed we now proceeded to take a leaf out of Charlton's set-piece book. The chairman has heavily criticised our execution of set-piece situations. He's dead right. A major portion of today was spent attempting to improve the quality of the balls delivered from free kicks. We got that improvement. Today. Today's entire session went very well. It always does in training. Four hundred and fifty minutes-plus without a goal, maybe, but I finished the session feeling that, from a coaching point of view, I had done my week's work thoroughly well. Sadly, as regards team selection, I was once more going to have to be confined to the side-lines as a definite non-starter.

In the middle of enthusiastically orchestrating the players, I instinctively controlled a miskicked ball. Jesus! There's no way this could be down to just bruising.

Agreed, said the physio. The most likely diagnosis was a hairline or stress fracture. We'd best get it X-rayed.

Friday 29 November

Information as to the outcome of last night's EGM was scant but one item of hard news spoke volumes. We're operating at a running loss of £3,500 a week. The implication is starkly simple. As night must follow day, cutbacks on the size of our already shoe-string squad are inevitable. And imminent. The dream of a glorious first management season promotion has faded. Four weeks ago we were all celebrating Hodgie's Manager of the Month award. Now that seems like an old dream too, or, at best, a gift from the wicked fairy. Fantasy has flown out the window to be replaced by the repeated blows of reality trying to hammer sense into my head. In the last few weeks it has several times been in my hands. A few more and it could be in the chairman's.

Saturday 30 November

A bad, bad day. A woeful, an abject performance. Ice in the pit of the stomach time. My irrational surge of optimism at our potential for overturning Swansea has proved … irrational.

Theoretically it couldn't fail. And in fairness and fact for the first 15 minutes of today's game the practical wasn't that bad either. Then the inevitable, as it's now, alas, appearing to seem. Someone forgets to do their job defending a corner. The ball falls to the one unmarked Swansea player on the edge of the box. A shot. A cruel deflection. A goal. In that 'I feel sick' moment I knew that the excellent week's work we had put in had been for nothing. The result here was as good as done and dusted.

It was what ensued, though, that was truly ominous. Win, lose or draw there had always been question marks, of course, about our collective experience, our technical skills, our cohesiveness. But never about our attitude, our – I have to use the word – commitment. Now for the first time I could unquestionably see heads dropping. The team in blue and yellow stripes had taken on an air of 'born to lose' acceptance and were going through the motions. Another goal for Swansea before the game's end: never a sniff of one for us.

The coach ride home promised to be dire. In the event Providence of a sort provided a diversion. The supporters' club coach having broken down, the travelling army petitioned a hitch back home aboard ours. It was hardly a problem. Glad as I was of our fans distracting presence I could only wince at the number. Twenty-two. Not so much an army, more a trickle of refugees.

By Torquay standards the journey was short. Mid-evening found three ashen-lipped men sole occupants of a pub at that epicentre of riotous West Country roistering, Chudleigh. Shaking our heads in repetitive turn we peered forlornly into the flames of an artificial log fire in search of a no less synthetic hope. None was forthcoming.

I shivered as I remembered. In mid-August the three of us had sat along with wives and a few friends in the garden of a pub idyllically out of a British Tourist Board brochure. The setting sun was still warm, the evening air swollen with the scents of two-dozen species of softly glowing flowers. And Torquay had just won their opening game of the season. Ah! Just to be there now! God was in His or Her heaven and in the Plainmoor boardroom too …

And now. Cold and dark. Doom and gloom. Was it only a month ago since Kevin was named Manager of the Month and the team on the verge of surpassing last season's final points count in the course of just 16 games? No, not a month, a lifetime.

No points. No goals. November.

Monday 2 December

Things can only get better. Or not. No crumbs of comfort were to be garnered from a demoralising early meeting with the chairman. He delivered an ultimatum. Given the weekly running loss of £3,500 the wages bill has to be cut. Players have to be let go. In this context enquiring whether we could bring in Scott Partridge as a loan-signing – Bristol City are willing; he can play in three different positions – was always going to be a futile exercise. Out of loyalty to ourselves we put the question anyway. The response was not unexpected.

Most unpleasantly, no, not surprised, but disappointed to find his darker expectations confirmed, was Ellis Laight. Kevin had called Ellis in to tell him he'd been axed. So much for our recent request that he be patient.

He can, I believe, consider himself very unlucky. Retained on no more than a series of month to month contracts, he's easily dispensable. In hard financial fact the £200 a week he is on is going to make only the tiniest dent in the outgoings column. There's a harsh whiff of 'to encourage the others' about his being elbowed. He's no Robbie Fowler, yet; not even, dare I say it, a Garry Nelson. But in the five months we'd been working with him he has clearly improved and learnt. If we and he had continued at the same rate I believe he might next season have been challenging for a regular first-team place. He's really a victim of our currently drawing crowds of 1,500 rather than 3,000.

To say that he was now disconsolate is to give no impression of how he felt – and how I knew he was feeling. He's 20. A trap door had just opened under him. But he's a smashing lad and the character he now showed in gulping down his anger and chagrin is precisely what will have him coming back for more, developing and, in time, knocking in more than his fair share of goals. The most well-meant advice I could give him now was to get placed with, say, a Conference or ICIS team: to get into the *habit* of scoring and so relax into improving. We shook hands.

One down. How many more to go? At present our first-team squad numbers precisely 16. Of those two, Jon Gittens and Charlie Oatway face longish suspensions (four and three weeks respectively) and three players, myself and Steve McCall included, are injured. To fill the bench against Rochdale on Tuesday night we'll be dipping into our YTS reserves. It could be argued that axing Ellis now is akin to ditching an engine on a 747 to conserve fuel.

Those who are fit are now made to pay for their last Saturday's spinelessness. Making our position clear ('We're prepared to accept a poor performance but never a poor attitude') we take them to Easterfield. The surface of this 'rec' is moon-like. But that's irrelevant. They're only there to run and run. And run. And – 'Give us a break, boss' – run.

The form book affords us one glimmer of hope to hold onto. Tomorrow's opponents haven't yet won away. We can keep it like that by putting the squeeze on them. We'll field a back-three formation with Paul Mitchell sitting just in front of them. This will allow the wing-backs for this time around, Ian Hathaway and Rodney Jack, to push on and, we devoutly hope, deliver good quality crosses into the Rochdale box. We've always looked our worst when the game has been stretched but this line-up will condense play. We'll do battle on our terms.

Tuesday 3 December

A cold gale is blowing in from Nova Scotia the length of the Plainmoor pitch. And straight down the icy streets of Torquay. Newcastle–Metz is on the box sitting beside several million cosy fires. Our gate tonight is precisely 1086. When Torquay United have 60,000 of Rupert Murdoch's readies thrust into its hand at one fell swoop it seems like high rolling times have come. But how many tens of thousands of spectators do Sky-televised matches keep away from mid-week grounds over a season? Comfortably enough to leave us out of pocket. Where is Ellis Laight tonight? Where were the Football League when the mid-week fixtures and the European Competition dates were being set in stone? I'll have to look the answers up in *1086 And All That*.

And where, at the evening's end, were our good intentions of yesterday? Early on, as so often with us of late, all seemed set fair despite the wintry conditions. We had the wind behind us. It made crowding Rochdale back the easier. Once again I had that now to be suspected 'they're there for the taking' feeling. Chances came our way. To Neil Gregory's way. Deadly in training, a textbook finisher, he muffed them. Once again at half-time a 0–0 score failed to reflect our superiority. The gale remained constant. In the second half we had it in our face but still we carried the fight. Paul Mitchell was down in my book as a Man of the Match candidate. Two more very takeable chances went begging but, going for the three points, we still looked to create and convert a third. We brought on an extra attacker for a defender. Tony Bedeau came on to replace Scott Stamps. In the 70th minute Tony won the ball cleanly in a sliding tackle and cleared. But the whistle had sounded. Harshly, erroneously probably, his challenge had been judged a foul from behind. Protest. Whirling arms and gesticulating hands. And a quick Rochdale free kick while half of our defence is still arguing. Discipline gone. Free header. Goal. All our strategy blown away on the wind.

The changing room afterwards was desolation row. Seven successive defeats. Ten and a half hours' play without a goal. I can sense an irrational logic possessing each and every one of us. We haven't scored in living memory. We can't score. We're never going to score again. There's nothing to say that we ever will.

'We shouldn't have changed the line-up,' someone says.

Oh – that would have prevented everyone forgetting page one of the Discipline Manual, then, would it, I think to myself.

'See you all tomorrow,' Hodgie orders. 'Sod your day off.' For the apparently condemned there is no such thing as a day of rest.

Wednesday 4 December

Twelve short and I would like to think sleepless hours later the players were back in the home team changing room wearing a standard issue training strip that looked as washed out as they felt. To make certain they were in no mood for what they thought they were about to receive we let them stew for a quarter of an hour or so longer than they might expect. When at last we deigned to join them we entered upon a degree of silence utterly in keeping with the commencement of an inquest.

To intense collective relief but not, thankfully, to anyone's smirking, embarrassed, indifferent amusement – the faintest suggestion of a smile would have triggered a 'run 'til you drop' session – we announced that our immediate plans did not include a forced labour period of PE. Instead we would ask them to exercise their minds – novel experience though it might prove for most of them – before engaging their tongues. In a positive attempt to pinpoint exactly where our ongoing problems lay we wanted to initiate a talk-in.

As is so often the case with group therapy what followed threw out a welter of individual input but very little in the way of genuinely insightful substance. Lee Barrow did advance the opinion that we, the coaches, had turned our back on the defensive basics – showing attackers inside, for instance – that we'd majored on at the start of the year. A grain of truth here, as Hodgie and I acknowledged. Our own defence was that given the current goal drought, the relatively steady performance of our rearguard, we had made remedying our attacking deficiencies a training priority. Another halfways fair comment was that we had juggled overmuch with our playing formations: a constant 4–4–2 would have got everyone into comfortable habits. Or rut, we countered. You wouldn't bat against Shane Warne the same way you bat against Wasim Akram. Should we play against Fulham the same way we played Lincoln? At Torquay – as was in their interest – changing personnel wasn't an option. Varying tactics was. Being able to play in more ways than one – it was called 'professionalism'.

Two hours brought us to the point of completely diminished return.

'OK, lads,' Hodgie said, 'on your bikes. Have a nice day.'

He and I remained behind to pick over the bones. Yes, we should go back to basics. We must again cover the ground that we'd beaten flat during our pre-season. Perhaps the euphoria generated by our comparatively good early results had led us complacently to believe this management caper was a right cake walk. If we ever had, we'd since learnt otherwise.

One compelling reason to sort it out was Rodney Jack. Potentially he was a trump card. His skills on the ball, his speed, his finishing (sometimes!) could make him a match winner. But problems were built into his natural game. He wasn't an out and out forward. He wasn't good at creating space for himself off the ball. It wasn't his style to get involved in a losing game. At the risk of sounding incredibly grandiose, we must in future gear the team up much more to getting the ball to him in the same sort of optimum positions where Liverpool feed McManaman.

Driving home I found myself modifying my disappointment at the squad's reluctance to admit responsibility, aka blame, for some of our shortcomings. It's asking a lot to finger yourself and colleagues in a group situation. Over my own career I'd many a time said to a manager informing me I was being dropped, 'Fair enough. I haven't been doing much of a job lately.' But that had always been one on one. In similar group breast-beating sessions – and I've known my fair share, believe me – I'd never made a public confession. Not so surprising really. When it comes to balls and bucks, footballers are generally vastly more skilled at passing the latter.

Later in the day a distant result was cause for guarded satisfaction. In Vienna, Manchester United, aided by Juventus doing the decent thing in beating Fenerbahce, succeeded in qualifying for the play-off section of the European Cup by overcoming Rapid. Next spring, supporters of the 'English' game can look forward to involvement in Europe's most prestigious competition. Torquay United can confidently expect more diminished mid-week attendances. The more I reflect, the more I'm convinced the Football League chairman held out their hands too readily for Murdoch's 60-grand pittance.

Finally on a variously crowded day, sad but not altogether unexpected news. The Brighton board have given Jimmy Case the bullet. Given the anarchy shaking the club to its foundations, the demotivating malaise swirling about the Goldstone, you would have to say this once great player was on a hiding to nothing as a manager. A cynic would say he did spend a lot of money – £250,000 or so – in the transfer market to little concrete effect, but I can't help think that given the present Seagull climate he could have bought George Weah and not got much of a return in points.

169

Thursday 5 December

Failure to progress beyond the first round of the FA Cup is not, perhaps, the most coveted way of earning a mid-season break but we'll take what spin-off benefit is going. The second round gives us a weekend off, very welcome in the light of our need to regroup. In particular it made implementing yesterday's good intentions that much easier. Committed to getting back to basics, I took the squad through a sustained two-and-a-half-hour session that bore down on showing inside, winning the ball back, using the ball with maximum speed and simplicity.

From little local difficulties to universal implications. A viable and even civilized compromise seems to have been hammered out by all interested parties in respect of *Bosman* – the European Court's ruling that a player, once out of contract, is by definition a free agent. Now, the suggestion is clubs should continue to own a player's registration, regardless of contractual status, up to the age of 24. On the one hand, the accommodation runs, players won't remain chattels, wage slaves of clubs throughout their working lives. On the other hand clubs will not run the risk of discovering and developing a youngster, teaching him everything he knows, only to see him wander off towards the money-bagged horizon the maturing moment he becomes a hit property and/or some cigar devouring agent pours poison in his ear.

For the Torquays of this world there is still a considerable risk element. A likely lad of 17 steps across our threshold and right away there's a problem. Do we offer him a long-term contract (to discover six months later he's a flash in the Plainmoor pan) or do we play safe with shorter terms (to discover that, kissed by genius, he strolls on to Arsenal within a couple of years)? Well, it's what happens at the blood-stock sales and it's for us to prove ourselves good judges of horseflesh. Speaking as somebody with a foot in both camps (just about) I would say a '24' threshold is an equitable one.

Friday 6 December

More concentration on our trade today in the form of two training exercise games aimed at improving basic technique. Both are played in a 60 x 20-yard corridor. The one is structured around a team of four taking on one of eight with instructions to close them down. The more elaborate other involves three teams of five, the third occupying a 'piggy in the middle' position between the other two. In time as they successively lose and win back the ball, all three sides change position. In (literal) practice there's a fourth participant in the exercise. The playing area. We've drawn the very short straw today of the Centrax rec. Not only is its surface another backside of the moon job, it's on a pronounced – and therefore never rolled – slope. The section we mark out gives new meaning to the pace bowlers' expression 'corridor of uncertainty'.

Saturday 7 December

Luxury. A winter Saturday at home. It does give me time in which to assess the almost complete lack of improvement in my ailing left foot but, hell ... I'll worry about that next week.

Monday 9 December

Is it possible to coin a new proverb? If so, how about: 'a rest is as good as a change for the better'? The mood in the changing room today is surprisingly 'up'. It could, of course, be that the presence of new sets of civvies on three pegs, three new faces alongside them, has given everyone else a Monday morning jump-start.

Our persistence in attempting to blow the breakers on BT's circuitry has brought us the reward of three trialists with a bit of 'previous'. First is the wonderfully named Llewellyn Riley. Introduced to us by the good offices of the same former Torquay resident who brought Rodney Jack to the club's attention, Llewellyn comes from Barbados' Lambada Club. If he can manage flashes of brilliance that anywhere match his smile, he'll do nicely for us.

Coming from closer to home is Stoke's 19-year-old midfielder Aiden Callan. He's here for a week's assessment, courtesy of Lou Macari. The third hopeful is Robert Calderhead. Currently of no fixed club he was formerly with Watford. That suggests he might have something to offer beyond the potential convenience of his currently living just up the road in Exeter.

In an ideal world we would have had all three in a couple of weeks ago and involved them in a Reserve game. The one factor making us hesitate over this plan has been the real world absence of any Reserve game. Now, rather than continuing to keep everyone dangling on the end of umpteen 'well yes, in principle ... maybe a little later' phone calls, we've called the three in anyway. We'll think of some way of running a rigorous rule over them.

The lack of any fixture for our stiffs is also bad news for Steve McCall and me. We both need to play 90 minutes of 'in anger' football if our fitness is not to dip appreciably after our three weeks of injury-enforced sidelining.

In my case, however, this soon proves a purely hypothetical set-back. Gingerly kicking a first ball in training I rediscover that it's a case of in agony as before. The problem is clearly more deep-seated and persistent than squares with a diagnosis of heavy bruising.

Ligaments maybe. My morning's misery is completed by the decision that my mandatory next step must be an appointment with Spear. Doctor Spear, that is. Really. Suiting his actions to his name the good doctor will be only too delighted to plunge the needle of a bicycle pump-sized syringe into the bony heart of the problem.

Tuesday 10 December

If a job is worth doing at all, it's worth doing well. As best as we can. Lacking a Reserve fixture we pay our three trialists the compliment of selecting two 11-a-side teams and sending them out on to the Plainmoor pitch for a 90-minute 'give it all you've got' match. Mind you it's a somewhat dubious compliment. The selection process has made use of every one of our fit full-time pros, all our youth team lads, head coach Hodges and two school kids.

The proceedings did momentarily turn farcical when the referee trotted out but yellow carding Alex Watson for dissent during the tossing-up convinced everyone that Mr Nelson (Braintree, Essex) was in no more of a mood for messing than linesmen Trevor and Neville (groundsman and odd-job man respectively) or fourth official Algernon (club mascot).

The whistle blown, the game was taken with all appropriate seriousness. The players got a lot out of it and both in terms of tactics and talent-spotting the exercise fully justified itself. Young Callan impressed everyone with a classy display and a cool finish.

The final score of 3–0 to the probables was a fair reflection of the game and, possibly, of the gap between our first team and the rest. But this 'form' result did throw up a genuine cause for concern. The striker's crisis of confidence shirt now has the name Ndah clearly stencilled across its back.

Pairing Jamie with Rodney Jack and pitting him against Hodgie and two 16-year-old schoolboys should have been a heaven-sent platform for planting strike after strike in the back of the net. Sadly, save for one moment of pure Hot Rod genius, it was a case of miss upon miss upon miss.

In football there's nothing sadder than an off-form striker not scoring goals. Having spent more private post-mortem mental replays looking for the one that got away than I care to admit to, I now really felt for Jamie. After today's game I took him to one side and reminded him that it's something all strikers experience and the only way he'll get through this rough patch is by hard work and getting himself into scoring positions. But it's all so easy to say that when it's not you. A Dwight Yorke, a Les Ferdinand might have been able to end their droughts, Jamie will be thinking, but what iron-clad law exists proclaiming that Jamie Ndah ever will? It's so hard for him to take the long-term view. He must sense that, short term, today's session has probably cost him his first-team place: that if things don't improve, there may not be a long term.

Wednesday 11 December

At first rosy glance it seemed that Santa Claus had prematurely tipped the contents of his entire sleigh down the Premiership chimney. Fending off intense competition from several other blue-chip companies, the brewing giant Bass has bought the right to sponsor the Carling Premiership for the next four years. The price tag was an ice-cool £36 million.

But not the half of it. Lob in Sky TV's recent multi-million pound investment and the big fish in the English leagues would appear to be swimming in a fiscal pool awash not only with dosh but also countless wannabe sponsors stumbling over their wallets and each other as, in an age when pro football's marketability is hotter than at any time previous, they try to link their breakfast cereals, their pizzas, their film stock, oh yes, their football boots, to the beautifully high-profiled game.

Christmas, then, has already come home for the Premiership and its goose has got so fat that in a fit of seasonal goodwill the caring and sharing Chairmen of the elite clubs are talking today of carving a £30 million tranche from their golden bird for charitable distribution among their cash-strapped brethren, the 72 poor bastard teams of the Nationwide.

Goodwill? The little boy in me that still believes in Father Christmas, also wants to believe that the fortunate few haven't lost touch with the also rans after all: that they fully appreciate the need to make a positive contribution to the maintenance of quality control in the domestic game, the subsidising of emerging teen talent, ongoing investment in soccer ground real estate and construction.

But a *free* lunch? Are you sure there's a Santa Claus, Virginia? That this isn't humbug? The Scrooge in me cannot but wonder: where's the catch, the ulterior motive? Those profit-motivated business supremos are not readily renowned for giving away something for nothing. What are they really after?

It couldn't be, no, surely not, that this gift is actually proffered as a sweetener, a none too virtuous attempt to buy the silence of the minority when, as might just conceivably come to pass, the talking turns to bigger and better pay-per-view deals? Better, that is, for the couch potato. I've already suggested that, grasping before properly considering, the lower leagues have already been short-sighted in snatching at Sky's £60,000 per annum offer rather than calculating the fall in turnstile revenue over the five-year period the agreement covers. This gift from the Premiership could obliquely lead to more short-changing.

It might also be the case that some of today's open-handed Premiership clubs would rather like a change in the rule-book which would allow wealthy directors of one club to become more openly involved – surface back to us , Robert Maxwell, all is forgiven – in the running of another.

The day wears on and I find still more reasons to beware the Premiership bearing gifts: £30 million, 72 clubs. But who says the division of the spoils will be equal? I can already anticipate as we lurch into 1997 the voices of the bigger clubs, Man City, perhaps, Wolves, maintaining that they deserve more than their fair share of the cake because they are … well, bigger.

Who says I worry too much? Worry? Me? If I'm being guilty of too much suspicion, I've picked a good day for it. There's a little appointment today that will take my mind completely off the sordid question of money. It's that appointment with Dr Spear, a session guaranteed to replace cerebral agitation with pedal agony.

'Hello, Doctor,' I say. As he turns to pick up this *thing*, I lack the nerve to ask him if he's in joint practice with Dr Jackson. He motions me towards a couch – I must take this medicine lying down – and I discover I lack courage of absolutely any sort whatsoever.

'This may sting a bit.'

The hypodermic is a prop from a hippopotamus clinic. It will be delivering cortisone. It will be delivering cortisone to the bony inside of the foot just forward of the ankle. The interval between the initial insertion of the needle and the plunger finally completing its travel lasts two whole minutes. Give yourself a break from reading and count off 120 seconds. You'll find it takes about a fortnight. No, you don't want me to go into further details.

Thursday 12 December

Nine able-bodied men this morning. Even Hodgie and I can work out that it doesn't add up. We scrap plans for a five-a-side session. Training becomes a token work-out.

There's one bright note, however. Local bruising around the needle's entry point apart, Dr Spear's initial thrust seems to have been to the point. I tap a ball or two around and there's no deep-seated reaction. A few more days and I could be back in business.

Back in business – for how long remains to be seen – is my former boss Steve Gritt. Stepping in where many another would fear to tread (although he won/lost out over some 49 other candidates) Steve has accepted the managership of Brighton and Hove Albion. Too little too late? In wishing him all the best, I only hope that his general eagerness to get back into football, his particular determination to confound the Gritt-doubters, have not led him to take on a mission impossible with no potential whatsoever for a happy ending.

Friday 13 December

John Carpenter day is lucky for some. The virulent bugs that invaded the immune systems of seasonal – but not altogether seasoned – revellers Stamps, Barrow and Hathaway have proved to be only of the 48-hour variety. Variety is what the Torquay management find themselves blessed with. We need 14 players for pitch and bench tomorrow and, low and behold, here is the sudden luxury of being able to select from a fully fit first-team squad that numbers no less than 15. The only confirmed non-starters are the still convalescent Messrs McCall and Nelson.

Our first 15 does include former star schoolboy fly-half Kevin Hodges. It has been drawn to his attention that his terms of employment clearly state him to be still registered as a player. Needs must. Hodgie has callously evicted the family of spiders from their squat in his 'Protected' boots. He's sticking himself on tomorrow's bench the better to act as childminder to Wayne Thomas and Michael Preston who, at 17 and 18 respectively, can't quite combine to outscore Hodgie in years.

The numbers game continues to be a daily constant. Scott Partridge, for instance, seems fated never to become a welcome addition to our columns. Our hopes of finally bagging him took yet another snipe-like twist today. Joe Jordan has given the green light to Scott's flying the Ashton gate coop but a night at home with his macaws has mysteriously caused Chairman Mike's enthusiasm for the signing to evaporate. We no longer have licence to target our man. The negative impact of this decision on our playing complement is all the more cruelly underlined by the sequel to our three trialists' command performance game. We would have liked to persevere with two.

Odd man out was Llewellyn Riley. He can certainly play a bit and his acting unpaid 'rep' Kevin Millard was certainly anxious to see his latest find sign a Plainmoor contract. My view, though, was that, very English in style, the lad wasn't an improvement on what we already have. This time, the trial offer completed, the goods would be returned.

Exeter is not Bridgetown. But it is home to Robert Calderhead and it is only up the road. We might have thought that as regards Robert continuing in our midst, geography was on everybody's side. In effect it's proved a stumbling block. Robert, unpaid trialist, asked us for £40 travelling expenses to offset the, say, 225 miles of his week's motoring. He was told that, if pushed, troubled Torquay (and it's a measure of our day to day economic desperation) would contribute £20 towards his out of pocket expenses. He told troubled Torquay that, thanks but no thanks, it didn't seem as if it would be worth his while to stick around. He'd get a job.

Considerably more of a disappointment was Aiden Callan's decision to return home. For a 19 year old he looks a class act.

To Aiden, however, Torquay looks about as far away from home as, well, Bridgetown – a long way, that is, from his family and friends in Stoke. Quite far enough away to get fed up in. He's still got six months to run on his Potters' Contract. For the moment he'd rather continue strutting his stuff in their stiffs hoping to catch the eye of an adjacent Burslem, say, or Walsall suitor.

No additions to our playing strength, then. And here's some more negative number crunching.

Believing that a total gate of 1086 is scarcely worth opening up the ground for, Mike Bateson announced a week ago that he was relaxing his hitherto firm stance on pricing and that admission for the traditionally poorly supported last home game before Christmas would be dropped from £8 to £6. The arithmetic means that we'll have to pull in 600 spectators more to reach the financial square one of our seasonal low 10 days ago.

Saturday 14 December

Statistics day. First the crowd. Mike Bateson's disappointment must have been considerable when our ever cheerful PA announcer broadcast that today's less than densely packed spectators totalled 1,586. Against Scarborough we pulled in exactly 500 more spectators than against Rochdale on a Tuesday. We're out of pocket on our bargain offer. Probably the people who took advantage of our December sale were the loyalists who would've come anyway.

But I'm not bitter. Frankly, my dears, I don't give a damn. The key statistics of today were that after 658 minutes of play, we scored a goal: after seven defeats on the trot we nicked a win! Torquay 1, Scarborough 0. And the day's local hero is Scott Stamps who, on the spot like a good attacking wing-back should be, got in on a rebound to deliver a first-class drought-ending strike.

Ecstasy multiplied by rarity! The parched desert patrol had found the oasis at last! The doomed feeling that we were predestined never to trouble the scorer again had been blasted in to touch. The relief was orgasmic. In holding on with thorough professionalism against a useful Scarborough side committed to second-half attack we'd not only gained a deserved win but also burst through the ceiling of Torquay's all-season points total of last year. For many, I think, this arbitrary benchmark was beginning to assume hoodoo qualities. With it breached, we could now switch instantly from bleak despair ('our jobs are really on the line now') to sky's the limit fantasy ('a good run now and we can make Wembley').

What kids footballers are!

Sunday 15 December

A win! A win! Any fan knows that the warm after-glow generated by a Saturday win always makes the Sunday stroll through the sports pages so much easier. A win means you can once again face doing all those mental arithmetic gymnastics that games in hand, forthcoming 'six-pointer' encounters, 'goals for' tallies demand. So it was with me today. It's a comment on the Third Division (though the others are no different) that after seven losses in a row, Torquay are still only three points off of a play-off spot. Gradually, though, as today wore on, my good mood became distinctly qualified. I increasingly focused on a 'result' of a far more profound and complex sort than any in today's soccer pages – the recent court decision against the chief constable of the South Yorkshire Police.

The judge had found in favour of John McCarthy – not the former Beirut hostage, not the classy Port Vale winger but the step-brother of a Liverpool supporter. A dead Liverpool supporter. A Liverpool supporter crushed to death at Hillsborough. This John McCarthy had sued the police on grounds whose relevance would immediately be apparent to them – PTSD.

They might perceive the grounds. They did not concede them. Although not denying liability for the Hillsborough disaster (how could they after the Taylor Report?) the South Yorkshire police did contest Mr McCarthy's claim. Their reasoning for doing so seems to me obscenely contemptible. It rested on proximity. The alleged lack thereof. Neither in terms of consanguinity or topography, they argued, was Mr McCarthy close enough to his relative. The thinking goes like this. He was, we submit, m'lud, only a *half* brother. He was, we would point out, m'lud, at the other end of the stadium, a matter of some 90 yards away from the, er … the regrettable incident.

Let us set aside the undisputed fact that Mr McCarthy's afternoon at a footy game ended up with him weeping over his step-brother's corpse as it lay stretched out on the Hillsborough turf. Do, however, let us bear in mind the proven fact that the two young men were good mates. Let us then proceed to put ourselves in the unbearable position John McCarthy's found himself in. In the Leppings Lane End all hell, it was increasingly becoming clear, was breaking loose among the press of people who couldn't escape. He was powerless to do anything but watch. Distance protecting him!

I've not the slightest doubt John McCarthy would rather have been nearer to his step-brother; that he would rather have taken his chances on the Leppings Lane terrace with the opportunity thereby of perhaps saving him and, perhaps, other 'brothers' than as a passive spectator, being slowly impaled on the spectacle from a distance.

The judge was commendably short with the South Yorkshire police's case. He awarded Mr McCarthy £200,000 compensation. Technically the chief constable concerned is liable for this sum. In practice it will be furnished by tax and rate payers everywhere. So what? I hope this is a first worthy foot in the doorway that the fat blue line has had its beefy establishment shoulder to these past seven years. May there be many more such civil actions.

Or so I would hope. There is an almost inevitable sting in the tail. The South Yorkshire police – proven great second-leg specialists in the PTSD Cup – have indicated that they will appeal the decision. The legal processes could take months. Years. In the meantime the award is likely to be frozen. Information as to the condition of Mr McCarthy's grief and ability to function normally is less cut and dried.

So, too, is the cost-effectiveness of the basic police stance. Saving hundreds of thousands of pounds otherwise paid out in damages may well be a huge divisional accountancy triumph. But what will be the cost to police credibility and budgets right across the country that this despicable post-Hillsborough South Yorkshire stance will finally run to?

Monday 16 December

The first headache of the new week is finding somewhere to train. The school field we've been using lately has cut up rough. I wouldn't like our lads to become discouraged by a random crop of true bounces.

The windswept and seriously soggy Clennon Valley then. Load up! Bibs, balls, cones, portable goals all present and relatively correct, it's, 'Hi ho, hi ho, it's off to work we go … ' or not. As charged with life as Frinton after dark the van's battery isn't up for it. Neither, when, after endless faffing about forming a caravan, we did get to train, were many of the players. Saturday's win had not only relieved a good deal of collective tension it had, incredibly, all by its single self, bred complacency. Not for me. Not only did I know one summer doesn't make a swallow, this was my first foray as a participant in training for four weeks. Rain. Gale force wind. Logistical cock-ups. Boy, do I know how to pick 'em, I began by thinking. Half an hour later I was into it and all enthusiasm. Business as usual for the left peg.

Come afternoon it was my untroubled right ear that experienced a work-out. The voice of a man far more dramatically back in business than I am was audibly beaming down the phone line. Ostensibly Brighton's new boss, Steve Gritt was calling to check on the progress of his claim for the expenses he'd incurred while executing the occasional covert scouting mission (the last, ironically, a check on Brighton!) at my behest.

'In the post tonight,' I said. The fact he was now competition had no bearing on a job well done. I knew in any case that this cheque chasing was all foreground flim-flam. Brighton had got Scarborough next. Steve was phoning to get the low-down on our last opponents.

I gave him my read-out. He'll be desperately hoping for a similar result to that of his first game in charge, a 3–0 win over Hull. The perfect start to an anything but perfect situation. I hung up very much hoping that the nightmare scenario being played out on the Sussex coast will benefit from its injection of true Gritt.

Wednesday 18 December

Not the correct day of Christmas but, who cares? The Chairman having kept his pledge to sleep on it, we've his formal blessing to adorn the Torquay tree with Scott Partridge. My spirits as I left Plainmoor in the early afternoon (technically this was a rest day: I'd come in especially to help cross the 'T' on the transfer) were those of a lord a leaping. Twenty minutes later they were those of an oven-ready pheasant. The phone was ringing as I came through my front door. On the line was a Kevin Hodges as exasperated as dejected. His news was simple. Middlesbrough had called veteran Clayton Blackmore back to Teeside. His loan period at Ashton Gate was to be neither extended nor converted to permanency. Consequently Joe Jordan felt he had no choice but to retain Scott Partridge's registration. The bird almost in the hand had never quite left the bush. I think if Judy Garland's *Have Yourself A Merry Little Christmas* had been coming out of the radio at this moment I might have slashed my wrists.

Friday 20 December

The game's afoot! Rather than awash. A 10.30am call from Feethams confirms that rather than experiencing another football-free weekend, the Gulls must fly north at once to our Leeds hotel. It's a distinct luxury. The state of our mid-season finances makes deciding whether to overnight or travel on the day harder than ever.

Facing a difficult enough decision of his own is the head coach. Both his assistants have declared themselves fit. Physically, that is. Match fitness, though ... now that's a different matter.

Saturday 21 December

Darlington today. It was only as spring was turning to summer last year that I saw them at Wembley but it seems a lifetime ago now. What a wealth – and otherwise – of experience and incident has since flowed under the bridge.

In classic fashion (Brentford and Blackpool provide other recent examples) Darlington have been in a state of severe shock since that game. Losing the play-off final by its only goal after a mere draw instead of a win in their last League fixture had snatched the nerve-shredding lottery of the play-off from the jaws of automatic promotion. They have been in trauma ever since.

So near then and now so far! As that final Wembley whistle sounded I had joined with the 30,000 other Plymouth fans in an exultant victory-saluting roar. Then, as prompted by the booming no-time-for-losers sound system the massed choirs of the West Country united in rendering a far from accurate *We Are the Champions*, a very different set of feelings swept through me.

In the face of all the green and white audio-visual ecstasy 14 forlorn white-shirted figures summoned the last of their energy, spirit and dignity to embark on a tear-stained but still proud circuit of the stadium. I didn't know any of them personally then. But as they passed I found the hairs on the back of my neck standing up. My own eyes grew moist in sympathy. I'd been overtaken by an incredibly poignant mix of emotion. Perhaps only another player could have felt it. You would have to be a fellow pro, I think, wholly to appreciate the bitterly distraught feelings of that entirely admirable Darlington team.

Now all is changed. Jim Platt, their Wembley manager sacked, their best players sold on to offset dire economic necessity, saddled with an ageing ground in urgent need of improvement, reeling from the Football League's announcement there is scant money left in the much abused reparations kitty, they have plummeted to second from bottom of Division Three. Changed utterly.

Not quite. To their great credit Darlington have not deviated from the credo of playing cultured, to-feet football. For that they deserve great respect both in a general sense and, narrowing down to today from us as, our formation modified to counter their diamond line-up, we run out at Feetham. Since we'd rather out-play than overpower opponents the portents are for a tasty encounter.

But don't bet on it. What ensues is a mediocre mish-mash.

Watching from the bench I've just begun to congratulate our coaching triumvirate on a tactical triumph when it becomes apparent that both Lee Barrow and Alex Watson, consistently excellent and vice versa all season, are having mega off-days. Our defending is punctuated by poor collective covering and personal errors. That we go in at half-time with a 1–1 score line – Stevie Winter getting forward to equalise – hugely flatters us. With halfways decent finishing Darlington could have been 4–1 up without us having cause for complaint.

This will be Neil Gregory's last game for us. During his loan period he's got perceptibly fitter but never once got on the score sheet and we can't justify retaining him longer at the asking price. It's sharply ironic, then, that amid all the half-time fire-fighting, I'm able to smile at him and say quite genuinely that he's saved his best performance for last.

With the resumption comes hope. Moving in on a short corner Mark Hawthorne stunningly crashes home a volley of Terry McDermott quality. 2–1 to the good guys. For a while we settle. But as Rodney Jack is injured, as Steve McCall tires, we fail to kill Darlington off. They push forward again and as chances are cackfootedly spurned at either end the possibility of an equaliser is very real. Then the goal comes. But it's ours! Popping up in the 81st minute to make it a personal scarlet letter day Hawthorne does it again. Embracing, Hodgie and I dance as if we'd won the Cup. Torquay have hit three in a league game for the first time. The game's won! We can relax.

In the 86th minute Darlington get a second.

Five minutes of hell ensue. It's panic stations in our defence and in the coaches' hearts and minds. With nothing to lose the Quakers surge at us. They create still more chances. They must score there … here … now. Somehow they don't. Holding out in spite of ourselves we've won our second game in a row.

Sunday 22 December

Not so much Sunday as Shilton's day. This afternoon the ex-England he-ancient ran out at Brisbane Road to take part in his 1000th league game. Even allowing for his one-off position it's a record as incredible as magnificent. I don't expect to see it equalled. I've been playing for 18 years, half my life. I'd have to go on well into my forties to come anywhere near Peter's all matches aggregate. That's just the quantity. As to the quality factor ... Cheers, Shilts. There's no question who's the main man King of Orient this Christmas.

Tuesday 24 December

He must find it perilously close to Christmas Eve in the work-house but today we made a signing. On a non-contract and (to the chairman's delight) no wage basis, we've registered former Charlton, Gillingham and Southend striker Steve Crane. His name was first drawn to my attention in the summer by my former navigator and co-driver, Steve Brown. A couple of months later ('I'd given up all thoughts of ever hearing from you, Nelse') we were finally able to follow up on the tip and for the past six weeks an overweight and ring-rusty and acting all-unpaid Steve Crane has been training with us. In contrast to the indifference of the two youngsters who gave us the cold shoulder recently this stickatitability has been impressive: so, too, as Steve has got back into shape, his skills. A little more perseverance and I think he has chances of making it all the way into the first team and gainful occupation.

Wednesday 25 December

Peace on earth, goodwill to all men. Unless, perhaps, the man is a soccer coach and you're a player. Not a quarrel but a grown-up difference of opinion. I was the dissenting minority voice in a 2–1 coaching decision to bring the squad in for mandatory Christmas Morn training. In the course of my past 17 professional soccer years, insistence upon this practice has hardened into a sacred tradition (aka bloody imposition). I've always thought it a counter-productive blow to team morale.

We went for a five-a-side session. Having made the effort, I thought, Nelse, you might as well give it your best. Again I was in the minority. Most of the squad visibly begrudged being ordered to jump through the hoops today. Reserving, as ever, all their enthusiasm for the sprint to be first in the showers, they only confirmed my belief that the day – in this case a whole 45 minutes – was nothing but going through the motions.

A year ago to participate in a similar tokenism cost me three hours of round-trip driving. Today, thankfully, my new set-up and the deserted roads took only a sixth of that time out of my life. It was still just about morning when the Nelson's bread-stuffing winner crossed the family threshold and Carly and Christopher's self-imposed restraint could explode in a whirl of major present opening.

Thursday 26 December

As it will always be, today is the short-changed Christopher's birthday. It's hard to combat the inevitable sense of after the Lord Mayor's Show but, just stopping short of his annual suggestion he be given a second on June 26th, we do our best. Not such a good best in my case, alas. I'm out the door first thing for the game we've so keenly honed ourselves for.

Cardiff City. And perhaps we've got chances. We beat them at home. We're coming off two wins. They're on a losing streak at their place. The trip isn't such a complete ball-breaker.

On the other hand, as umpteen other games across the country are cancelled South Glamorgan is an icy waste. The Ninian Park pitch is about one up from permafrost. Tundra testing suggests it offers just enough give to allow the shortest kind of stud. This decision brings us to the day's second equipment problem. Cardiff play in blue shirts, white shorts. All we've packed is our away strip – blue and white shirts, white shorts. It's not deep and crisp and even but there's plenty of snow and frost lying around. Sensing he's close to having to search for an albino in a snow storm, the ref, quite properly, isn't having any. He glances at Kevin who is in a first-team shirt.

'You'll have to play in your other strip,' he says.

'Fine,' says Hodgie, 'we'll just nip back and get it.'

Cardiff knocked the problem on the head by loaning us a set of their change strip. Yellow shirts, psychedelic black dots merging into white shoulders, black under-sized shorts, dark blue socks. They must have a side in the Cymru Punk League. Oh well, needs must ... looking in the shorts like we'd all over-eaten anyway, we took to the field.

Lurid the shirts might be. The Gulls, sadly, were a pale imitation of our recent selves. In due course we conceded yet another goal from a second ball to the far post and yet another from a free header from a corner. As the game went on slip, sliding away I thought wistfully of Boxing Day last year when against Portsmouth at the Valley I got my last goal for Charlton, a 90th-minute match winner. No smell of a repetition today. We'd handed Cardiff three points as readily as they'd handed us their kit. Ah well, it is the season for giving.

Friday 27 December

'What do you want first – the good news or the bad?'

The scene is the cramped management cupboard. Youth Trainee Matthew Wright confronts the massed ranks of Torquay's coaching strength.

'The bad,' he boldly goes for.

'OK,' Hodgie says, 'you're dropped for tomorrow's game.'

Wright's face doesn't fall that much. On current form his downgrading would be hard to justify. He's played not only solidly but also with considerable aplomb. He knows, though, we've got an embarrassment of equals in his position. He's been sacrificed on the often used altar of 'we've got someone with more experience'.

'What about the good, then?' Wrighty pursues.

'The good news is you've done plenty well enough to earn yourself a professional contract until the end of the season. Sort your terms out with the chairman. He's expecting you.'

The grin split his face from ear to ear. Sharply in contrast to Ellis Laight, Matthew Wright floated out of the office. A not wholly insignificant rite of passage.

Saturday 28 December

There's one consolation to this time of year. It affords minimum time to dwell on defeat. Just 48 hours after losing to Cardiff our seasonally maladjusted players have to do it again at home against Cambridge United.

Although we made them fight hard for it, their 1–0 win was thoroughly deserved. In particular the objective part of my brain was much impressed by the performances of Cambridge graduates, Messrs Joseph, Beall and Hyde. They've all clearly benefited from the teaching skills of experienced pro David Preece and new manager Roy McFarland.

As for us – chances not taken, unpenetrative possession, yet another set-piece goal against ... We slumped disconsolately in an eerily silent home team dressing room as the 'still got an awful lot to do' end of year report silently sunk into each and every one of us. The high spirited, shot through with relief 'we're going to jingle all the way' celebration of a short week ago has been drowned out by alarm bells.

I was able to grab a tiny personal crumb of comfort from events. I might feel utterly drained now but after a five-and-a-half-week lay-off I'd gone through two games in 48 hours without buckling on the field. I dredged up a last cup of energy with which to rally the troops. Sort of. Echoing the words of another seasoned old campaigner I offered the home team the best advice for the advance into the New Year I could muster – Corporal Jones' 'Don't panic!'

Monday 30 December

Almost the year's end but we don't seem to be turning any corner. What to do? We've tried running them. That didn't work. We've tried building up corporate self-esteem. Neither did that. We've tried a heart-to-heart talk in. That, if anything, put the management firmly in its place. What now? Good question. And the simple answer is there isn't anything. You're left looking at patience and application and the constant use, if you can come by it, of countless little local dollops of intelligent advice. In other words we've got to keep on keeping on and doing the best we can. Today, then, let it be hard work and a type of session that all pros enjoy – finishing.

The hard effort consisted of a sharp, endurance-testing sequence of short sprints aimed at getting hearts thumping and feet featly moving. Then, momentum generated, we channelled it into a 40-minute phase-of-play exercise designed to re-emphasise the type of delivery and maximum opportunity areas – whence and whither balls should be played and players arrive. *This is what you do/where you should be now.* Get the idea this time? On Saturday let's have the theory turning into practice.

Tuesday 31 December

Last year when Scunthorpe thrashed Torquay 8–1, 6'3 striker Andy McFarlane accounted for four of the goals. The experience seems to have seared itself into Mike Bateson's memory bank. Switched back on to a positive 'you have to speculate to accumulate' current, the chairman, of his own initiative, is proposing we acquire this haunter of his dreams to answer our running need for a do-the-business target man. Good thinking. Only … Andy McFarlane has been marginalised at Scunthorpe by their acquisition of a six-foot striker named Paul Baker – yes, the doing-the-business target man we sold to Scunthorpe three months ago!

Nevertheless … Neither Hodgie, Macca or I have seen enough of what

186

certainly won't be a gift horse so we suggest looking him in the mouth during a loan period. Scunthorpe manager, Mike Buxton, however, is understandably reluctant to deal in half measures. His opener for a full transfer fee is £20,000. A similar figure to the one we let Paul go to Glanford Park for. What a pity nobody then had seen *Trading Places*.

Groundsman Trevor Webb looked out on the eve of New Year. He found Plainmoor anything but even. He found it distinctly uneven because the big freeze had started hard on the heels of last Saturday's players before the divots had been replaced, the furrows filled. Frozen solid is how it remains today. So as to get some kind of an acclimatised grip, we train on it but very gingerly. Without exception all of us are reluctant to play on so treacherous, so easily injurious a surface. Time to call in a local ref for an inspection.

Hold on. A dissenting voice. Our views cut no ice in one quarter. The chairman, who has already bent a fork testing it, deems the pitch playable. There's no need to summon a second opinion, he opines. After all, Brighton have already set off for their overnight hotel.

This is a little more than *Gardeners' Question Time*. New Year's Eve may have produced some cold long tines but the Football League regulations clearly state that, in the event of insufficient notice of match postponement being given, the costs incurred by the visitors are to be met in full by the home side. Chairman Mike had already personally picked up the tab for our overnight in Leeds. I could sympathise with his wish to avoid similar largesse towards Brighton. It becomes clear that Hodgie and I have the job of getting our players' minds fully focused on the certainty they will be playing. Meanwhile grudging credit where it's due: working hard on the pitch our forking chairman is out with groundsman and school kids putting his back into it.

Wednesday 1 January 1997

Overnight -5°C added its own syncopation to those icy intimations of mortality that run their fingers up and down our New Year spines. Nevertheless, with Mike Bateson devilishly poised in the background with his pitchfork, referee Wilkes passes the surface as playable. Our first footings of 1997 are going to be anything but sure. Happy New Year.

But likely to be unlucky for some. Today's absolute cracker of a fixture sees last year's wooden spoonists by a country mile entertaining the side who are straining every over- stressed nerve to capture the dishonour this season. Or, rather, were. Under Gritty the Seagulls have not only flown in a different formation (the Charltonesque 4–4–2: what's new?) but taken on a goodly pinch of resilience. They're still seven points adrift but in their last five games they've only lost once. We only managed a draw at the Goldstone and there's a tightrope feel to this one at the back of my mind. This game is a psychological biggy. Lose it and we might find ourselves dropping faster than a Richard Branson balloon.

Suspensions cleared, Jon Gittens and Charlie Oatway are back. No one's nose, however is much out of dropped joint because Steve McCall is again sidelined by his troublesome Achilles and Jamie Ndah's resolution to stay fit and healthy this year has succumbed after just one hour to a bout of microwave flu. That's right. It's all over in a minute.

Remembering our Ninian Park slip-ups we glided across the rink and, in the fangs of the 'shut that freezer door' blast, dominated the first 30 minutes. Then, mounting a rare sortie, Brighton snatched a corner. Danger! Danger! All hands on deck! Red alerts were flashing. But a poorish ball in. Stationed in front of the near post I headed it away. Wind-assisted the clearance would have found touch. Against the wind the ball barely cleared the 18-yard box. Corner taker Paul McDonald seized on it and hit an inswinger to the far post. It floated towards not one but three totally unmarked Brighton players. It was Phil Andrews, scoring his first league goal, who clinically accepted the gift-wrapped chance. *That's just what you don't do there!* Up-thrusting hands appealing for offside (but not in the least to me!) sheepishly became downwardly mobile as a certain coach bade fair to thaw the pitch with the steam issuing from his ears.

Somebody did take it to heart – and himself to where he should have been doing just what he did. Despatching an exquisite volley (no mean technical feat on this death trap surface) stand-up Scott Stamps got us back into the game two lightning minutes later.

In the second half the wind filled our sails. Brighton were no longer breezy as we totally dominated ... and failed to capitalise. The temperature was sinking with our hopes as the clock ticked away. Damn! Psychologically, a draw would do Brighton far more favours than us.

A hit and hope clearance. It was chased down by unpaid sub Steve Crane still giving it his stick-at-it best. He surged lurchingly forward. Now the ball was lodged in a frozen no-man's land between eager forward, panicking defender and unnecessarily advancing keeper. Something had to give. The ball. Squirming away at an awkward height it bounced even more awkwardly in front of veteran striker, the previously dubbed Goldstone Gaz. No time for a setting up touch. Precision was a more pressing requirement than power. I took considered but right-footed aim. The ball rolled directly towards the far stanchion. Slowly. It rolled and it rolled. Suddenly, agonizingly, the long legs of Peter Smith were extending to ruin the slow-motion sequence. Out-pacing the ball's progress he would surely slide in to hook … What's he doing? Oh, he's trying to stay on his feet! He's in the net! He followed the ball into the net! He missed it! We've scored! We've won!

Joy. Unless you're a Brighton fan. Despair if you're Steve Gritt. You have to divide by a factor of about 1,000, but, as my second reaction was to feel for Gritty, I must have experienced something akin to Denis Law's feelings when, in a blue Maine Road shirt he back-heeled United out of the First Division. The Torquay fans in their relief were according me rapturous applause. But as I turned towards the away end and the fans of the side with whom I had enjoyed my never to come again scoring salad days, I had a sinking feeling that the adjective placed before 'Garry Nelson' might be other than 'One'. I wasn't doing them justice. My 'sorry, lads' shrug and wave at the final whistle were greeted not with the finger but, good on them, a chorus of 'well done, Nelse'. They deserve far better than they're being given.

Not exactly applauding was a clearly miffed Brighton manager. But credit him too.

'It had to be you. Well done, mate.'

'Sorry, Gritty.'

'That's what you're there for.'

'Fancy a beer?'

No chance he'd refuse. Our parting handshake was warm and firm. With Gritty there, Brighton still possess a ghost of a chance of avoiding the lower depths.

Saturday 4 January

I'm not involved today. None of the Torquay team is. The third round of the FA Cup finds us with time on our idle hands and, come late evening yesterday, Carole and I ensconced in a West London hotel. It's combining business with business time. Today Carole will execute a forced march through the Sales. Tomorrow I'll be earning a bit of pin money (well, it'll subsidise the hotel bill) summarising the big Cup tie at the Valley for Radio 5. It's all come together beautifully, because on Tuesday evening we're up at Vicarage Road in the Auto Windscreens Trophy. Until then, ice-age conditions permitting, I'll stay up in town smoking out potential Torquay superstars from the plethora of Avon Insurance Combination games on offer at the start of next week.

Sunday 5 January

An excellent day. An easy morning saunter across London got me to the Valley in plenty of time to wish my old Charlton mates the very best before climbing up to the cribbed confines of the Radio 5 cabin.

Too many unforced errors on both sides prevented the ensuing Charlton-Newcastle clash attaining classic status but end to end passion gave me plenty to talk about. With Phil Chapple delivering a probable career best, Alan Shearer failed to get on the score sheet for the third time running against Charlton. Robert Lee, my Man of the Match, enjoyed a huge 'welcome back' reception and, if his opening goal was the outcome of a double fluke, not too many of the Charlton faithful would have denied that he'd earned his luck.

One goal never seemed as if it would be enough and when Mark Kinsella delivered a long-range strike worthy of Waquar Younis in its use of reverse swing, it wasn't. The diving Shaka Hislop played well outside the ball's final line – a classic example of a keeper's reach exceeding his grasp.

One all at the death, then, and an interesting post-script to the match. Asked if rumours that his lessening commitment to the Newcastle cause might be true, Kevin Keegan got somewhat sniffy and … walked away. In such cases, of course, it's sometimes the first step that counts.

Monday 6 January

The best-laid plans. Weather that would send Ranulph Fiennes scurrying for cover has frozen the balls off no fewer than five targeted Avon Insurance Combination matches. I'm faced with pressing the 'abort' button on my extended spying mission behind enemy lines after just two days. Decisions … indecisions … Tomorrow's away game at Watford has not yet been ruled out but all sane meteorological indications are that it will be another frost-bitten non-starter. 'Get the hell out of there while the A303's still drivable,' is my self-arrived at verdict. Mission unaccomplished I point the car westwards.

Tuesday 7 January

Sod's Law has a long arm. It reaches all the way from Torquay to Watford where tonight's game is on.

Re-arrival in London brought no relief. The Vicarage Road pitch was essentially frozen but the large quantity of rock salt which Hodgie now employed was rubbed not into its surface but my open mental wounds. When he announced the starting line-up the roving radio correspondent was accorded missing in action status. Hodgie felt that I needed a sustained period of recuperation to recover from the stress of engaging my brain on Radio 5 air.

Then again, team selection could have had more to do with our earnest wish to see non-contract trialist Steve Crane operating on a higher plane.

In easily our most accomplished performance for some weeks, the team played close to their best and Steve was no conspicuous weak link. The one major blot, I'm afraid, was born of an old shortcoming.

A minute before half-time Torquay casually conceded their second corner. Watford played it short. Object of this manoeuvre, of course, is to vary the angle of the inswinging cross by a couple of unsettling degrees. Unsettled we were. The Hornet's number 5, Page, powered a quite unstoppable header into our heavily protected – or otherwise – net. I thumped the dug-out in frustration and knew at once that I could now deliver my half-time team talk on automatic pilot. The five goals we have conceded in our past four games have all been down to our inability to defend at corners.

Our generosity again proved decisive. A questionable penalty decision in the second half saw us go down 1–2. Against higher-leagued opposition it had been a creditable effort and, back in the changing room, there was no problem about praising the players generously for their commitment and skill. All the same, they all bore the aura of men about to be sentenced to the galleys. I knew that they knew that up ahead was a force-fed repetitive diet of defending set-pieces, defending more set-pieces, and then defending yet more set-pieces. We've got to plug the set-piece leak. But what might it cost us in morale and open-play inventiveness?

Wednesday 8 January

The shock announcement rocked the very foundations of English football. The (almost) out of the blue withdrawal of Kevin Keegan from the court of St James? Nothing so commonplace. Today Torquay entered the transfer market.

Semi-obscure object of our desire is the aforementioned Andy McFarlane – unknown quantity enough, be it noted, to make the delay getting back to Scunthorpe since preliminary talks a fortnight ago readily comprehensible. The hesitation of the Torquay coaches – in particular my hesitation – before committing the chairman's money was no direct reflection on Andy. It stemmed entirely from a lack of first-hand knowledge of his strengths and weaknesses. My one close encounter with him had been of the adversarial kind way back in August. Certainly he is big and strong and possesses the physical presence we've sorely missed since the much mourned departure of Paul Baker. But his performance that day was inconclusive and our less than complete intelligence gathering net has provided little in the way of 'go-get-him' data since.

On the other hand … at least a score of already targeted strikers have proved to be either unavailable, unenamoured of Torquay or, should a six figure fee make the difference for their cash-strapped owners, liable to bankrupt cash-strapped us … Further, the fee received for 'Bakes' is a plus on what we had to play with at the season's start. It could be argued Andy's cost is nominal. With only the price of a moderate secondhand car the stake money, the odds available to the newcomers to the poker school, were not wholly unattractive. Then again, we can all remember sweet-talking ourselves into buying a car that wasn't quite right. The key feet on the ground question that any management team must address before deciding to add to their squad is actually, let us not forget, very simple: does he give us more than we already have?

The answer in our case is, 'Yes'. Mike Bateson picked up the phone and dialled his opposite number at Scunthorpe.

Thursday 9 January

Hour upon interminable hour dragged by. When the hot line at last glowed red the delayed suddenness took me completely by surprise. As did the caller's identity.

'Hello, Nelse, Mick Buxton 'ere. What's happening to the lad McFarlane?'

'I don't know, Mick. He's supposed to have called to let us know he's on his way.'

'Can you keep me posted? If he doesn't sign, I need him for Saturday's game. I've only got 14 players who are fit.'

'I know the feeling. As soon as we know something, Kevin or the chairman will get back to you.'

By three o'clock my day was done. My yes vote cast, there was nothing further I could do to seal the deal. I left an anxious head coach manning the recruitment desk.

There is always something in the antics of our (alleged) elders and betters that grants us relief from our own cares. This is why against all good taste, the Royal Family still succeeds in commanding such widespread support. As I drove home, my journey was enlivened by a radio discussion speculating about who was most likely to succeed King Kevin.

Ah, yes! The abdication! In the past 24 hours rivers of ink, infinities of radio waves have been dedicated to analysing the impact Kevin Keegan's departure will have upon Newcastle. Scarcely a word seems to have been written about what sort of impact Kevin Keegan's departure will have upon Kevin Keegan. Wholly beneficial, I'd be apt to believe. Getting out while the game was still (just about) football and before he'd become a pawn in that game excluded from the heart of decision-making, he's potentially done wonders, I suspect, for his equanimity and the retention of his 'own man' status.

Football is no longer simply a game, a sport. It hasn't been for years, of course, but now more than ever the real name of the game is money. As this little or large piggy goes to the Stock Exchange market, millions are at stake. Further millions will be staked. The time may not be far away when share prices rise and fall in direct response to every result. As the old saying will soon go: when United sneeze, London catches a cold. It is to that square mile the goal posts have now been moved. For fans up and down the land the expression 't'City' is in the process of ceasing to mean the club up the road and to signify instead the pitch where outrageously shirted players (aka dealers) have but one goal in their hucksters' sights – to make even more serious money for themselves and their already seriously rich clients. The name of their game is risk elimination. At any price!

It was no less evident that, less than fully committed to John Hall enterprises – he wanted to quit come the end of the season – Kevin Keegan was just such a risk. His imminent departure might make severe inroads upon the estimated opening offer price of Newcastle FC plc. Can't have that, young man. Thanks for all you've done but stay not upon the order of your going. Clear off quick. Don't hang about because if you do, it'll cost us all a bomb. What? Bobby Mitchell? Which brokers is he with? The Robledos? What's the current rate of exchange?

Thousands of true supporters incapable of such misunderstandings, will want to think seriously about risking their hard-earned savings in buying a defined share not only in their club but also in their dream. (With the bidding opening at £500, mind you, the vast bulk of the Toon Army will have to think very seriously. Knowing the game so well, they will appreciate just as perceptively as the fat cats that teams, like shares, can go down as well as up.) But the money men will plunge. Once on the market the shares will shift as fast as Wor Jackie. ('Who, old boy?') With such heady investment will come heavy pressure. As the financial barometer rises so will the wild expectation. I would guess that Keegan had come more and more to appreciate that such mania could only end by coming between him and his true interest – putting together the most efficiently attractive portfolio of football players he could direct.

Steve Coppell, already yesterday's man, got out at the right time. So, it would appear, has Keegan. If his decision to walk was born, as it should be of the belief that, Sod that for a game of accountants, there are more important things in life than maintaining the company's share price, then he's made one of his canniest moves yet. Good luck to him. What I do, however, very much see as a down side is his loss to the game. Soccer, let's face it, needs all the honest and humane, all the feet-on-the-ground characters it can lay its increasingly greedy hands on. Sad. I don't think that come the next revolution of the merry-go-round Kevin will be that eager to climb back on.

But who will now? Such has been the rapid (Kevin-fuelled) rise of Newcastle over the past five years that in *realpolitik* terms the short-list of candidates to replace Keegan must be very short indeed. There can't be too many managers around who, hand on heart, feel they have the on-field reputation to earn the respect of such a star-studded squad, the charisma to satisfy the supporters' desire for a high-profile replacement and, as well, the marketable potential to calm the City's fraying nerves and thus boost the flotation price. For the foreseeable future the 'boss'-ship of Newcastle is going to be soccer's ultimate pressure cooker.

Or perhaps penultimate. Following three hours of relentless contract discussion, wor Kevin was finally able to proffer a pen. Andy McFarlane became our first cash-signing. The fee works out at .0003 per cent of Keegan's £62 million transfer outlay. There's pressure and ... there's pressure.

Friday 10 January

Hit the road, Jack, black ice warnings though there be. Our one consolation was that we didn't get far. Ninety minutes into our epic journey to the West End of Hadrian's Wall, the 'match off' mobile call made audible connection with the northbound team-bus. Executing as tight a U-turn as is legally allowed under motorway rules, our driver hastily rearranged his destination cards in the front window. Torquay replaced Carlisle and we could head for home.

Realisation soon dawned that five or six players were parked up at various locations between Taunton and Exeter. To bring them back in for training now would not only be a logistical nightmare but also, more likely than not, provoke a 'you're being petty' reaction that could potentially damage rekindled team-spirit just at a time when we are in most need of everyone pulling in the same play-off direction. For the sake of future harmony and unity, the decision was taken to give them an extra couple of days off.

Delight was unconfined. They were distinctly more underjoyed, however, when I announced that Monday would be a double-header, with the second half entirely devoted to endurance-based fitness work.

'Enjoy your weekend off, lads,' I meaningfully finished with. The lads responded in kind. You didn't have to listen too hard to make out that it also included the word 'off'.

Monday 13 January

Winter's worst seems to be over. (I'm talking climate here, not wing-backs.) The almost despaired of thaw surfaced this morning and allowed us to experience our first full bore session on (almost) green grass since New Year's day. The bleak interim has fully tried the improvisational skills of the 'what the hell shall we do with them today' coaches.

The past three weeks have dragged by in a weary succession of mind and bum-numbing delays for the players. At the lowest points the nearest they've come to an aerobic work-out has been the thumb-twiddling exercises they've had all the time in the world to master while, in that cramped cupboard at the end of the corridor, those responsible for honing their skills and fitness to unbelievable heights have placed ever more frantic calls to the booked-solid sports halls of Torbay.

There's no question that fitness has suffered. What is a question is how best to retune. With the visit of table-topping Fulham now only five days away, my delicate priority is to make sure that the extra running sessions we'll need to top up our stamina reserves (which always ebb rapidly if neglected) don't take the edge off individual sharpness when Saturday comes. I've also got to structure things around having new boy Andy McFarlane in our midst. Much to the Old Guards' relief today's session very much revolved around our Leaburnesque acquisition and, contrary to cynical expectation, did embrace the comfort aid of a ball. Concentrating an attack v defence phase of play exercise on the forward aspects of our game plan, I reminded everyone that while we were still wedded to playing the ball to feet, the long pass (not to be confused with the long ball) was now a far more realistic option when time and space were at a closed-down premium.

'Not that I want any responsibility shirking,' I made clear. 'Just because we've now got a Blackpool Tower target man doesn't give you the easy way out of pumping endless high balls up to him.'

Developing the session further, I politely (enough) requested the midfielders to unload the leaden inhibition they'd been running out with in their boots of late and be prepared to take the gamble of making more forward runs into space. Sure, I agreed, given that our two most recent strikers were no taller in aggregate than one Big Mac, their misgivings over cavalry charging upfield were understandable: yes, too often the bloody ball had been instantly returned with interest. Now, though, there was a far better chance of hanging out in the opposition's back yard.

We stuck at it and, as tends to be the training ground norm, the balance between short and long was pretty much achieved. The pretty patterns didn't disguise, though, the still serious shortfall in the number of quality crosses, shots and – gulp! – goals.

Tuesday 14 January

It's a funny old game. History, that is. In the close season of 1977 Kevin Keegan quit the newly crowned champions of Europe, Liverpool, to join the *Bundesliga* side Hamburg SV. Who on earth could fill his classy, 'irreplaceable matchmaker' boots? No problem. He was replaced by someone with an even classier pair of feet: one Kenny Dalglish.

Fade out on the Mersey. Fade in 20 years later on the Tyne and history repeating itself. The king is dead: long live King Kenny. Dalglish's genius as a player was to be in the right place at the right time. *Plus ça change.*

First to wish him success in his new career – indeed, to help engineer, it seems, his entry upon that career – was Alan Hansen. On BBC's 'Match of the Day' Kenny's golf partner and bosom buddy told the transfixed nation that, as a championship-winning manager with both Liverpool and Blackburn, his former team-mate 'was ideally equipped, had a marvellous track-record and is itching to get back into management.' Quite an endorsement at a time when names such as Robson (Bobby) and Cruyff (Johan) were still being bandied about … Curious, too. I always thought that you couldn't advertise on the BBC.

It's not all about repetition. Sometimes history opens a new page. Usually an ironic one. With sardonic juxtapositioning, another former Liverpool star and former Dalglish colleague today made a far less covetable appearance before the cameras. Today the 'match fixing trial of the century' (what short memories the tabloids have!) kicked off at Winchester Crown Court. As the formidable list of charges was read out, Bruce Grobbelaar sat impassively in the crowded dock alongside the similarly accused Hans Segers, the tall John Fashanu and the short Malaysian man, Heng Suan Lim.

Early days though it is (given the slowness of due process of law and the case's complex ramifications it will be weeks before a verdict is brought in), the overall shape of the trial is already evident. The defending counsels will be trying to offset some very heavy duty looking circumstantial evidence by seeking to discredit utterly the already very discreditable chief witness for the prosecution. Has this anything to do with the game my son has come to enjoy playing so much? I'd like to be able to answer with an unequivocal 'no' but I simply can't. Like all true football fans I'd like to be confident that this particular trial will produce only a 'we find the defendants not guilty on all charges' verdict. Anything less and the image of the game, its very spirit – of 'may the best team win' – will have been sullied still further by greed. Perhaps irreparably.

Thursday 16 January

If you reach the stage of having to make a threat be absolutely sure you are capable of making it good. I've thus been at great pains to underline through action that there was nothing idle about my 'promise' to spend much of this week working on defending against set pieces. The squad will be of the opinion that, to this end, they have been put to considerable pains too. By knocking off time yesterday I would have said that they were getting there. Today, though ...

Five minutes into a First Team v Youth Team practice 'match' the youngsters were awarded a corner. Given our immediate 'previous', alarm bells should have triggered in the minds of all grizzled seniors. Grizzled or complacent? Free as a far post bird, fledgling Froud headed the kids in front from six yards out. An aberration? A last getting of old bad habits out of the system? Not quite. Several retakes later two other beardless youths again escaped the attentions of the ball-watching back five and, meandering gently to the same spot, engaged in a diplomatic exchange over who should take precedence in despatching the ball home. Red-faced with anger and embarrassment the first-team coach immediately despatched his charges to the running track.

Saturday 18 January

Well make mine a double! It'll be my first of the year – just as today was Torquay's first of the season. Our 3–1 win over league leaders Fulham was all the sweeter for our having to come from a goal down. Another (open play) sticky moment at the back put us behind but from then on we hit our stride. The score was a fair reflection of the game's shape. Making his home debut Andy McFarlane impressively combined brain with brawn giving me an unopposed cranial tap-in towards the end. From eight inches out I'm still deadly.

Tuesday 21 January

We are Millwall!
We are Millwall!
No-one likes us
We don't care...

Unless, of course, that no-one is a someone who is something in the City. Then the Lion rants a different tune. Not even the most tungsten-skinned Spanner will be indifferent to the announcement that, following the revelation the club is in the red to the further tune of £10 million and losing a steady £250,000 more each month, Millwall's price has been suspended on the Stock Exchange.

In the red! The true-blue Millwall fan will be asking some justifiable questions. It's only a few years since the directors sold the old beloved Tip – sorry, Den – and moved to the Senegal Fields stadium purpose-built on a site which, despite its several million pounds price tag on the open market, they received scot-free from Lewisham Council. Whatever happened to the multi-million pounds that must have been racked up through the selling on of Sheringham, Armstrong, Thatcher, Cunningham, Goodman, Cooper, Kennedy, Keller and the certainly not free Scot, Rae?

All right. There are obvious entries in the debit column. The sterile state-of-the-art ground is arguably ill-conceived for Millwall's culture and profile. The small crowds are lost in it and it must be literally unattractive to the 'may be' fan. Certainly whether for the floating, potential spectator or for the staging of other events the location is an out of everybody's way disaster. Then again, balancing the transfer monies in, there are the obvious transfer fees and wages that have gone out. Until quite recently Division One Millwall indulged the luxury of a squad numbering well over 30. Large sums were disbursed on some near-insane acquisitions – on some Russian 'superstars', for example, whose ever rarer appearances went a long way not only to substantiating the 'never the twain shall meet' theory but also to embodying the practice of taking money under false pretences. But all the same ...

The suspension of trading in Millwall shares seems to indicate that the City believes the club guilty of mismanagement – not in a McCarthyite or Nichollian manner on the field but in terms of its overall operation as a business enterprise. Who, for instance, ever believed that a soccer club – or its shareholders – would make money investing £10.2 million in a chain of pubs, a species of business requiring hugely different know-how?

The Millwall experience, it has to be said, contrasts ill with the tight ship run by their South East London neighbours and rivals. After years of frugal self-denial, of getting both their manpower and their stadium structures right, of not trying to run (either off or on the field) before they could walk, Charlton are now solvent and at last able to think bigger. They are on the point of floating shares to the value of 49 per cent of the club's worth. The money raised will be invested not in the acquisition of the new Uzbekistan Maradona but in the completion of rebuilding the Valley. Enlarged stands will bring its capacity up to 20,000.

I learned much of the small print on this straight from the chairman's mouth, so to speak. Taking the 200-odd mile trip in his good-natured stride, Martin Simons was spelling it out this evening in a Taunton hotel in a meeting of West Country Addicks – an occasion that I proudly attended in my newly elected capacity of branch vice-president. Martin's bottom line message was that, making hard-headed, sometimes unpopular, business decisions, the Charlton board had given priority to building as permanent a foundation as possible for the club – one not likely to crumble the instant that performance on the field suffers a temporary blip. It was a message not received with universal patience.

- 'When are you going to buy a decent striker?'
- 'Surely your priority has got to be spending out on a good team?'
- 'We need to spend a couple of million on two new forwards.'

Fans! You can understand their impatience. But their insistence on a Spend! Spend! Spend! spree in the transfer market (whose money is it, anyway?) is exactly the run before you walk policy that threatens to destroy Millwall and not a few other clubs. Lazio wasn't built in a day, either.

I had nothing but admiration for Martin's legging it all the way down West to us country hicks. Part of Charlton's fiscal revival has been due to sustained preaching of the Valley gospel in the community; getting locals to vote with their feet. Five-figure crowds at the Valley are now the norm. Once, of course, in the '40s and '50s the norm was a gate, drawn from the cheek by jowl population of the thriving docks, of 50,000-plus. Many of those spectators are still alive, well and elsewhere. As Britain ceased to be an industrial power and became instead a leisure centre, they moved away from the dead docks to service industry pastures new. But part of their hearts remains for ever Charlton and the club enjoys a surprisingly large following right across the country. Pilgrimages are still made to the Valley; new generations introduced. Many other clubs, of course, can lay claim to the same traditions of nostalgic loyalty. But I wonder how many of their chairmen take the trouble to return the compliment of their long-range visits.

Wednesday 22 January

Three weeks into the year and the Reserves' first outing. The game at Crediton results in a 4–0 win but, tempering superiority with mercy, our lads got very little out of the game beyond a fitness top-up.

Thursday 23 January

And another two bite the dust. First was Alan Buckley, the now ex-manager of WBA. It's strange and sad that, having for years fashioned wholly admirable teams at Grimsby, he was unable to transfer the knack to the enhanced arena and resources of the Hawthorns. Alan's talent should rescue him from limbo before too long.

Because it happened in our own backyard, the set-back to Matthew Gregg, our apprentice keeper, seemed far more dramatic. He was a fraction late in reacting to a volley struck perfectly from 18 yards out. He was still good enough to get his fingers to the ball and prevent a goal. But at a cost. His wrist jack-knifed back at a ridiculous, hence a horrendous, angle. It was immediately clear that he had sustained serious damage and X-rays confirmed the worst – a clean break to one of his wrist bones. He could expect to be back in playing action again in some 10 weeks.

Not the end of the world you might think. But put yourself in his gloves. You're 18 and entering the last few months of your apprenticeship with a professional contract almost in touching distance beyond. Now, in a blink of an eye, such dreams might be as shattered as his bone. Ten weeks! Matthew knew only too well that the review on which extension of his apprenticeship depended would fall within the healing period; that Torquay United FC were not in no way legally obliged to retain him.

Legally, not, no. Morally, of course, was another issue altogether. But so too for Torquay were the financial implications ...

Almost succeeding in masking his teenager's misgivings Greggy entered the coaches' office to learn his fate. All three of us were in residence. To his eyes we could hardly have appeared other than a trio of hanging judges. But callous, cash-driven rejection had never been on the cards. Youth-team supremo Steve McCall informed Matthew that, quite simply, his apprenticeship would go into cold storage: time lost now would be regarded as suspended time. The assessment clock would only start ticking down to judgement day again once he had regained full fitness.

Greggy's joy made him like his wrist. Less than fully articulate. But his grin split his face from ear to ear.

Friday 24 January

Gone but not forgotten. Fondly remembered in fact. Terry Bullivant, his one-time manager at Kingstonian retains such happy memories of Jamie Ndah he'd like to renew the acquaintance. Since Jamie has become pretty peripheral to the immediate Torquay scheme of things we agree to forward him onto the joys of Underhill for a week's trial and game. We speed his departure with the no-nonsense interim report that while we haven't written him off totally, he'd be doing himself a big favour if he could use this opportunity to kick-start his career back into consistent form and, indeed, participation. If not …

The big external event this week – it has implications for so many clubs and could be the tip of the chilliest of icebergs – is the passing into the hands of the receivers of AFC Bournemouth. The club has debts in the region of £4 million – largely to Lloyd's which, 'hiss, boo', have now stepped in to foreclose.

Among the almost endless welter of reactions this crisis conjures up is the thought that this debt is only somewhere around one-twelfth the amount Newcastle, which operated at a loss last season (and whose multi-millionaire chairman has just been allocated one-third of the latest boardroom 'wage' of £2.45 million) have just announced themselves to be in the red. For clubs, it seems, as with individuals. Owe a Sir John Hall's ransom and you're still a most valued customer: owe a tidy bit that people can still relate to and you're a bad debtor.

All the same, I've some sympathy with Lloyd's. If an engineering company goes bust, a jobbing printers, a picture framers, investors have a right to recover what they can. Why should a mismanaged football club – for in common with dozens of others, that is what Bournemouth appears to be – have a God-given exemption from paying its dues? In the '80s, under Harry Redknapp, Bournemouth were on the ascendant. Plans were laid to sell and expand – are you watching Newcastle? – into a larger state-of-the-art stadium. It never happened. Upward mobility became – why? – downward plummet. Serious debts were suddenly being countered by the selling of a roster of players that today's Premiership supremos would kill to have – Jamie Redknapp, Joe Parkinson, Efan Ekoku, Shaun Teale, Mattie Holmes, Keith Rowland, Gavin Peacock. How much did their going realise for *Bournemouth*? As with Millwall, you get a sense the vendor failed to get full money for value.

I appreciate that Bournemouth or Brighton or Millwall going out of the Nationwide League would be a cause of dark heartsickness for all their faithful. For that very reason I'd hate to see it happen. But I don't think that it would be the beginning of the end of the League. Waiting just one tier lower down the pyramid are a stack of well-run clubs – Yeovil, Woking, Kidderminster, say – often with superior grounds. Progress to a Nationwide made up of semi-professional sides, with a consequent loss in scope for agents, might be accelerated but the basic shape of today's league structure would essentially remain.

In their current throes Bournemouth wrote asking for a hand-out to all of the Premiership clubs. They didn't receive so much as a reply from many. This doesn't surprise me unduly. But it does strike me as being an attempt to thrust an unofficial toe in a distinctly dodgy door. A solution that financially beleaguered sides have been increasingly prone to invoke of late is the concept of the farm club. The aristocrat will give succour to the subsistence level peasant by stepping in to pick up the tab. Henceforth the *droit de seigneur* (a medieval custom allowing the rich to rather literally screw the poor) will apply.

It seems that there's a growing swell, perhaps even a majority, of smaller clubs in favour of the feeder team solution. The new nine-man Football League board is seriously considering the potential merits of such an approach. Perhaps because, unlike the board's chairman, I am in no way a bit of an aristocrat myself, I have to say I have the gravest 'where will it all end' misgivings.

For a start there's the less than appealing potential for dozens of His Master's Voice scenarios. That's to say somebody such as myself becoming the tactical glove-puppet of a Premier manager. ('We'd just like to see how he shapes up playing in the hole, Nelse.') Bollocks. If I fancied playing 2–3–5, that's what I'd want to be allowed to do. But that's just for in-the-family openers. What about the legalities of the proposed system? It would be the end of the FA Cup.

Consider. Torquay are Everton's farm club. Then we are drawn away at Goodison. Both boardrooms, both changing rooms would be swarming with 'Short Men'. Torquay, the logic has to run, would not be eligible to enter the game's most revered competition.

Equally – being utterly fanciful – supposing the Gulls were to fly upwards through the Nationwide and gain promotion to the Premiership. Could they take advantage of it? Not under the present ruling that no chairman or board can hold an interest in more than one club. Suppose eight months later, threatened by relegation and BSkyB revenue loss, Everton came down to the new 60,000-seater Plainmoor ... who would ever believe that their hard-won away win was purely a matter of merit? The logic now is that Torquay would not be admitted to the Premiership in the first place. That means, to bring it back to the place where it should always start and finish, the Torquay fan would have to be resigned to supporting a side that he or she knew would never qualify for the best division in the country and so never qualify for Europe. Don't begin to ask me what would happen when Torquay got promoted and Everton relegated to the same division in the same season ... Heaven forbid either happen but, economic push coming to shove, I'd rather be part of a wholly independent club in the Vauxhall Conference or Dr Martens than coaching a 'kept' team in the Nationwide.

Saturday 25 January

I've spent half my lifetime in this game and today it threw up a footballing first for me. Thirty-seven minutes into today's match with neat, skilful Mansfield, referee Rejer blew a long blast on his whistle, picked up the ball and went home. Why? I can't say. I haven't the foggiest because we were all in a mist. There was no doubt where he was coming from even if, thanks to Nature's dry-ice effect, we couldn't see where he was going. Later he pointed out that he had no option but to cancel the game on account of fog as, unable to see across the pitch, his assistants (aka linesmen) couldn't do their job properly. It's never stopped them before.

Sunday 26 January

Very occasionally the main event actually lives up to the pre-match hype. Today before a crowd of 28,000 shelling out record Stamford Bridge receipts of half a million and a subscription-paying Sky audience of many million more, Chelsea and Liverpool proved that professional football can still be the ultimately satisfying entertainment.

Skill, endeavour, athleticism, goals. Passion, pain, reversal of fortune, tragedy, triumph. What a game! What a comeback! God, how I can still love this game sometimes! What a way to earn a living!

Monday 27 January

'Sometimes...' I wrote yesterday. Yes, there's football and there's football. Several million miles away from the Kings Road two puzzled professionals spent the first chunk of today searching for an adequate-ish bit of turf on which to train their team.

Finally we got a result of sorts – an *almost* flat area of some 70 x 60 yards that was largely free of dog crap and hadn't been churned up yesterday by another epic encounter in the local League. Here we would attempt to emulate the skills of Super Sunday.

This lack of a decent practice ground is a stumbling block (sic!) that gets harder to get over every recurring time. It's a real killer for group morale and it doesn't do much for individual tolerance thresholds either.

Full credit to the lads today, then. They get enthusiastically stuck in to the drills and took everything, surface and slope included, in their stride. We'll have to find another cabbage patch for them tomorrow. Their whole-hearted input had ploughed up this one beyond all immediate repair.

Tuesday 28 January

More little local – and thoroughly depressing – difficulties at the coalface. Sixty minutes into our home reserve fixture against Plymouth, 19-year-old winger Michael Preston crashes to the ground under a heavy challenge. When he was halfway down you could already tell it was a bad one. A knee. Sure enough, guest sponge man, Jack Pearce is immediately signalling for a stretcher.

'Stretcher,' I order.

'It's in the First Aid room.'

'So get it.'

'It's locked.'

'Who's got the key?'

'Dunno.'

Dumb blank looks stared apprehensively back at me. Grim as they were they had the edge over the stoically tooth-clenched Michael Preston's. An enforced impromptu game of hunt the key lasted for a whole bloody 10 minutes. It culminated in door-jamb splintering forced entry. Only now were three over-stretched bearers (me, Jacko, Plymouth physio Norman Medhurst) finally able to carry Michael to the treatment room. Play had meanwhile resumed. During the 10 minutes of sweaty 'hurry up' Plymouth succeeded in coming back from two down. It's the final result – in the amateur night context of a 'Dad's Army' cock-up like that, who the hell's bothering to count!

Wednesday 29 January

Black, black news for Michael Preston. Damage to his cruciate ligament and cartilage will require a minimum of two operations and sideline him for months. It makes my knee problem seem very minor.

After only exercising my coaching larynx all day I decided I'd finish with an extra-curricular work-out. Head coach Hodges was on the fully pressurised ball. He fizzed it in to me. Eat your heart out, Zola. I gathered myself to thunder a half-volley home.

Laugh your head off, Zola. Fractionally late to a ball sticking in the glue-pot ground I only made contact with the forward part of my foot. The shock-wave ran straight up to the medial ligament in my left knee.

Friday 31 January

At the endless journey's end not a pot of gold but a fast, gutsy, sometimes classy match. In a goalmouth to goalmouth encounter both sides showed a lot of enterprising running off the ball and the ability to pass with accuracy and vision. As half-time approached, however, it was clear that Colchester were that little bit better in both departments than Torquay.

Having watched fast rising Colchester three times we knew that they'd come at us from the off, frequently bordering on a 4–2–4 formation. Our counter was to string a five man wall across the midfield and press. As the first half progressed, however, and we made chances, the tendency became for some of our midfield to linger too long in attack. Still, with 40 minutes gone, the game was goalless. Then, 'Mayday! Mayday!' we had conceded a corner. Over it came. A Colchester head rose to the ball and hurtled it straight to the inside of the post where Scott Stamps, playing a stormer, magnificently blocked and cleared it! Glory hallelujah, I thought, can it be we've cracked it!?

Vain hope. Half a minute from the interval Colchester arrowed in another corner. One of our midfield was improvising on the edge of the 18-yard box instead of picking up his man in the six. Up rose Tony Adcock. In went the ball. I'd been 30 seconds from talking three points in the half-time changing room. Now objective one had to be salvaging the draw.

We rearranged. I'd been playing in the hole but now I went up front. The iffy knee was just about justifying the gamble of my playing. It was all irrelevant anyway. A few minutes after the resumption saw Colchester make a swift break and Tony Adcock finish with an elegantly precise deflection from a diving header. Game, set and match and the best team overall winning.

Half an hour for a shower and a rehydrating beer and then hit the road time all over again.

As we droned westwards it came to me that one distinct contribution to the game had been the atmosphere generated by the lively, vocal crowd of nearly 4,000. Such a number at Plainmoor would mean a bit of profit for the day and might even be worth the occasional goal start. I think the case for regular Friday night lower league football – all concerned parties being agreeable – is unanswerable.

Friday night fixtures face no competition from the big club down the road or televised European clashes. For the fan they offer a nice focus to the Friday night start to the weekend. A few beers, the game, a curry. Saturday afternoon can be dedicated to such 'new man' activities as pushing the pram round Tesco's or watching the racing on TV. Friday night matches are one positive way of starting to win back the missing generation of 20-somethings forced to jettison football as Life's more fundamental demands gang up on them.

So, between chatting and cat-napping, I mused. There was fog part of the way back. I got home at four in the morning.

Monday 3 February

Chalk up another plus for Friday night kick-offs. After two days uninterrupted rest and recuperation I felt really up for it as I drove in this morning. Maybe, mind you, it was simply because it was a beautiful morning and I knew all the kids were going to the seaside.

Necessity is the mother of finding an adequate practice pitch. *Eureka!* We'd go to the beach at Paignton. Goalkeepers could safely dive into the sand but the surface would be firm enough for outfielders. To give us maximum time and space for going up and down the strand, Hodgie would clock the tide on his way into the office … 'Just on the turn,' he announced as we gathered at Plainmoor. 'Be dead right by the time we get there.' No buckets or spades but cones and posts. Off we went. 'Hmmn. Taking it's time to go out,' our salty old Head Coach said as we arrived. 'Tell you what, we'll set out the cones and go for a warm-up jog and by the time we're back we'll have all the space we need.'

Off we went. Back in due course we came. The remorselessly incoming tide was already floating several cones out to sea from the rapidly diminishing strand.

'Come unto these yellow sands,' (William) Shakespeare wrote. 'Or jersey,' we amend. Only halfway through its first morning and the week's yellow jersey award was already decided.

There is, it transpires, a coastal resort theme to the day. By way of compensating the squad for their disappointment over not being able to train, we're able to announce that on the 23rd we'll be flying out to, inevitably, Jersey, on a busman's holiday weekend. The cost will be met by our taking on a select Island XI (colour of strip as yet unknown) the next day. It's an attempt to combine pleasure with business – a bit of reward for everyone at winter's end and an attempt to put a spring in everyone's step as the bell for the season's last lap sounds. There are no initial complaints.

This evening as I was in the middle of writing the above, the phone rang. The caller was Plymouth resident, football 'civilian' and long term friend, Ken.

'You hear the news yet?' he asks with a degree of portentousness.

'No … ' I guardedly respond.

'Warnock's out.'

'Really? Did he jump or was he pushed?'

'Pushed. He's got the chop.'

Neil Warnock was dismissed by the Plymouth Board of Dan McCauley and Peter Bloom. No great surprise given the recent highly public wrangle over the spending/non-spending of still more money on players; but piquant it should have happened just after Sam Allardyce has moved into Neil's old berth at Notts County.

'You've got to be in the frame, I suppose?' Ken fishes.

'I don't think so,' I truthfully answer. 'This is the first I've heard of it anyway.'

We chat on about this and that. But part of my brain is weighing immediate personal consequences. All three Torquay coaches are ex-Pilgrims. Ken's the first of umpteen. Tomorrow at work the rumour mill will be turning at warp speed.

Tuesday 4 February

Was I right or was I right? The first person to cross my Plainmoor path this morning is Gull director Merv Benney.

'Hope you boys'll still be talking to us when you go to Plymouth,' he says with a nod and a wink.

'Thought you'd work a bit harder than that to keep us here, Merv,' I reply.

Meeting up with Hodgie and Macca I speedily confirm that Neil Warnock's dismissal was as big a surprise to them as to me. But 2+2 adding up to 5 soon receives quasi-official status. Mike Bateson summons us to announce that he's been on the line to Dan McCauley.

'I wanted to end any speculation before it got out of hand by asking Dan if he had any interest in any or all of you lads,' he told us. 'The short answer is no. He's got it all sorted down there and – for the moment – Mick Jones is being offered the job.'

By evening 2+2 is popularly adding up to about 17. There's a sharply sardonic twist to the day's tail in that our reserves are away to none other than Plymouth. All three of us attend to watch our lads classily turn on the style to win 3–1. But I think as many pairs of Pilgrim eyes as watched the game were focused on Hodgie and Macca on the bench and me in the directors' seats. We old Home Park lags must have seemed like inwardly cackling vultures.

Friday 7 February

A two-fold parting of the ways. The one involves Jamie Ndah. His trial time at Barnet has persuaded Terry Bullivant that Jamie can do a job and we have forwarded him on a free to the metropolitan (well, Northern Line) joys of Underhill. It wasn't a hard decision but, for all concerned, a positive one. Jamie has been inconsistently out of sorts at Torquay. A new setting should kick-start his buckling down to acquiring the commitment and fitness that will do justice to his talent. We wish him well.

The other decision was far harder. Hodgie and I found ourselves faced with having to do something professionally that on a human level we didn't want to do. Informing Steve Crane we wouldn't be persisting with him could only leave a nasty taste in our mouths.

Steve has been with us for three months at his own on-the-dole expense. He arrived short on fitness but, even at first glance, rather longer on ability. We gave him the benefit of the doubt and, fully focused, he steadily lost poundage and gained stamina. By Christmas time he had worked his way up to the subs' bench and those couple of late first-team appearances.

Unfortunately he has seemed to stall on that plateau. His attitude is splendid but, that once acknowledged, we found ourselves applying all those second degree adjectives to him – not bad, worthy, got an idea, a bit of something. He could probably get a mid-term nod right now from some of our Division Three rivals but the sad, home truth is that he doesn't seem to have enough right now to tip the balance with us. We felt that, being cruel to be kind, it was fairest to acquaint him with this assessment and give him a chance, faint though it is, to hang his 'Have boots, will travel' sign on the grapevine while he's still back up at match fitness. It was an impossible message to convey with any kind of positive undertow. Making it worse was the knowledge that Steve had heard it all before, give or take, from both his previous clubs. Hodgie did his best by stating, most genuinely, that the decision was by some way the most difficult and heart-wrenching of our fledgling managerial experience.

In a sense it may have been easier for Steve than us. Familiarity had perhaps bred dignified restraint. Slowly getting up he shook our hands and thanked us for giving him a sustained opportunity. Then he was gone. I stared at the door which had closed not only on his back but also, probably, on his prospects in professional football, and wondered how I would have coped at receiving the same thumbs down when I was 25.

Saturday 8 February

Something of a downer of a day and of a game. A 0–0 draw against the 'O's', appropriately enough. Although we had a break-even at the gate crowd of 2,600 the whole side took its time to get up any perceptible fire. I've heard of a flat back four. This came close to a flat outfield 10. Not that I can cast the first stone. A heavy, uphill struggle of an out of sorts training session on Thursday seemed to still be exercising its draining effect. I was certainly not firing on all cylinders myself and a black-eye in the first five minutes did nothing to readjust my timing.

Twice, though, I beat the jabbing pain in my knee and offside trap to nip through on to balls over the top. On a rain-slicked pitch the ball might have skidded through nicely into my stride. But today – excuses, excuses – the ball took an awkward hop, skip and a jump and I lost vital yards controlling it. Then, finally, with seconds to go, I cracked it. Timing my run to the split second I was through on to another ball, the bounce was kind, my touch good, the one-on-one chance converted. Turning arm aloft I was greeted by the sight of the linesman in identical pose. Only he was holding a flag. He was wrong, I swear. But even though the rules now ask assistant referees specifically to favour attackers in case of 50–50 decisions, offsides in soccer remain like lbw's in cricket. It's easier to say no.

Not an afternoon to leave me chuckling, then. But the chairman seemed reasonably buoyant. We're 13th in the table now amid a pack of clubs all within a narrow points spread. I think that after the trauma of last year Mike is beginning to settle for this. A couple of wins, though, could still see us, mathematically, back in the play-off scrap. I hope that, despite outward protestation to the contrary, the players aren't thinking, 'Well, we've done well enough, considering.' I hope the chairman isn't thinking he'd rather avoid the additional financial stresses and obligations that play-off involvement or – even! – promotion would bring. I've got this vague but persistent feeling that now that we've climbed halfway up a 24-rung ladder somebody has taken the top 12 away. Before I become too sorry for myself let me feel happy for Steve Gritt. Brighton are closing on the pack. Today they thumped Hartlepool 5–0. An 8,000 crowd packed the Goldstone. The huge increase was made up of fans from dozens of other clubs arriving to display solidarity with the Brighton supporters.

Monday 10 February

The receivers are putting a bit of stick about at Millwall. Some 20 admin staff are being elbowed in a move that, interestingly, will cut the wages bill by £1.5 million a year. The casualties include the chief executive and, inevitably, Jimmy Nicholl, the manager and his assistant Martin Harvey. Twelve of the players have been listed. Contract renewal will now seem an impossible dream. Further, all players have been asked to take a 10 per cent drop in the wages that their existing contracts specify. This is tough one for the PFA. They clearly don't want to see Millwall founder but if its 10 per cent at Millwall today, it could be 50 per cent at Stamford Bridge the year after next. Fearing a precedent be set, the PFA have told the Millwall players not to co-operate even though the dorsal fins of the creditors circle ever nearer in the Financial Straits.

We, meanwhile, are one Rodney Jack lighter. Just for a few training days, initially. Having gone up to the North East to strut his stuff in black and white stripes, he's returned to do it again in red and white. Peter Reid is interested. The source of that interest is keenly interesting. The Sunderland manager had a friendly dinner recently, it seems, with the ex-Newcastle boss who warmly recommended Jacko as a prospect. Nice aspect of the story is that it rather indicates recent experiences haven't dulled Kevin Keegan's interest in or enthusiasm for the game.

Tuesday 11 February

If good management is the art of being in the right place at the right time then Hodgie and I were in the Plainmoor box today looking for a cross being hit at Ibrox. Mind you, it's a chairman's art as well.

Last Friday, having shed Messrs Ndah and Crane from our anorexia-courting squad, Hodgie and I petitioned Mike Bateson for permission to re-engage our pursuit of the again available Scott Partridge. Yet again the chairman said he'd like to sleep on it. He'd let us know after the weekend. Today he phoned from his office with the desperately depressing news that we'd expressed our interest too late. This time the bird has flown for good. A player genuinely able to do a class job for us in several positions has just signed for head-to-head, play-off chasing rivals Cardiff! Red faces all round. Ours with anger.

Wednesday 12 February

England 0, Italy 1. Victory justly went to the better skilled, better drilled and better selected side. Why play two clones in the midfield? If you're (eventually) going to play your two Newcastle top guns up front why omit their week-in, week-out ammunition provider?

Friday 14 February

The injury list has left us with the wrong bunch of survivors for our preferred 3–5–2 formation to remain a realistic option. Worse – with nowhere left to run, let alone train, we lack the practice-ground wherewithal to familiarise said survivors with the game plan hastily cobbled together to see off Hartlepool. All that's left us is another session of well-intentioned blackboard theory.

'Let's be solid early on. Full-backs, stay tight alongside your centre-halves. Midfield, be prepared to sit until we get our own game going. Rodney is the out ball. Get the ball to him and let him run at their defence …'

Well, we know what good intentions pave the way to.

Saturday 15 February

The luxury of overnighting in Leeds may have performed the function, we can but hope, of bonding our makeshift line-up a little closer and allowing yesterday's team-talk instructions to sink in. In the changing room Hodgie and I seek to administer the final massage to morale.

'If we're disciplined and determined, today can be a perfect opportunity to pick up three away points. Hold your shape.'

Initially we do. For the first 25 minutes Torquay give what you would have to describe as a textbook, even blackboard, performance. But – as so often before – all the superiority and concentrated effort reap no reward. Four chances came and went. As did something else. With each agonizing miss our collective and individual belief levels slid almost visibly further down the scale. And then off it altogether. From nowhere Hartlepool kick our teeth in with a scrambled goal.

How to respond? Scream blue murder was Hodgie's half-time reaction. 'If we shot at goal with the accuracy and regularity we shoot at our own feet,' his argument as amended for polite society ran, 'we'd have the three points safe already.'

He'd hit a nerve. Resuming, we tore into Hartlepool with self belief restored. The equaliser was going to be a formality. Yes! Before doubts had time to work their treachery again, Rodney Jack had fired home an opportunist's strike from 18 yards.

Sadly, that was the sum of our efforts. In November Hartlepool had done for us in the 90th minute. Today time was called without us being able to return the insult. 'An away point,' informed opinion recites. 'You've got to be pleased with that.' Yes? Opinion as often as not gets it wrong. On the latest version of the unvaryingly identical journey home, I had no illusions that, rather than a point gained, this was two lobbed casually into the North Sea. At season's end when we're all playing the mindless, inescapable game of 'if only' our one point from six Hartlepool experience will bulk large and black.

Tuesday 18 February

At the end of the day, this day to be faintly original, the end of the dream. Come *News at Ten* time that glowing 'glory, glory' fantasy which you don't let on about much to anyone for fear of seeming a right plonker had been beaten so thin by reality that, utterly transparent one moment, the next it was no longer there at all. Outright promotion? Making it to the last play-off place? Dream on, if you still can, Nelse, but do it in your own time. Life and Mansfield Town have got an alternative scenario.

The cold facts first. It's Mansfield at home, Act 2 – minus nature's dry-ice this time. A knife-edge fixture for us. Six points from successive Plainmoor fixtures and we'll still be up, just, with the play-off chasing pack. All of which equally applies to Mansfield. No-one's saying it's going to be easy. Steve Parkin's growingly confident side are neat passers, quick on the break and marshalled dauntingly at the back by that big bastion Brian Kilcline. We'll need to earn a win. In the pre-match briefing Hodgie emphasizes the need for us to come out of the blocks fast and impose our rhythm on the game. Message received and understood. When we win the toss we have the elements to give us wind assistance.

We don't quite make the most of things. The received, understood message is immediately ignored. Two minutes into the game we're a goal down. Just the one, I tell myself, still 88 minutes to put things to rights. But a black-capped statistician at the back of my brain is coldly whispering to me that Torquay must be the worst team in the division when it comes to playing catch-up football.

Unless, that is, somebody gives us a helping – or even misdirected – hand. It must have been the rarity of my trying a long range strike that flummoxed Ian Bowling. The shot wasn't that hard and closer to him than not. All the same he misread it. His CV won't have been enhanced by allowing himself to be beaten by a G Nelson right-footer from outside the box. One apiece, then. We have caught up. For 20 minutes we are worth the draw. But that was as good as it ever got. Four minutes into the second half breaking from their own penalty area, Mansfield performed a convincing imitation of Man U in smash and grab mode. It culminated not in an immediate goal but an unnecessary lunge by Jon Gittens. Penalty. Johnny Walker stepped forward and scotched all hopes he might bottle it.

The decision seemed to throw Jon Gittens for a total loop. Denying there'd been any foul, denying his responsibility if there had been one, he proceeded to throw 'a right wobbler', ignoring his positional duty as he pushed irresponsibly forward. Exasperated beyond endurance Kevin substituted him. Off came the player, off came his shirt, off to the changing room stormed our allegedly senior professional. It's just what you want when asked to claw your way back into a game for the second time. We never did.

In a changing room aftermath Hodgie tore seven different sorts of strip off the team in a verbal assault that combined ice-cold chapter and verse analysis with more passion than most of his audience displayed all night. He had every right. I, meanwhile, sat trying to maintain a beady-eyed, dead-pan maturity. But in my heart my head was in my hands. A sour, presumptuous joke now, the dream was gone. No rose-coloured fantasy any more between me and reality. The scales dropped from my eyes I could see there was a large sore on the body of the season that I wouldn't be able to prevent myself picking at. Starting now.

STAYING ALIVE

Wednesday 19 February

Was I right or was I right? Take two. Tired muscles, aching heart but a brain still working overtime. It cost me my usual good night's sleep. I must have dozed a bit from time to time but for most long periods I couldn't help but pick at the scab. Each flake that broke away revealed another cock-up cameo from our season's 'previous' – a selfish shot with a team-mate unmarked in space; an 'after you, Claude' hesitation; a failure to pick up the only man the set-piece defence plan said you should pick up; a failure to cover back, to overlap, to move up in a line … My brain, the Torquay season to date, was somehow scrambled together in a little shop of horrors. Today is a rest day. When I got (rather than woke) up I knew I had to stop the mad roundabout continuing to circle in my mind by exhausting it before it exhausted me. I called in the black-capped statistician to impose some order on the crazed kaleidoscope.

With fearful symmetry our away 2–1 win at Mansfield and our home 1–2 defeat at their hands were respectively the 16th and 32nd games of our league season. Of those first 16 we won eight and drew four: of the second we have won four and drawn two. Our win at Field Mill was the culmination of the run that saw Hodgie named as October Manager of the Month. We then immediately plunged headlong down that black November chute of seven defeats in a row. Our first 16 games saw us keep six clean sheets and fail to score only four times. In the second sixteen we kept only two clean sheets and failed to score no fewer than on 11 occasions. In open play our defence has looked largely competent. All the same, during this second batch of games we conceded the first goal 13 times. Since we managed to score only 11 goals in the same sampling, it's no surprise that our conceding the initial goal has usually been decisive. Negatively so. The statistic – no the actuarial probability – that we'll concede the first goal and struggle to score ourselves means that we're in a pressure situation from the kick-off. Tense, we lack that touch of laid back confidence which lubricates a team's smoothness. The last 16 games have brought us just 14 bloody points. The raw truth is that if the season had started on 1 November, we would now be at the bottom of Division Three. Torquay would be right back where they left off.

By afternoon I was confronting the cold, hard, fact that I'd been trying to keep locked away in the back of my mind for weeks. Strip away all the surface naffnesses – lack of funds, lack of anything approaching a decent training facility, lack of Paul Baker (and these are all strokes of ill luck or ill circumstance nine out of 10 other clubs have to contend with) – and you're left contemplating a plain unvarnished truth. Too many of our minimalist squad aren't up to it. We don't have enough good, no, *useful* players. We aren't capable of sustaining a level of performance that is consistently acceptable. If Torquay are to do anything other than run on the spot on a back-sliding travelator, Hodgie and I need to institute a wholesale clear-out at the season's end and, as of right now, start rebuilding from close to scratch. Always supposing, of course, we haven't been cleared out first ourselves.

A fair question. Is my disenchantment with a sizeable proportion of the squad no more than the whinging attempt of a poor coach to protect his back? Is it a disgruntled passing of the buck? I honestly don't think so. Time and time again the cock-ups on the field have arisen when this player or that has strayed from the straight and narrow path of basics. I don't – eventually! – mind any lad missing a sitter. Who am I to cast the first stone in that respect? What isn't on is leaving an opponent unmarked at a set piece; a left-sided midfielder ignoring the game plan instructions to drift inside to cover colleagues advancing up the right. A missed sitter is one thing. A consistently duff first touch, the inability to read the game and anticipate, the continuous inability to hit a short pass in the right direction at the right pace, these are something else. If a 'professional' can't do this at 20, he's not going to do it at 24. Would fear make the difference in our case? Should Hodgie and I have ushered in a reign of terror? I'm not even going to consider that option. Any side that I have a part in 'bossing' however small, is going to be a *team* – working their guts out, yes, but because they care about the game, because they respect and want to work for each other, because they respect themselves, because they want quality for its own sake. Slave driving isn't my style. End of story. But then again neither am I an advocate of suffering gladly those just going through the motions.

The season's remaining weeks are going to be crucial. If we're to rebuild Hodgie, Steve and I must short-list and vet a seriously viable clutch of players. Yet again it will be no peace for the match-covering wicked. We know just how successful we've so far been in this department. Identifying players of adequate calibre, though, is going to be the least of our problems. It's attracting them to Plainmoor on terms that won't make our fiscal noses bleed that's going to be the bastard. It's not just our necessarily low wage structure. With all respect to the local chamber of commerce it's been a while since Torquay was on the front of *Time* magazine as capital of the coolly swinging world.

And there's a mega complementary downside to this. Poor clubs essentially try to avoid signing players for the incoming season towards the end of the old. To do so is to commit to paying their wages through the summer. But if we don't adopt a gung-ho attitude by the time we eventually come to market, the players truly worth having will have been snapped up by the handful of more forward-looking clubs. That's another fine problem Hodgie and I are going to have to run past the chairman.

Meantime, in every sense, we have been here before. The pair of us went straight back into stake-out mind-set at the Park of St James (the Lesser). Where no fewer than six Exeter players have been listed. Speedily, alas, this half-dozen confirmed themselves as superfluous even to our requirements. Like the game they were absolutely average.

Thursday 20 February

My chief mission this morning was to build upon Hodgie's Tuesday post-match tirade. Coming straight from the heart what he'd said would have to have rung true for any listener with a shred of conscience.

Today my pre-planned input was designed to be more rational and analytical. All the same I've no doubt that it emerged less as brain-waved wisdom than heart-felt feeling. By its end no player could have been left in two minds about what's required between now and the season's end.

What Kevin and I were looking for today was that an 'adult' reaction to Tuesday's 'discussion' would prompt not only an upsurge in collective passion but a determination on everyone's part to take on more individual responsibility out on the park. Starting on Saturday against Hull, we were saying, show us you still want it.

I'm still not sure we got more than lip service. I've never truly felt the squad to be alive with unqualified commitment. Around Christmas, say, January, when a play-off berth seemed at least on the cards, everyone was saying, 'Yeah, sure, gotta go for it. We can do it.' But the words always spoke louder than the actions. Now when, such is the point spread across the division, last place is at least a mathematical possibility, nobody, I sense, is *that* fussed. Neither the prospect of Wembley glory nor anxieties over contract renewal (currently approaching over the horizon at a rate of knots) seem able to jolt the squad out of a 'mid-tablish is all right; we've done a job' frame of mind.

Saturday 22 February

Home to Hull and, early on, as we buck the statistical trend, it's all going right. This time, after just 10 minutes, we get the opening goal. The wind's in our favour in more ways than one. But except against Torquay 1–0 is never enough. Repetitive strain syndrome weakens our downward pressure on the accelerator. Gradually, steadily, Hull get back into the game. Eight minutes to go and we're hanging on by our fingernails – body parts our supporters have long since chewed away. In comes another cross. Up goes a Hull head at the far post and ... Saved! Thank Christ. All hands back for the corner.

It's an inswinger to the near post. My defensive patch. I press my tired legs and aching knee into upward action to head the ball, as all good coaches preach, handsomely high and wide. But I hadn't been listening to myself. The ball's that vital, teasing fraction higher than I read. I don't head clear. Instead, in a manner Steve Bould would envy, I flick on. The ball flashes directly to an incoming Hull attacker. He makes a pig's breakfast of his volley. The ball bounces once, twice, bobbles between umpteen pairs of legs. Then it's motionless. It's nestling with disastrous neatness in the back of our net.

Ten pairs of eyes turn accusingly in the direction of the wise old coach. I saw them as I lifted my head out of my hands. That gesture had said it all but I made it official.

'My fault. Sorry, lads.'

Another draw. Another single point in place of three. In another deflated changing room I sit drained and contemplating the built in hazards of the player-coach role. I don't need players to like me. It's nice if they do but it's not essential. But I do need their respect. Not commanding that I've got nothing. A Shankly, a Stein, to take two supreme examples, drew their latter-day respect from being such three-dimensional human beings and from all that, they very evidently masterminded from the sidelines. But I'm just a beginner. And I embody two functions. Two jobs, one person. When as a player I screw up it's instantly obvious. When I goof it's all but impossible for the rest of the team not to think, at least subconsciously, 'why does he ask us to do stuff he can't deliver himself?' All right. That's not logical. I know that if I think about it calmly I can win back that territory. But right now when I'm essentially trying to get the squad to acquire the enhanced respect for themselves that will maintain our mid-table safety, it's a right bugger that I came off today feeling like a right plonker.

Sunday 23 February

Exeter Airport. It's crack of dawn but nobody's got a long face. We've got a collective 48-hour pass and at 7.30 am the night looks very young indeed. Sensing they've got off the treadmill, a couple of the squad already clutch open cans. They don't contain fruit juice.

Nelson turns his blind eye. The underlying hope here is that a change will prove as good as a rest: that we can break the habit of shrugging away points. Let it, then, be party time. But not for the coaches. We won't get any nearer to relaxing than those middle-class hosts for whom the strain of seeing everybody else is having a good time/behaving themselves never quite abates. The trick is to avoid coming on like a party-pooper.

In a 36-seater, in the gustiest of conditions, the Gulls take to the air. The conditions are particularly tough on Andy McFarlane who, despite his everyday proximity to the stratosphere, is one of those people with an innate fear of flying. Still, he survives. We all do. All's well that arrives well. Jersey proves to be quite green. Everyone behaves in exemplary fashion. It's not a match to be played in anger or for high stakes so Kevin and I impose back at the hotel by 11 and in bed by midnight curfews. To the best of our knowledge and belief they are scrupulously observed.

Monday 24 February

The wind is gusting up to gale force but it hardly matters. The rain-slicked Springfield pitch is in magnificent condition. It will be a pleasure as well as something of a novelty for a Nationwide Division Three team to keep the ball on the floor tonight. If we've got a team. Of our touring party of 20, just 14 are able-bodied and fit enough to play. Sort of. The count includes both physios!

In the event it's not a problem. The Jersey XI afford no chance for any instant recruiting and the game develops into what Rodney Jack would doubtless call a 'Torquay shoot'. We win 4–0 easing up, with both physio's getting on.

Wednesday 26 February

We were back in Devon early yesterday morning. Training would have been possible but, after a quick appraisal, Hodgie and I went for another ration of goodwill sustaining carrot rather than slave drivers' whip. Even today we trained lightly. Our physical fitness isn't a problem. It's our mind-set that keeps putting our consistency over ninety minutes in question.

Forty-two points. We need 50 to feel confidently safe. Eight points, then, our minimal target from 13 remaining fixtures. Achievable, surely, provided ... I go down with a sharp, sudden attack of manager's speculation syndrome. It leads me to commit another mistake. Opening the *Rothmans* I check on Torquay's points tally from their final thirteen games last season. They totalled ... three. Irrelevant, I hastily decide. Ancient history. Nothing to do with us, squire.

Thursday 27 February

By the close of some days I'm amazed that I'm still without grey hair – that I've any hair left at all. Today we enjoyed the necessity enforced luxury of training on the Plainmoor pitch. And how did players allowed to cruise in second gear for four battery charging days acquit themselves? By bringing to training a rampant apathy. The collective disinterest made it clear that on their arrival at work each superstar had expected his individual sun lounger to be already set up complete with initialled towel and tall Cinzano. Threaten, cajole … I'd have been better off trying to get shit from a rocking horse. I mean, where do they think they are going to be in 10 years' time? Where will Ian Hathaway and Rodney Jack be next week? Offers have come in for both of them. Exeter want Ian on a free. Earlier in the season it would have been a question of weighing the welcome shaving of a few bob off the wages bill against his intermittent contributions to our game of a bit of finesse. Now, though, the blue and yellow line is stretched so thin we can't even indulge in a moment's indecision.

Plymouth (unlike Sunderland at the moment: 'We'll continue to monitor him') want Rodney but the offer of £75,000 (plus two potential £25,000 top-ups) from a club that has just sold a no better player on for £500,000 is derisory, especially when coming from near 'We love to hate them' neighbours. Rodney at Home Park would be perceived as a 'Judas' and Torquay no less disloyal to its faithful. Mind you, the upping of the offer into six figures might give us serious pause for thought. It would tip our season enough into the black to give us a war chest from which we might fund the acquisition of the three or four stalwarts the club needs to put backbone into AFC Sunlounger.

Friday 28 February

A day in which the macro largely overrides the micro. The UK professional game today is both subject of and arena for a welter of rumours-cum-arguments. One school is predicting that to protect their place at the television trough Premiership clubs will buy a Premiership-Nationwide promotion-relegation system of just one up, one down. The asking price will be the money they shell out to rescue the Bournemouths of the lower Nationwide from bankruptcy. These grateful poor relations, the scenario then elaborates, will then become, yes, their saviours' respective farm clubs.

A counter projection foreshadows a world in which the Premiership consists of just 16 clubs (as on the Continent), as many as four coming up each year from the Conference and, for minnows, the evaporation, post-Bosman, of all transfer fees. Even, it's forecast, the PFA sanctioned 'tied until 24' agreement will prove legally unviable.

Neither blueprint bodes anything but bad for Torquay and the latter comes with a frighteningly persuasive dimension that theory will be translated into practice. My source is Mike Bateson relaying the 'minutes' of the new Ron Noades chaired Nationwide Football League Committee.

Take Torquay as a not atypical example. The chairman's view is that if we are to attract four, say, decent pros with more to offer than most of our present lot, not only will we have to let around six of the squad go, we will be unable to avoid asking the survivors to accept a cut in wages. For some that will mean drawing the same take-home pay as a parking meter attendant: £10,000 is hardly an inducement to remain in a physically arduous, short career-spanned occupation. Without the sale of an occasional home-produced Lee Sharpe to subsidise the merely competent squad members' wages, Torquay, as one of many, could well modulate into a semi-pro side competing more likely than not elsewhere than in the Nationwide.

Not that salaries and job opportunities are a problem everywhere. Ask Steve Coppell if you don't believe me. Or Frank Clark. Or Dave Bassett. Today it's been announced that Steve will essentially be replacing Dave at Palace since Dave has moved to Forest to replace Frank who left there to go to Manchester City to take the place of Steve who had resigned after a brief spell in the Maine Road job that Dave turned down so as to stay at Palace before leaving for the City Ground rather than City's. Who says British football is incestuous or lacking in powers of lateral thinking?

Saturday 1 March

Thirteen years ago I developed clinically diagnosable hypothermia while playing on the wing in a sleet storm at Spotland, England's highest and hence potentially coldest ground. Today the ice was internal. It lined the chambers of my heart.

Then, Spotland was a tip. Now, it's getting slowly to be a spick and span set-up. Ground-sharing with the Rugby League side has reached the parts of the facilities that single operation wasn't able to. But it's done bugger all for the pitch. Credit Rochdale for the gentrification but you've still got to say their playing surface does little to encourage a flowing, to feet use of the spherical ball. Nor did the (high altitude) hurricane. Today's game was dire.

We went down 1–2 surrendering one point for a draw in the, natch,

89th minute. Battling against the wind in the first half we gave as good as we got but the wind at our backs saw us guilty of believing that we would breeze the second half. Rochdale won because they wanted it more. End of post-match analysis.

Almost. We did genuinely draw the short straw on injuries. As early as the ninth minute Rodney Jack hobbled off. We were thus, dammit, without either a quicksilver foil to Andy McFarlane or 75,000 Plymouth quid. (Short-term this proved a blessing in disguise: moving up from the left side of midfield I almost at once fired in an equaliser.) On the hour we lost central stalwart Alex Watson. Fifteen minutes later Steve McCall finally capitulated to the Achilles that has been giving him gyp all season. By this time Paul Mitchell was a limping three-quarters hamstrung passenger with no option but to stay on.

About 20 minutes from the end I hit the post from about 25 yards out. That would have put us 2–1 in front and we might then … forget it. On the way home it was their winning goal that kept elbowing itself to centre stage in my mind's eye. It kept alternating there with a far less vivid fuzziness. An incomplete team sheet. What the hell sort of a side were we going to run out with for our next game on Tuesday?

Sunday 2 March

A day on the phone. Object of ironing my ear flat was to pick up some spare parts for the disintegrated Torquay vehicle. It was less a case of trying to wallpaper over the cracks than to buy cement to fill the fissures. It being a Christian Sabbath was no help at all. We always develop raging toothache when the chemists are all closed and the dentists are playing golf. At close of phonic play we had one acquisition – Danny Hinshelwood of Portsmouth, brought in on a month's loan. He's 21 and his first-team involvement tallies precisely five appearances.

By nightfall he was heading westward. Uppermost in his mind must have been that he was assured a Torquay debut away against Carlisle – league leaders and the tightest, most accomplished side in the division.

Monday 3 March

What a bummer of a start to the day. Clearly, even Torquay have to overnight for an away fixture at Carlisle. Only too soon we'll be dragging through eight hours of coach-ride monotony. The idea is to spend the morning on some light training, walking through the positions and formations we'll be deploying tomorrow. Given that we'll have three virtual newcomers in the line-up it seems an essential bit of common sense.

Others have different ideas. The groundsman for one. Plainmoor is venue tonight for a South Devon League Cup Final. That makes the pitch sacrosanct. We must get our priorities right. Unaccountably – we could go through the motions (not to mention the introductions!) in trainers – the chairman concurs. All right, we'll do it at a bloody service station on the M6!

Tuesday 4 March

News by midday that the Grobbelaar and Co trial has ended in an irreconcilably hung jury leading to the judge calling it, 'No contest'. Certainly the *footballing* video evidence was utterly inconclusive – never beyond a reasonable doubt. If Brucie were to be hung on the strength of those lowlights the rest of us would have to be slow roasted on a spit for the gaffes that we perpetrate week in, week out. After more than two years and better (i.e. worse) than a £1 million spent on the due process of law, it all has to go to a replay. I don't suppose the briefs fancied a penalty shoot-out. There wouldn't be enough in it for them. Interesting to ponder how Brian 'Grobbelaar has played his last game' Woolnough and his *Sun* colleagues are taking this 'not proven' interim verdict. Perhaps still more nice little earners for my learned friends are in the litigation pipeline.

Not that we don't have our own little local difficulties to face up to first. Or massive handicaps. Without an alternative all we can do is look on the bright side. If we have to go into action with a skeleton crew, it might as well be Carlisle. While we usually raise our game against better sides, the overwhelming form-book probability is that we'd lose tonight anyway, even if we did have Messrs Watson, Jack, Mitchell and Winter in our first-choice line-up. Instead we have overnight arrival Hinshelwood and Anthony Thirlby, let go some time back by Exeter and not under contract to Torquay. We've plucked him from the dole queue straight into our midfield. On the subs' bench is YTS rookie Wayne Thomas. Further, although he's more injured than not, we're fielding Steve McCall. He comes from Carlisle. He senses, I'm sure, he may never have another chance of playing in his home town. Also, we've got nobody else. Welcome to the Third Division, Danny boy.

Not that, when we run out, it seems we are at a Third Division venue. Brunton Park has a capacity pushing 17,000 and the memories of Carlisle being in the top division still hover here and there. In envy-provoking contrast to the Torquay subs' bench, our hosts' provides a viewpoint for players of the calibre of Rod Thomas and an on-loan Chris Freestone, a lad with Premiership first-team experience this season for Middlesbrough.

Before half-time we're two down and lucky to have kept it to that. But this statistic is soon made a marginal consideration by an extraordinary changing room outburst from, guess who ... Inexplicably over-reacting to the enjoinment 'get back out there', Jon Gittens is suddenly foaming at the mouth as, *fortissimo*, he slags off his head coach. Along with the rest of our lads – and the entire Carlisle team! – I was best part of the way down the long tunnel that leads from the Brunton Park changing rooms to the pitch. But I could hear every word quite clearly. We all could. There's no point in going into detail here but I could see the eyes of the Carlisle lads glazing over with that 'I'm not really listening' embarrassment we all try to convey when a family row erupts in a public place.

Short term it seemed to knock them out of their stride more than us. Soon after the resumption I pulled one back with as well taken a goal as I've snapped up in a Torquay shirt. But it was just a brief variation on the night's overall pattern and not a good career move. Stung, Carlisle moved up through the gears to pull us apart and add three more. 1–5. Lucky to get the one. All the same, let the record show that, given the in off the deep end hiding to nothing they were on, neither Danny Hinshelwood, Anthony Thirlby or Wayne Thomas had anything to reproach themselves for. Having found themselves out there, they did what they could.

Prompted by 'auld acquaintance' Jonathan Fuller, Charlton's director of finance until his recent move back up to his first love team, I was invited into the Carlisle Boardroom after the game. We were merrily recalling the way he used to delay honouring my invoices when Carlisle's coach, Joe Joyce, approached us.

'Fair play to you and your lads, Nelse,' he said. 'You never stopped trying to get it down and play.'

Between leaving Carlisle at half-ten and getting home at gone five in the morning I found it the kind of remark that sticks.

Wednesday 5 March

A day with all my nerve ends itching. The latest confrontation with Jon Gittens kept playing itself over in my mind like a road accident you can't forget. Throughout United's scintillating 4–0 performance against Porto in the European spotlight, it kept returning to poison my pleasure. I went to bed still hearing what he'd said to Hodgie. I suppose I did get some sleep eventually but when the morning came it didn't seem as if I had.

Thursday 6 March

A wasted morning in a sense. Instead of training and coaching Hodgie (blearily confessing he'd hardly slept either) and I spent our time in a five-way discussion with the chairman, our PFA representative, Rhys Wilmot and, walking agenda as well as participant Jon Gittens. Hanging in the air between us was the common awareness that he is still less than half-way through his two-year contract with Torquay.

What passed between us must largely remain confidential.

Suffice it to say that the defendant, as in effect he was, kept claiming over and over that there was no problem and he had no problem with Torquay. No-one else saw it that way.

I can appreciate that the cut in his wage-packet, the involvement with a (by his standards) indifferent team, the Mickey Mouse excuses for proper training facilities, the heavy commuting and the loneliness of playing in a 'foreign' town can all have got to him. But most of us have been there. I don't see that these tiresomenesses add up to a justification of his behaviour. I do see why Jon ended up being marginalised by Portsmouth. Indeed, in an attempt to jolt him into turning over a new leaf I concluded my observations on his attitude by telling him to his face that from where I sat he was one of – perhaps *the* – most difficult players I'd ever had to co-exist with on field and in dressing room. I was speaking, I stressed, not only as a new-to-job coach but as a former long-term PFA rep who'd been involved in many a divisive, morale-sapping, behind the scenes confrontation.

Had it been a voting matter it would have been a clear-cut 4–1. Mike Bateson was solidly behind his two coaches. Finally he asked Kevin straight out if he wanted to have our senior pro paid off. What we want and what we are able to do are seldom one and the same. A short, silent eternity passed. I knew what was delaying Kevin's reply. Yet again he was counting our squad numbers, our points total, the potential cost of further confrontation.

'Let's see how it goes,' Kevin had no real choice but to say.

Yes, let's! Half-a-dozen more in the bag and we'll be in the comfort zone. From a team selection point of view the target seems more desirable than ever.

Friday 7 March

Back to the drawing board. Joe Joyce's compliment is continuing to ring in my mind. But not quite as he intended it. If it's safety we're after then – much as it goes against the grain, much as it's prejudicial to our long-term development – we've got to stop trying to play elegant, pattern-of-play football and start scrapping. It's just like Life, really. With experience comes compromise. With us that means first things first. To pull out of the downward spiral we've got to cut out the would-be frills. We've got to press up and condense play. For the defenders 'anywhere will do' will do. The midfielders have got to stop trying to bring the ball down and play to feet. For players with their confidence close to rock bottom, the passing game just doesn't work. If they're at all under pressure they must simply think in terms of hooking it forward first time. Between now and the end of the season survival is going to be ten-tenths of survival.

One of our number, mind you, has the opportunity of making an instant great escape. Colchester (he had that impressive game up at Layer Road) have come in with a bid for Scott Stamps. It's all of £12,500 and there's no way AC Milan will come in to better it. For the moment it's irrelevant. Stampsie has rejected the offer. I have to believe that it's less out of undying loyalty than a calculated determination to up the ante by playing hard to get.

The timing, though, is unfortunate. Exeter are still anxious to take Ian Hathaway on loan to the end of the season. Normally we'd think very positively about making the savings to our wage bill. But if both players went simultaneously we'd look very thin down our left side. Until Stampsie answers the 'should I stay or should I go' question we've got to retain Ian.

Was I always this twitchy? Friday night games are threatening to disturb my beauty sleep between now and the season's end. This evening the Ceefax legend read: Doncaster 2, Wigan 0. I went to bed thinking, 'Oh Christ, they've closed the gap.'

Saturday 8 March

Darlington at home – and the best of starts. After just four minutes an anywhere will do clearance takes on the more positive form of a rugby up and under. The Darlington keeper comes to gather it but gets his penalty box co-ordinates all wrong. Andy McFarlane's head makes it to the high first bounce and breaks his Gull's duck by looping the ball over the keeper and into the net. I could hear Charles Hughes applauding the length of Route One.

The shape of the goal was the exception to the game's rule. Thenceforth, right back to their stylish neatness of last season, Darlington took us apart. They had us draped on the ropes metaphorically stretched across our six yard box. A boxing ref would have stopped the fight to save the underdog further punishment. Incredibly, at half-time we went in still that goal up.

Changing-room orders were to restore our shape and find our rhythm through pressing up. Orders are not achieved results. Six minutes into the second half Darlington executed a move the puritanical Mr Hughes would have deprecated in his classroom but which the five Quakers involved relished immensely since it produced an equaliser.

What a curious game this football is! What strange group dynamics it produces! With a reeling Torquay there for the taking, Darlington became inhibited – obsessed with defending one point rather than seizing three. In the face of all logic they proceeded to sit deep and allow us to 'impose' our game plan. Then, three minutes to go, a further twist.

We gained a corner. Danny Hinshelwood hit an inswinger to the near post. My territory. As I went up for it their novice stand-in keeper came impedingly right across me, half knocking me aside. I missed the ball completely. So did he. It swung straight in to the net. 2–1 to the Gulls. Or not. The whistle had sounded only to indicate a free-kick. Totally passive though I'd been, I had been adjudged the sinner. How does that song go? 'Nobody loves you when you're down and out.' The next whistle confirmed the draw.

Sunday 9 March

No true romance for Torquay this season but bucketloads for Chesterfield. Their 1–0 win over Wrexham sees the Second Division club into the semi-final of the FA Cup and cocking a snook at all but three of the Premiership millionaires. Hats off to Johnny Duncan and his Green Grass Boys and, indeed, to Wrexham and the season's third in-depth surprise packets, Stockport, who have created their own recent glory days by combining passion with style and intelligence.

All three clubs exist in the immediate shadow of giants but are able to attract a good percentage of those people to home games. In return they have put a distinct spring, so to speak, in the step of the town they've also put on the map. The creation of this general and genuine 'feelgood' factor underlines the importance of looking after clubs of this size: they should not be allowed to be crushed or swept into the margin by the inexorable advance of the Premiership juggernaut. Just one danger threatens. If Chesterfield overcome Boro at Old Trafford the people of Wembley may wake one morning to find that in sympathy and congratulation the twin towers have grown twisted overnight.

Tuesday 11 March

After thoughts of Chesterfield, the actuality of Chester and a mid-week evening fixture in the Deva Stadium. It really is amazingly soulless for a recently built venue. It's literally an extension of a contemporary trading estate complex and the breeze-block construction must have set the club back pounds.

Back in the dear dim days of almost beyond recall things were very different. In 1980 I travelled with Southend to Sealand Road, their former ground, which boasted a massive stand whose proportions were worthy of a far bigger club. I remember the occasion well because it was the swan-song home appearance of a young lad transferring upwards, a certain Ian Rush. He scored that afternoon but subsequently disappeared into obscurity – at least as the memory banks of Evertonians would have it.

Sooner rather than later that massive stand was demolished and Chester decamped to play at Macclesfield. Something of an anomaly, really, because more recently, when Macclesfield FC topped the Conference, the Football League deemed the ground unfit for Division Three games. I suppose there was a crowd control safety factor built in to the posters that Chester used to stick on the Moss Rose walls.

Tonight we could do with a subliminally subverted Chester squad. They haven't got Rushie but they've gone nine games unbeaten and currently ride fourth in the table. We go out with a 4–4–2 formation and, truth be told, not much in the way of hope in our hearts. It doesn't prove, though, to be another Carlisle. Danny Hinshelwood is comfortable at right back and Jon Gittens and Rhys Wilmot nothing short of outstanding. Our midfield – where I'm playing on the left – shows it can exhibit workaholic tendencies and, keeping it simple, scraps away. Only our blunt attack looks out of sorts. When I try to get forward in support I find that my aching right knee is travelling quite a few significant notches further up the pain scale. Whenever I start to mix it in a challenge, tackling or resisting a tackle, a stabbing jolt excruciatingly travels down to my right knee. But not to change a non-losing game. We soldier on and, hooray, with our second clean away sheet of the season, grind out the draw.

No need to round up the usual suspects this time. Our spirits were high on the way home. But this was one coach whose departure I would have been happy to delay indefinitely. Immediately after the game I had found myself chatting with Chester manager, Everton legend Kevin Ratcliffe. He was brilliant. I became the archetypal fan again as making me feel like we'd been mates for ever, he opened the conversational door on a wealth of 'school of science' nostalgia. I could have listened all night.

It was as well I didn't. As I was finally dragged away I was greeted by a sub-section of the Merseyside Nelson clan. Quite unbeknownst to me, they'd come to the game – and then waited a good half-hour outside in the cold. I held things up another five minutes while we chatted but it would have been so much better if they could have benefited from Kevin's wit and wisdom rather than my family chat.

Wednesday 12 March

Another day at the desk. This time with a succession of ice packs on my troublesome right knee. Damien Davey and I try to assess the potential longevity of the problem. Should I see a doctor for another jab? It's not *that* bad. I've struggled with it since Christmas. Another 24 hours isn't going to make any difference.

Thursday 13 March

Permission granted to train on the pitch today so there's a modicum of feeling that we're proper players again. No significant change in the knee. I can run without undue bother but any bracing of the thigh muscles triggers that grinding jolt of pain. I've got to weigh the short-term against the long-term now. I could offer the knee up to a hydrocortisone jab tomorrow. That would rule me out for Saturday but, fingers crossed, make me available for the week after and the season's remaining games. What the real long-term implications are – are you listening Malcolm MacDonald, Tommy Smith and countless other partially crippled ex-pros? – I'll pretend not to be concerned with.

One call among the many is interesting and faintly bitter. Danny Hinshelwood's father, Martin, rings from Fratton Park. Terry Fenwick is letting young midfielder Jamie Howell go on a free. He came to Pompey from Arsenal at the start of the season. At the time we expressed provisional interest but the lad opted for the far better set up South Coast club. Now it appears he's back where he started with a year largely wasted. Oh to see ourselves as others see us.

Friday 14 March

For the mid-term better, the short-term worse, the decision is taken. I face another instantly granted appointment with Spear. In so far as the knee is fractionally fleshier than the ankle the agony is marginally less. It's almost bearable. The next time I watch *Zulu* I'll definitely be in the home team end.

More lastingly bruising is today's training session – the attitude shown to same, that is. If we were out on some blasted, dog-turded recreational pitch as usual, there would be a collective moan-up I couldn't much quarrel with. But today, once again, we have the relatively grown-up luxury of the Plainmoor pitch. Since the Chester dog fight was our most spirited performance in weeks, this is a first-rate opportunity for the lads to remember they can play a bit (some of them) and to set about building on the sliver of consolation Tuesday brought. Is that their attitude? Is Vinnie Jones a PhD? Casual to an unprofessional fault the squad makes it all but explicit it doesn't want to know. I get the sense they'd better have enjoyed the flat-out moan up; the rec would absolve them of any need to deliver. I join Kevin in getting heavy but within I despair. I've no intention of allowing my future lifestyle to centre on a perpetual bollocking of the apathetic up to the level of mediocrity.

Around midday we mount up for the coach ride to Yorkshire, Although tomorrow's opposition is Scarborough we'll as ever be overnighting in the Jarvis Hotel, Leeds. We stay there for all visits to our friends in the North and two reasons explain the 'as ever'. One: it's not at all a bad hotel. Two: the manager offers us bargain basement rates. It's either because he believes our patronage boosts the status of his establishment or because, coming from Torquay, he's a fan. Check one.

With us as we plough forward through the darkening evening is a passenger whose presence among even our lot must be causing him a deal of private grief. He's 18, an Australian and we're giving him a lift halfway to Glasgow because that's where he has the few belongings he needs to take home to Oz and he's too broke to pay for the fare. Thereby hangs another sour tale from the Nationwide's scrap heap.

At the beginning of the year Kevin and I had been routinely sifting through the welter of faxes cluttering up our desks. There might just be some hidden gold among all the agent-hyped dross, we thought. Indeed there might! With more than routine quickening our attention focused sharply on the CV of a teenage Australian, Drew Lawrance. The fax was from Motherwell FC where he had until recently been on trial. Too cash-strapped to offer the wannabe wallaby a contract, the Scottish club had done the best they could on his behalf. They had penned him a rave review.

We didn't hesitate. There was pedigree here. Drew Lawrance's father had been a potent force with Aberdeen. Torquay were doubtless operating even more under the financial cosh than Motherwell but if young Drew was up for coming to Plainmoor to trial on a non-payment basis, we were certainly up for him. Thanks to our hostel we could at least offer him comfortable bed and board and relative proximity to his home town of Melbourne. Relative to Motherwell, that is.

It all happened. Eye-catching early performances in Macca's youth team exercises showed Drew matching our second year YT's stride for stride, touch for touch. Only ... a midfielder, Drew was as yet too slight to mix it in the hurly-burly of first-team play and, cruelly, nearing his nineteenth birthday. Life had him between two stools. Arriving one year earlier he would have been offered a trainee contract his first morning. Now his age made him ineligible. And, try as we did to twist our own judgement by the arm, his physique made him a non-runner for the immediate future for the fully grown game. He was clearly a fine lad – if my Christopher had chosen him as a role model I'd have had no problem – and potentially an excellent influence on any side's younger set. Kevin, Macca and I gritted our teeth. A few thousand at our disposal to speculate with, we could have offered him something and been fairly confident we'd made a canny investment. But as things were and are …

Another poignantly distressing encounter ensued. Less inured to rejection than Steve Crane, Drew made only a token attempt to hide his huge disappointment. For weeks he'd been living on the poverty line, no spending money in his jeans, this chance the one golden opportunity in his life. At 18. Now he was being told that through a malign set of circumstances, rather than any real fault of his own, his chance of following in his dad's footsteps was fool's gold. Perhaps we did him no immediate favours telling him that he had failed at the last hurdle by the narrowest of margins. So near, so far – and the unfathomable depths of his young despair very evident from his surface reaction.

Where do you go when no-one else wants you? Home. Drew told us he had no choice. He called Melbourne while we had a bit of a private whip round and a discussion as to how best to get him on his way. Hence his presence – so near, so far – on a coach among a bunch of professionals who, so-so as their own abilities might be, he'd currently give his eye-teeth to join. We said goodbye to him in Leeds and the chairman sorted his fare up to Glasgow. He might yet be a name to conjure with. Filled out, back in the swing of things in Oz, he'll not only enjoy his soccer again but, perhaps, re-emerge as a genuine prospect. He thanked us as he left but if he felt bitter, I wouldn't blame him. Virtue hadn't found its true reward and unlike the countless pub loud-mouths who falsely complain their brilliant careers with City or Town were blasted by a bent talent scout, Drew has legitimate course for grievance. I don't know …Ellis Laight, Steve Crane, Drew Lawrence – that's the beginnings of a tasty side.

Two other downers closed out the day. One was a Friday night result. Cardiff 0, Doncaster 2. No! They've closed up some more! The second was my knee. The pain is still there and, worryingly, coming from a different area.

Saturday 15 March

A non-combatant I sit in the stand thinking that we must have chances today. Scarborough have lost their last two matches 0–4 and 1–7. Their collective morale can't be at an all-time high. Twenty-five minutes later I'm on the touchline screaming and damn near kicking. Our brave band of brothers have done everything in their power to restore Scarborough's confidence. We're displaying the verve and resolution of a beached kipper. There's no suggestion we can play as we did four days ago at

Chester. Scarborough take a throw-in. It's Wimbledon-style long. Longer. Rhys Wilmot misses it completely. 0–1.

At half-time Kevin and I play 'nasty cop, nice cop'. He justly roasts the 11 guilty men; I then outline some constructive tactical games. Start to. I'm interrupted by a Scott Stamps' whinge. 'The ball's not coming to my feet.'

Not nice to know now, I go ballistic as I turn on him. In toned down summary I point out to him that there are 10 men in red and white shirts trying to stop the ball coming to him at all; that he's paid for more than expecting waitress service – if the ball's not coming to him he should go looking for it, *make* it his; that shirking responsibility ('It's not my fault. The others aren't doing it right') is the malaise that's dragging us further and further down the table. I storm troop at them that the good pro doesn't sit back waiting for the tasty bit: he works to create it and for his mates as much as for himself. Nothing I say is original or anything they haven't heard before, but our first-half showing makes it the hottest news in town.

The coaches' double whammy works. Pleasingly it's Scott Stamps who gets forward to equalise with a good goal. The second goal is always more significant than the first. Yes, we've got chances.

Don't you believe it. Scarborough get a free kick. Gary Bennett, ex-Sunderland, wily veteran, makes one of the late runs from deep for which he's famous and which our team in the pre-match briefing were specifically told to watch for. Well, he's not that famous for late runs, it seems. As Jon Gittens inexplicably allows the ball to sail over his own head there is the aforementioned Mr Bennett in space accepting the free header. Goal.

Fifteen minutes to go. Hodgie with nothing to lose goes for the old triple substitution ploy. Off came McFarlane, Hawthorne and Hinshelwood. On go McCall, Hathaway and debuting YTS lad Wayne Hockley. At once Kevin is vindicated. Stampsie breaks forward on the left and brilliantly draws defenders and keeper before timing his pass inside to perfection. It comes to Wayne Hockley six or seven yards dead centre out from an open goal. His first touch in league football is a tap in! Or prod wide. From the touchline I could register the split second in which tension, responsibility, inexperience reduced his body language to a clutched-up stutter. End of story because Scarborough's third goal came when we had Uncle Tom Cobbley and the kitchen sink in their half.

Afterwards Hodgie again read the riot act. I held my peace. Or would have had I had any. Truth is I was too angry to trust myself to say a word. We had nervously clocked the other Division Three results. I don't know why. It's what we do we should be interested in.

Grim days. On the way home I asked myself over and over if there's a basic trick I'm missing on the training field. I don't think so. This is a squad that shouldn't be expected to walk the ball into the net before it can run. As the old Navajo proverb has it: 'You can lead a donkey to water, but don't bet it'll remember how to drink.'

Monday 17 March

St Patrick's Day and for the Chelsea fan strolling forth from Number 10 Downing Street to confirm the universally known secret that the General Election will be held on 1 May every apparent need for even more luck than the Irish are said to command. I can sympathise. I'm not a Blues supporter myself (although I applaud John Major's saluting the day honouring International Labour) but I can totally sympathise with anyone wandering around repeating 'Mayday! Mayday!' while trying to impose a continuing semblance of shape on his disintegrating team. Whatever the 1st's result, let's hope we can keep some clear blue and yellow water between us and last place come 3 May.

The clock is ticking louder and faster for all parties. Deadline for the freezing of transfers is only 10 days away. After Thursday 27 March no club will be able to take on a new player until the season's end. I drive in to Plainmoor knowing that I've every prospect of putting in several hours of on paper and on telephone FA musical chairs. So it proves. I spend hours pushing umpteen of the names of the game around my desk.

The home front, first. Exeter are on to say they again want Ian Hathaway. Scott Stamps tells us he reckons he'll be staying at Plainmoor. There's no more ringing conviction in his voice than in his body language during a training session. We resist the urge to give Exeter a green light right away even though – possibly along with my neck – there are two new kids on the Plainmoor block today. Pompey's Jamie Howell is here for a week's trial, as is Birmingham's Dean Tilley, a YTS midfielder crossing our path thanks to a grapevine tip from coach Ian Bowyer. We'll have a fair chance to weigh them up on Wednesday when they'll start against Elmore in one of our Reserves' rare as Christmas in July friendlies.

Away name games now as Hodgie and I start networking. Trevor Challis at QPR and Jamie Clapham at Spurs are two recommended-by-rumour youngsters who may be looking for some first-team action. We're none the surer after due process of telecommunication relays because neither Stewart Houston nor anyone of decision making weight at Spurs is available to deal with country cousin enquiries. Nor is Alan Curbishley at Charlton but I am able to discuss with Keith Peacock our chances of taking seriously useful Paul Sturgess on loan. It rapidly emerges that to say those chances were slim would be gross exaggeration. The name Dean Chandler comes up in the margin of our conversation.

Hodgie, meanwhile, has been back on to Tony Pulis at Gillingham. Ian Chapman, long the object of our interest, is literally a non-runner now – he's injured. Jon Ford, however, might just be up for grabs. His current loan period out to Barnet is up any day now. At six-foot-plus (and a big plus at our level), with some 200 league games to his name, Jon Ford is exactly the sort of left-sided defender we searchers would like to see wearing a blue and yellow strip at Fort Plainmoor. To be continued.

Tuesday 18 March

Two depressing postscripts to yesterday's telephon. We're given a definite 'No' on Paul Sturgess and Jon Ford, it emerges, is not due to leave the Barnet fold until Saturday week. I sit pondering the implications and how my knee is going to be feeling *this* Saturday. Yet another jab? If I have it today I won't be able to train for the rest of the week and I *really* don't like these quick-fix expedients. They're not only pain but permanent damage masking. Physio Damien and I agree it makes more sense for me to see the consultant again tomorrow.

Enter Scott Stamps. The move to Colchester still might be a viable option, he tells us. They want him to go in and see them on Thursday to discuss terms. Can he please, pretty please, have the day off? Hodgie and I tell him that Thursday is our key day for focusing-in on Saturday's game. He's got tomorrow, Wednesday, off anyway. He should arrange to visit Layer Road then. The club who still own his registration must take precedence in calling his shots over the club who might. Permission denied.

'Oh,' says Stampsie.

In the evening two intriguing results. In Monaco an injury-ridden Newcastle try to overturn a 0–1 deficit by getting nine men behind the ball and are elegantly despatched by a side that would probably have beaten them at full strength. Better a great player, the long term seems to be proving, than an uninspiring manager.

I'm more worked up by a Division One play-off place six-pointer. Ipswich blast past Sheffield United on the back of a hat-trick. The triple scorer is Neil Gregory! I suspect the difference between his November sojourn with us and now is that he's simply that much fitter. But talking of differences ... if only he could have spread three goals through his games with us. Here we go again: if only ... if only ...

Wednesday 19 March

The day starts with a real bummer. Elmore phone to say, oops, they've double-booked the slot and, as we were the second in line, they'll have to elbow today's Reserve fixture. The news will set our wannabe stiffs climbing the Plainmoor wall. It's about six weeks since they played in anger and all motivation is being starved out of them. Two realities are head-butting each other here. We really do need to be part of a formal Reserve league. Like so many other have-not clubs we can't afford to be in a formal Reserve league.

I go off to see the consultant. In no time at all I find myself being intimately explored by an MRI scanner. Damien Davey has insisted my knee be accorded cordon bleu diagnosis. This is another ethical-fiscal stand-off. A National Health patient would probably have to wait in line a good six months for this high-tech chance. I've had to queue for no more than 20 minutes. Further, the cost to the private patient is a cool £500.

'Jesus, Damien, the chairman'll go spare.'

The immediate read-out is disquieting as well. *Degeneration of ilial-tibial band on or around the insertion and degeneration of retinacular vastus lateralis.* The rough translation is that I'm a freak: I've a long-established problem with the thick stretch of tendon which links the various big thigh muscles to the bones at the knee. It should be single continuous tissue. In my case there's a divide at its centre rather like a river flowing around a small island. The working upshot is that with the tendon showing signs of degenerative change – wear and tear – the whole area is now suffering the adverse effects of too much long-term stress. Hence permanent inflammation. Hence the almost electrical jolts I get random movement to random movement. What's more I've the same condition in both knees.

'I've never seen anything like it,' the consultant gleefully confesses.

'I could sew the split together but it's pointless. Any significant strain and it would all tear again. The best course for you is to rest the knee completely and allow the inflammation to die down.'

There's a translation for that too. Go on playing through the pain barrier.

Thursday 20 March

Guess who's absent without leave this morning. Right. Scott Stamps. How did you guess?

It's a right bugger in every way. Not only do we want to fine-tune our game plan to overturn Scunthorpe but, following the débâcle of yesterday's cancelled fixture, we need to give Messrs Howell and Tilley a searching simulation of the real thing. On the phone Colchester say Stampsie's not with them yet and with Garry Nelson definitely sidelined for today, we're obliged to push as many of our walking wounded as doesn't seem positively sadistic into active play.

Strangely everyone rises to the crisis and it's an 'up' session. Perhaps the format helped. Mixing and matching personnel we went for three 20-minute full game 'matches'. Jamie Howell showed up well throughout and in one set of variations we had the first team playing 4–3–3. We've had Scunthorpe watched and we sense they may be vulnerable to wide and sustained forward pressure.

In the afternoon, reading the worst into the AWOL scenario, we contact Exeter to say that pro tem, at least, Ian Hathaway is a Plainmoor fixture. If our Stamps is franked and my injury worsens we'd be denuded of left-sided players should Ian go up the road. It's as well we made the call. At five in the afternoon word comes in that Scott Stamps has shown up in Colchester. Well, he tends to play hard to get.

Friday 21 March

Still more negative vibes. Scott Stamps is no sooner in the gate than he's in the chairman's office being asked to explain himself. He's insouciance personified. As he can afford to be. Colchester have made him a good offer. He just wants the weekend to think over whether there's any reason he should refuse it. We know that the uprated transfer fee Colchester now propose is the unlikely sum, as bizarre as peanutish, of £13,500. We know that, both in terms of weekly wage and length of contract, what

Colchester have put on the table is markedly more than we could manage. Out of our league, I'm figuratively thinking, when the chairman bids to influence Stampsie's decision making by declaring that he'll be fined two days' wages for pissing off regardless. You can tell it is indeed decisive. Scott doesn't protest but at that moment it's clear to everyone he intends to jump ship.

I won't push the metaphor. At his age, in his position I would probably have done the same. Apart from the not to be sneezed at hike in income, with eight games to go we're ninth from the bottom of the league Colchester seventh from the top and in the play-off zone. Personally I have a three-way split on Scott. Socially he's great. On the field, when he's trying, he's got more than average touch and talent and when he needs to tackle hard he can. Finally, he's a rotten trainer. He's perhaps still young enough to suss that if he wants to make it really big two out of three isn't enough. Right now, though, there's a more pressing consideration.

'All things considered,' Hodgie asks, 'how'd you feel about Saturday?'

'Yeah, fine,' he says.

We'll see.

Stampsie's availability means we can go solid on our 4–3–3 strategy. This confronts us with a second unpleasant chore. We need to tell consistent Lee Barrow he's being left out against Scunthorpe. Model pro though he is, it's plain he feels his season-long consistency (a touch lacklustre the past few games) should have served him in better stead than this. We try to convey its overall strategy rather than personal form that drives our decision.

The day drags on. By its close we have said 'Thanks, but no thanks' to Dean Tilley.

Saturday 22 March

Not infrequently I'm accused of being over modest. I often think I've got a lot to be modest about but not this morning. Even with a dodgy knee I'm going to pose more problems to Scunthorpe than any replacement we could contrive to dredge up. Pain barrier here I come. By default I'm playing.

First, though, a pre-match catch-up with Paul Baker. He's not been playing for several weeks. *His* knee has required an operation. Strictly in terms of today I'm grateful for small (potentially large) mercies but his convalescence is all part of another swirl of soccer's never ceasing ironies.

Scunthorpe are the lot who did for Torquay 8–1 last season. That was the occasion Andy McFarlane collared four goals and the match ball. For us he's got one in 13.

Show time. It feels wrong from the start. Our communally choreographed warm-up is suddenly a shambles. There's no collective rhythm. Everyone's doing his own odd-ball thing at the wrong moment. If newish Scunthorpe manager (and occasional very fast food waiter) Brian Laws is watching this, I think, he'll twig at once we're waiting to be beaten.

Which is how it seems to me. There's a tension about our lot, a smell of fear that seems out of all proportion. Yes, we're on a downward slide. It's nine games since we won. But we're still 12 points ahead of the bottom side. We're playing not in front of 15,000 but 1,500. What are we, men or Mickey Mice? I try to boost the confidence factor in the last few minutes but there's no gainsaying it's an uphill struggle.

Off we go. Soon it promises to be our lucky day. We send a long throw into their box. Up go the heads and among these the arm of a balance losing defender. The ball strikes it. A harsh whistle and a pointing to the spot whence Stevie Winter duly despatches the kick. For the third game in a row we're ahead with the opening 10 minutes. Not for long, Stanley. From their first structured attack Scunthorpe equalise. A probe down the right wing exposes Stampsie, his mind away at the Colchester fair, forgetting the cardinal training ground rule of showing inside. Over comes the cross. Outnumbered on the near post, the one Scunthorpe attacker proves better than the two Torquay defenders he gets across. Not too long later there's a repeat performance. Cross. Goal. No. Thankfully, harshly again, a flag. Still 1–1.

What's becoming clear is that our 4–3–3 formation is misfiring. Scunthorpe have clocked that we don't have enough midfield vision or, indeed, basic passing skill to pull them about at the back. They've had us watched too and they know that Rodney Jack is going to start having to drop deep and forage for scraps any moment now. They're happy to mark three on three at the back and push men forward into our half. They've got the impetus and now – cross, goal – the lead. Twice we do work something highly promising. First Andy McFarlane, then Charlie Oatway go through one on one against their keeper. Both times brave closing down ends in less than cool shots hitting his body.

I'm less than on song myself. The pain in my knee isn't agonizing but it's inhibiting. I can't shake off the back of the mind feeling that with this lunge here, that tackle there, I'm going to find myself without a leg to stand on. Stow that, Nelse! It's half-time and we've got to reshape.

In the second half 3–4–1–2 steadies the ship an appreciable bit. They don't go further ahead. We attack from time to time. Now we've penetrated deep into their left corner. Softly, softly as I can, I pull off my marker on the far post. Yes! Here it comes – a high balloon of a cross falling out of the sky to me in this handy couple of yards of created space. It's a Craven Cottage rerun. Head? No. Too steep. Kill with first touch to make sure? No. They're turning back to close me down. Volley, then … NOW! Damn! The strike had been full-bloodedly malevolent and true. But the aim had been crucially awry. From six yards out the ball screamed over the bar. I screamed too, internally. It had fallen to me not only to salvage a point but also to prove one. I could have led by example: 'Look, guys, we can come back. We are survivors.' Instead, as I raised my head from my two hands I knew that the only message I had conveyed was the oldest in the soccer book: football is such a cruel exploiter of weaknesses.

Monday 24 March

Another watershed day. It begins with an expected early knock on the door from an eager and willing Scott Stamps – eager and willing to confirm that he is off. Hardly a surprise. Possibly a significant step. Given the luck I genuinely wish him, he could become upwardly mobile in quite a big way.

He's not going to be the only reduction to the Torquay numbers. A letter was sent to Jon Gittens today over Kevin Hodges' signature. If Plainmoor really was the clone of Downing Street it would have read something like this. 'I would like to thank you for your services on our behalf over the past eight months but must inform you that due to changes to our policy, as of today your services will no longer be required. As per your contract, your salary will be continued to be paid until the end of next season.'

Rightly or wrongly – he certainly felt that it was wrong – we're convinced that the rest of our squad would operate better as a collective whole without Jon in their midst.

Made, though, on the same day as Scott Stamps bidding us farewell, it's a hugely courageous decision. It drives us back down to 15 squad members with first-team experience. That grand total includes knee-knackered Nelson and two goalkeepers. It is thus also a potentially disastrous decision. If our results don't improve quickly, we'll be targets for the scorn of fans and 'experts' everywhere.

But by the same token, it's also a thoroughly handsome supportive gesture on the chairman's part. There are no ifs and buts about Torquay being stuck honouring that contract for the next 16 months. The club will lose more on the Gittens swing than it has just gained on the Stamps roundabout. Mike Bateson could well have cut up rough about having to amputate.

Fifteen men on a Plainmoor chest. The deadline four shortest days away. The sands of time are pelting through the neck of the hourglass now as if there were no tomorrow. We're definitely into 'last orders' time and, after all our fumbling attempts to transfer wheel and deal, we're more in need than ever. We're short of a left back, a left-sided midfielder, a striker, in a world in which the harsh reality is that there are only so many players riding on the footballing merry-go-round, or, as we term it at Plainmoor, treadmill. But onward and … onward.

I talk to Martin Harvey (elbowed by new, share-suspended Millwall but none the less canny for that) and, again, Tony Pulis. The door on Jon Ford may still be ajar. So it goes. Then, again, I'm talking to Curbs. Paul Sturgess is utterly off limits but Charlton can probably see their way to loaning out big young defender Dean Chandler. He's had senior team experience, just, but with four seasoned centre backs in the Charlton squad ahead of him, a permanent berth is most unlikely. He's probably hungry for a first-team shirt of whatever colour. My one faint ray of consolation.

Tuesday 25 March

'Dean Chandler wants to come,' Keith Peacock replies to my start of the day question, and the thin ray of hope at once widens to a broad shining beam.

'If you want to run the rule over him,' Keith continues, 'he's involved against Norwich Reserves tomorrow.'

'I've got absolutely no problems,' I say, 'but understandably Kevin would like another look. We'll be there and if we like what we see we can bring him straight on down to Torquay with us.'

Great! So far as it goes. As I yet again count up the bones comprising our skeletal squad, there's no avoiding the diagnosis that we still need to bring in another player. Kevin and I convene an urgent meeting with Chairman Mike. Smiling through his tears he finally gives a nod to our clasped-handed pleas.

'Lee Archer, Geoff – would you consider loaning him to us?'

It's me on the blower yet again. The lucky listener is Geoff Twentyman, an old sparring partner and now the assistant at Bristol Rovers. Not so lucky. I've dragged him to the phone from off the golf course.

'I'll have to speak to the gaffer,' he says, 'to confirm it, but my gut feeling is a 95 per cent 'yes'. I'll get back to you when I've finished the back nine.'

I'm holding my breath. Archer is a talented left-side midfielder who could give us much needed cover down that now distinctly denuded flank.

Nine snails pace (as it seems) holes later I learnt that Ian Holloway's consent makes it a 'yes'. Except it's 'no'. The player doesn't reckon Torquay. Proceed immediately to *Jail* and under no circumstances collect £200 as you're still the wrong side of Go. What – or, rather, who – next? Or even 'where'. The Conference, both Yeovil and Enfield are hoping. Their top-of-the-table ICIS clash tonight drew a crowd of no less than 8,000. Another 2,000 were locked out.

No problem attracting anyone there, it seems.

Wednesday 26 March

A breakfast news item that sends my appalled brain reeling. After eight years a Hillsborough 'survivor' – surviving, that is, in a diagnosed permanent vegetative state – has regained sufficient consciousness to be able to communicate with his loving, caring family ('No, we don't want him switched off, thank you ever so much') by means of a 'one press for 'Yes', two for 'No' touch pad. My aghast thoughts spiral away beyond logical ordering. From the practical care level (What made the positive difference?) to the ethical-legal level the implications are, well, mind boggling. *Eight years on!* I can only grapple with one consideration. In the 3,000 days that have passed since then how many hours in the sun, how many cool beers, how many hours of prime-time television have former crowd control supremo chief superintendent David Duckenfield and his South Yorkshire police colleagues enjoyed? More, we might guess, than the now 30-year-old Andrew Devine.

To return to the mundane, today is day before D for Deadline day. The clock is now ticking so loud and fast we're measuring time in hours and minutes.

9.15 – The office. I arrive to discover Hodgie already speaking on the phone to Jamie Howell. Clearance has come through for him to sign non-contract forms for Torquay.

10.00 – Mount Stuart Hospital, Torquay. Formal results of my scan. Yes, there's unquestionable degenerative change to the tendons. It's not career-threatening as of this very instant, but I've now got a deadline all of my own. My personal biological clock has gone into overdrive. Is it going to hurt me out there on the park? Only when I laugh.

10.25 – The office, take two. A hint of joy with Notts County's Sean Farrell. He's willing to come in principle, other things being equal. For 'other things' read money. As Hodgie and I left for Charlton, Chairman Mike and Chairman Pavis were playing the numbers game.

11.00 – Kennford Services near Exeter. The aching knee has absolved me from driving duties. The much-felt absence of a promised mobile consigns Hodgie to a run to a payphone. No updates from Plainmoor. No news is … no news.

2.25 – Late arrival at the Valley. We cheerfully take our seats in a surprisingly crowded directors' box. Dean Chandler performs well enough to make the long trip seem worthwhile.

2.45 – Half-time. Hospitality suite at the Valley. More phoning. Bristol Rovers have been on to offer Andy Gurney. Who he? A quick check of our PFA manual indicates a player who started 42 games last season. Can't be all bad. We cancel plans to visit Fratton Park tonight and book seats for Rover Reserves v Brighton instead. There's been no meeting of minds on the Farrell front but the chairman will give it another go tomorrow.

3.45 – A tangible result. A quick chat with Curbs and a quicker handshake. He's happy to lob us Dean Chandler.

4.00 – It seems we've sat and talked like this before. We're back on familiar territory – the M25 – but with extra baggage. Our loan-signing is the force perforce third member of our Yate Town scouting team tonight.

7.40 – Late arriving again but, at 10 minutes adrift, getting better at it. And worth the effort because both Andy Gurney and Lee Archer are playing. Gurney is essentially a wide-right player – not really what we need. Archer shows some neat touches and delivers a couple of excellent crosses but our appreciation is no little qualified by the Ambridge – sorry, umbrage – we've taken over his giving us a thumbs down.

8.15 – Second half-time of the day. A quick chat with Ian Holloway sets some of the lad's reasons for turning us down in a more acceptable light. It's been a long day. We decide to skip the second half.

10.15 – Arrive home with a lodger. The Easter weekend looming, the club hostel has a 'No Vacancies' sign clearly displayed in the front window. I wish the squad did too.

Thursday 27 March

Here it is. D-day. With two witching hours. Twelve noon for signings who want/are needed to play this weekend and 5 pm for those still able to register but ineligible for inclusion this coming Saturday.

We're still after Sean Farrell. Based on our season-long understanding that three loan players is the permissible maximum but – how puritanical – only two can play on any given occasion, our plan is to add him to the Hinshelwood-Chandler collection. If we get him, young Danny, as a defender, will be sacrificed for the games on Saturday and Easter Monday and, able to claim he did a job for us, return to Portsmouth at the end of his loan.

Such is the plan. I sped off for training leaving Kevin and the chairman (now resigned to meeting the, by our standards, hefty wages bill) to complete the paperwork. My presence at training was essential today. I had to familiarise Dean Chandler with his fellow defenders and vice versa and remind everyone of Lincoln City's single-minded airborne approach to the game. It was a good session. Dean settled in well. The tactical message got across. I was in good spirits as I piloted our over-laden van through the narrows of the Devonshire lanes.

Within moments of my returning to Plainmoor those good spirits had been replaced by the bitter flavours of frustration and anger I couldn't vent and black, black misery. Precisely four minutes away from the noon deadline, I was told, a message had come through to Plainmoor Control from the Football League. They were refusing to allow Sean Farrell's loan signing.

Their answer to the agonised Torquay squawk of 'Why?' was totally in order: two loan signings, two, period, was all we or anyone was allowed. What? No, of course not! Our intention not to use D Hinshelwood was utterly irrelevant. Case dismissed.

Stunned, shell-shocked, my disbelief only slowly dwindling I heard the not so everyday story of a cock-up of football folk in unbroken silence.

What was really getting to me was the amateur crassness of it all. Who are these clowns, the Football League must even now be thinking. Don't they have even an elementary knowledge of the rules and regulations? I knew that in any grown-up club a dedicated club secretary would have had the small print at his full-time fingertips. We'd been meandering along in a fool's paradise for weeks, months, even. Inexperience or basic incompetence? At 17th in the table, and with just seven matches remaining, the question will doubtless soon be resolved.

Friday 28 March

Easter pushingly early and the weather perversely glorious. All the same for Torquay a far from good Good Friday in prospect. As on Christmas Day pro football training takes precedence over the Christian calendar. No little good about this Friday though. On the warm, almost sultry Torbay breezes a distinct sense of that fear-generated tension which destroys timing and saps physical fitness before a muscle is moved. For the coaching staff it had to be make-believe day. Mask all suggestion of yesterday's admin cock-up and put on a happy face. Any panic signs of our feeling that we're in a pressure chamber might be the last straw on our camels' backs.

Training today was consequently pitched in a light-hearted key. The emphasis was on fun. This time we seemed to have got it right. I felt myself unwinding and realised it was because the squad's mood seemed definitely to have lightened up in the course of the morning. Oh to be on the same wavelength come five tomorrow afternoon!

Voluntarily plunging into the Third Division pressure chamber is Paul 'More moves than a pinball' Baker. A deadline swoop by Mick Tait, his good mate, has our early season target man now lining up in a Hartlepool shirt. Getting absolute value for money being a priority of the yet again relegation-haunted poor relations of North East football, Paul is also to be responsible for first-team coaching duties. Snap! Phoning to wish him well and give him the benefit of all my vast experience, I wasn't too surprised to detect his enthusiasm transmitting on a rather higher level than my own. After all, for him, it's two days: for me it's been, as it seems, centuries.

'Get stuck in,' I urged him, 'the best is yet to come.'

Saturday 29 March

We hit the low road for Lincoln at 8.00 am. The pundits all have the game down as a home-win banker – less than cheering background knowledge to carry with us. And indeed the prospect of non-stop high balls mortar bombing down into our penalty box is about as appealing as a day trip to the Gaza Strip. If we're going to bring anything home from Sincil Bank we'll need to take big hearts, strong wills and undivided attention out on to the park.

The initial impish tactics hardly surprised us. They know full well that 20-goal speedster Gareth Ainsworth on their right flank was up against a nervous 36-year-old debutant wing-back, Torquay's only left-sided player. It was this weak brick in our defensive wall they set out to exploit.

Inexperienced defender I may be but give the (old) boy a man's job to do and I can at least be counted on to give it my all. The brick, I think I can say, stayed cemented in place. Solid, too, was our total debutant Dean Chandler. For 20 minutes, that is. Then an accident in the finest traditions of black comedy made mockery of much of our loan signing toils. Another Lincoln ball into the box had new man and old keeper colliding at the far post. The good news: the ball bounced to safety. The bad: his match, certainly, and, possibly, his season over, twisted ankle ligaments had Dean heading for the treatment room's ice bucket. We reshuffled our thread-bare pack. Paul Mitchell dropped in to the back three to allow Mark Hawthorne to come into the so far bypassed midfield.

Unlike Dean we survived the first half. Fifteen minutes into the second, glory be, we were leading 2–0 as a result of converting our only two post-interval chances. McFarlane and Jack, that (on paper) dreaded strike force, finally realised their potential to cause chaos in the home defence. Two up but 30 minutes still left. The uniqueness of the situation could only have us fearing that we'd peaked too soon. Sensing our discomfort at being in the lead, Lincoln increased their Big Bertha bombardment. Something in the Torquay trenches would surely have to give. Something did. Yep, you've guessed it. From a corner. 2–1. Eleven long minutes to play.

Three more corners, four long throws, a couple of accurate long range strikes. It was heart-thumping stuff. And then heart-stopping. Another long throw hurtled into our six-yard box. A Lincoln flick-on. Harassed by former squaddie Phil Stant our keeper Rhys Wilmot came for what still seemed a safely claimable ball. Until somehow it wasn't and a nightmarish scramble was underway. The fumbled ball bounced, was hooked back by Stant, hit a post and, rebounding, struck the unwitting head of Stevie Winter in mid-tumble on the goal line. From eight inches out he's as lethal a finisher as I am. At either end. The ball barely had momentum enough to cross the line but cross the line it did. Lincoln arms shot up. Torquay chins hit the heavily watered deck. In another last minute we had thrown away two more priceless points.

As, horrified, I turned from the scene of the accident, I was confronted by a vision of beauty. The assistant referee was holding his yellow flag on high. I blinked hard to establish whether I should go on believing what I thought I might be seeing. But my eyes had not deceived me. The goal had been disallowed and we were still winning. During that brief moment of mayhem God had been in Torquay's heaven and there, bless Her, she stayed for the next 60 seconds to share with me the ecstasy generated by the sweetest sound I had heard in ten bloody awful weeks. The final whistle! How sweet the sound to those in front!

Orchestrating the celebrations in front of the magnificent 70 – our long, long ranging fans – cost me my first footing rights to the showers. Who cared? It had been a giant step for Torquay against the gravitational pull of relegation. I was as proud as punch of the team's performance – we had fought for the whole 90 with all the character required – and proud of my own performance too. The sweetness of the victory lasted all the long and relaxed way home. Consistency. The stubborn refusal to roll over and die. What's the secret? If only we could bottle today's spirit and draw inexhaustibly upon it.

Sunday 30 March

The win has cost us. Dean Chandler is definitely out for at least two weeks and so too, alas, is hamstrung defender Paul Mitchell. Our fully-fit complement of professionals now numbers 13. Only two of those, mind you, are keepers.

Monday 31 March

'A win today, lads, and we're there. Get on 51 points and we won't even have to bother about what the other teams do.'

Enough said, the assistant coach considered, as he hoped fervently that not all of Saturday's spirit had evaporated. Surely all that remained was to just go out and do it.

Others had other ideas. Ian Atkins has cobbled together a physically fit and, more to the point, strong Northampton side. This Easter Monday they rose to the occasion and straightforwardly overpowered a Torquay slovenly to a fault in their starting. Two set-piece goals in two minutes consigned us to a familiar bleak landscape. Just 20 minutes gone and here we were playing catch-up football.

We did pull something back. A speculative shot from Rodney Jack hit the side of one of several sand-dunes in the goalmouth. The ball was sent soaring high over the low and until then covering hand of the justifiably disgusted keeper. Back in the game we did not join in his complaints about life's uneven ups and downs.

Bucked up ourselves, we now put together a creditable performance but, however commendable, the surge in spirit and endeavour was too little, too late. And far from subtle. Having failed to fashion anything much in the way of goal-scoring opportunities, we heard the whistle – a sour sound this time – signal our eighth home defeat. Our mini revival had been a run of one whole game. I was 60 yards from the tunnel when the whistle sounded. Somewhere in my mind I was distantly pleased to have got through two games in three days without wilting but my knee was giving me gyp. By the time I'd reached the sideline the PA system had brought me more grief. Chasing teams Darlington, Orient and Exeter had all recorded vital wins.

Tuesday 1 April

One of the last ways you'd want to spend April Fool's Day is among a bunch of footballers looking to work off their chagrin over a bad result. We gave those of our squad still without Zimmer frames the day off. They could recharge their physical batteries and, it was to be wished, their mental ones too. Much to concentrate their minds should be Brighton's ninth home win tonight from the 11 Goldstone games since Steve Gritt took charge. If they continue to be driven on by 9,500 Sussex voices roaring incessant encouragement, it's not too hard to imagine the Seagulls soaring up, up and away out of trouble.

Wednesday 2 April

A win on Monday and the playing staff at Torquay – the eight currently standing, that is – would have been enjoying another rest day today. The loss has brought us together for business as usual.

With minimum room for the manoeuvring of manpower we opted to extend Danny Hinshelwood's loan period. I gave him full marks for his not being so churlish (not to say unprofessional) as to respond with 'Bollocks to that!' after our resting him for two games. His loyalty will be rewarded with a midfield berth in our derby encounter with Exeter.

Friday 4 April

A week can be a long time in football. This has lasted a month of Sundays. The anxious hours we've passed hypnotised by our minimal options have only served to underline the lasting seriousness of last week's administrative cock-up. Why did we get ourselves into such a fine mess? Retrospection has kept stealing out of the past to inhibit the present. Football's great 'Why?' question. Why so many chances conceded? How come so many points tossed away in the last, concentration-straying minutes? Why? Why? Why?

'Why not?' a stark but sense-restoring voice finally asks. With the retort we can, for the present, forget the past and focus on the future.

Exeter tomorrow just up the road. No coach marathon, then, but the fixture gives our nearest rivals the perfect opportunity to leapfrog us in the table. Judging by the probing, edged questions they're putting to Hodgie – particularly over the high-profile absence of Jon Gittens – the gentlemen of the Press are expecting the Gulls to be shot down. Just five games to go means the metaphorical heat is up, to levels far crueller than the brilliant 'too hot to play' weather we're currently suffering. Then again, Brian, a win will ensure our survival for another year. Where better to secure both than a packed St James Park.

Saturday 5 April

The game is a six pointer. Three for us will see us effectively exorcise the spectre of wooden spoon and lost Nationwide status. Three points will allow us to blood some of the youngsters and let me rest my leg until next pre-season.

On the other hand, three points for Exeter will see them leapfrogging above us in the last third of the table where all around have run into some form.

What better place to clinch it, I repeat to the squad, than at their place. Privately, though, I'm nothing like as bullish. If we were coming off the Lincoln win I'd have high hopes. But the relapse, the abject surrender to Northampton two days later has me fearing the worst. I clutch at the straw of consolation that the Exeter lads will be feeling no better.

In the event the game proves to be just what you might expect – a shocker. Long before half-time the crowd were getting on to both sides, as it 'encouraged' us to put something together by way of entertainment. A rock-hard pitch, near gale-force wind and a blinding, lowish sun didn't begin to help, but the real villain of the piece, of course, was fear. I've seldom played in a game where the fear factor was so close to the surface of virtually every player's skin. Literally uptight muscles, minds split into dithering fragments by the freezing prospect of making the calamitous error that would cost the match, destroyed touch and accuracy, inhibited initiative. This was professional football played by 22 men close to the breadline and scared into incompetency by a not altogether paranoid anticipation of dipping below it. Sod the crowd. Never mind the quality. Get shot of it soonest and let some other bugger carry the responsibility.

Somehow we got a goal. By half-time we still had a clean sheet. In the changing room I gave a performance worthy of John Mills in a submarine. We're going to be all right, chaps: work hard, work for each other, don't make the mistake of dropping deep. They're the ones in trouble.

Minutes after the resumption Exeter equalise. An icy new fear runs through my veins and camouflages the pain around my knee. The second goal! They were going to do us now, I just knew it. They didn't. In general, just like Darlington, Exeter failed to detect how far on to the back foot they'd pushed us and were too cautious to move forward for the knock out. In particular, that said, we were inestimably indebted to Ray Newland, recalled in place of injured Rhys Wilmot, who with brave brilliance twice got the better of Glen Crowe in one-on-one situations. The final whistle sounded with the travesty still at 1–1.

That'll do for us, was my gut reaction; we've kept the status quo with Exeter. We can be the happier. The thought helped me ignore the scornfully raised eyebrows in the bar afterwards. Then that same gut received a nasty pinch. Doncaster had topped Darlington 3-0 to close on us. It's not with one bound our Torquay heroes are going to free themselves from the drop but fighting desperately every inch of the way.

Sunday 6 April

The Coca-Cola Final. Millionaires versus menials. A dull game with Boro fools to their log-jammed season selves in allowing a deserved Leicester equaliser in the last couple of minutes. All to do again and Bryan Robson looking like he'd got flu.

Tuesday 8 April

Today's rec pitch is as rock hard as St James Park. After 48 hours rest my knee was feeling not at all bad; well up, surely, to the standard Tuesday operational procedure of some light training and a gentle five-a-sider. Oh-oh! Bad career move, Nelse. An attempt to turn on a foot maladroitly askew a divot has me hopping mad and in pain. Already I'm more out than in for Saturday.

Trying to stay in – and up – are Brighton. Formal national news channels today are stating that the Seagulls are taking 'court action' to have the FA's confirmed decision they be deducted two league points for a Goldstone pitch invasion declared illegal. Which court, I ask myself in genuine perplexity? Does any court or any other authority in the land hold jurisdiction over the FA in this context? Isn't this a within the family dispute – confined by working practice solely to within the footballing world? There isn't, as far as I know, a government-appointed tribunal instructed to hear claims against the unfair dismissal of points from your total?

It's a genuinely hard one, this. The fellow player in me feels instinctively that the deduction is unfair on the Brighton squad. Their points tally should be a genuine reflection of their achievement on the pitch. Then, however, you have to ask yourself what else the FA might do. A fine? Not really. A fine that would put Brighton out of business would mean nothing to, picking a club at random, Middlesbrough. A fining policy could open the floodgates, as it were, on pitch invasions when critical defeat was imminent or a dubious penalty decision seemed like settling a Cup semi-final. After all, whether or not a coded message was received beforehand, the Goldstone demonstration (not the first, in any case) came as the climax to clear advance 'publicity' from its perpetrators-organisers.

My foreground suspicion, meanwhile, is that this 'legal' action is more about Brighton trying to put the frighteners on the clubs immediately above them. Two points promise/threaten to make all the difference come this season's end as to who will get to go on dancing at the Nationwide ball at the start of the new one.

Wednesday 9 April

The Michelin Man was a wimp. His on the road mileage is speedily diminishing in our rear view mirror as Hodgie and I take off again for first Bournemouth v Swansea's and then Southampton v Palace's close encounters of the stiffs kind.

At the first fixture our interest is focused on Swansea keeper Lee Jones. In a dire goalless draw he never put a foot wrong. Since he also literally never had a save to make the Torquay tycoons forbore racing after him with open cheque books.

The Saints v Eagles clash was a better game – so much so that, although we'd been put wise that some of the lads might be foot-loose come season's end, its chief impact was to remind us that, not tycoons at all, us Torquay beggars can't be much in the way of choosers.

Better still, no doubt, was the Borrusia Dortmund v Man United game. United's 0–1 defeat (fair reflection, by most accounts) is salvageable; 1–2 would have been better.

The goal would almost certainly have been prevented by Peter Schmeichel had an 11th hour back injury not sidelined him. It's my belief the gods were punishing his hubris. Earlier he had declared that today's superstars would turn over those of a generation or two ago 10–0. A pointless high-profiling, truth be told, of the old pub discussion that invariably fails to distinguish content from form.

Thursday 10 April

Scouting may have done things for Baden-Powell but it's been bad for my knee. With the weekend in mind I thought I'd put it to the test this morning in the context of an All Stars clash – Garry Nelson's Famous Five versus the Alex Watson Quintessentials. At game's end Mars bars would separate the men from the boys. Not in my case. I was no sooner up and running than hobbling off.

Even in this state, though, I might have done a job for Liverpool this evening against Paris St Germain. Good, is not the word. They were appalling. Thank the Lord Ray Newland didn't have David James' yips last Saturday. Ninety minutes was sufficiently long enough to demonstrate they're contagious.

Friday 11 April

No training for me today in either sense. Hodgie took over the coaching while I submitted myself to a heavy-duty fitness test. No problems in motoring in a straight line but any attempt at turning, bracing my body weight on my right leg and … forget it.

'Forget it, Nelse,' Damien said. 'No way you can play tomorrow.'

In spite of the pain my mind still tried to reject the verdict. Our squad numbers are so down – lower than a snake's arse, as Sweaty Balmer would put it – that I know there's a quality control need for me to play tomorrow. Only … not wanting to, common-sense has to win out over wishful thinking. I nod agreement at Damien.

As I do, the chairman approaches. He's obviously read the message from my body language. 'You've been a good old horse, Nelse,' he says, 'but now we're going to have to shoot you.' Cheers, Mike. You're the boss. But I'll take the parrots with me.

Saturday 12 April

It's chiefly down to having moved on and across from just being a player, of course. In 18 years I've run out for nearly 650 league games and never in all that time have I felt the apprehension, let's face it, the dread, I've been experiencing these last few games. I've been in relegation and promotion and play-off climaxes to seasons many a time but, until now, only as a player. I'd turn up at the ground focused on just one responsibility – my own performance – and knowing that if it all went pear-shaped on the park there would be 10 others sharing the blame. I'd be nervous, yes, but in that positive, keyed-up way you can put to work. Now, responsible in large measure for the team's overall performance, knowing that jobs, even the club's future, could all be on the line, the nerves are jangling in a manner anything but positive. What's more there's not a solitary person with whom, in the hope of halving it, I can share this occupational hazard. The weight on Kevin's shoulders is heavier than mine and, where the other players are concerned, even if I do feel like a head to toe blancmange, it's my job to seem like a sunny Rock of Gibraltar.

And yet as I drive in I ask myself: could this be the day? Barnet are safe but out of the play-off fight. There's nothing specific to motivate them after their long coach ride. I'm out of the line-up today but, recovering fast from his ankle injury Dean Chandler, will strengthen our defence even though he's two weeks adrift in training. If the lads don't try to be clever-clever with the ball when under close pressure and just do the basics well ... at the bottom of the briefing notes I stick up in the changing room I print 'Determination: Attitude: Hard Graft = 3 points'. Then I am shown the 'Chairman's Diary' section in today's programme.

Writing about last week's Exeter match he openly wonders: 'Is that the worst game you've ever seen? It certainly was one of the least attractive football spectacles I've ever seen and if there was any justice neither team would have earned a point.'

As comment it's fair. As comfort on the afternoon of a crucial opportunity to banish all fears of relegation it's colder than a week-old cup of Eskimo sick. Now, as the players arrive I have another emotion to put alongside high anxiety as I go into my tower of strength impersonation. Mike Bateson psychologist extraordinaire? Possibly. *Just* possibly.

The teams line up. I'm on the bench feeling, as Hodgie has all season, like a traffic cop isolated in a bus shelter at the side of a derestricted four-lane highway. Not out there, I can't tweak, encourage, on the run. A deep breath. We need this more than Barnet. That's *got* to be the difference.

The whistle goes. We have the early better of it. In the 10th minute, yet again, we take a one goal lead. A through ball from Mark Hawthorne sees Rodney Jack scorching beyond a caught flat defence. Still motoring he steers the ball at speed past Lee Harrison. A fine goal – he had time to think about missing it – and a small landmark. A Torquay striker had made it into double figures for the season.

The game settles down. Danny Hinshelwood is bright. Dean Chandler is solid enough. Now we're a goal up someone putting his foot on the ball occasionally would steady us, unsteady them. No-one looks capable of doing it. We're still in front at half-time.

The team talk highlights a few specific instructions – we must start defending from the front, we have to get tighter in midfield, give nothing away at the back – but a general underlying message is designed to make the three points we almost clutch permanently ours. 'Just 45 more clean-sheet minutes and the season's safe. Your best shot now and we can breathe easily for the rest of our games. You're just inches away.'

As I say all this a cold part of my mind feels a perceptible jab of shame. I'm coming on hot and heavy to a bunch of players half of whom, in all likelihood, won't be with us in two months' time.

If shards of guilt were troubling me as I returned to the bench, the second half eased my conscience utterly. I'd wasted my breath. Up front Messrs McFarlane and Jack defended neither our lead by their work-rate or their reputations. Danny Hinshelwood faded. One of his fellow midfielders covered every blade of grass – we could have saved money by fielding a remote-controlled lawn-mower – but never came near to putting effective boot to ball. Barnet got on top. When Alex Watson belatedly went for, and missed, an awkward bouncing ball, a visibly tiring Dean Chandler found himself one on one with the nippy striker it had fallen to. Routine operation procedure as per training now was to shepherd him towards the corner flag. Instead, Dean dived in, got it wrong and allowed the forward to skip by him. Not exactly a textbook example of giving nothing away at the back. In came a low cross to a goal-mouth bereft of covering Torquay midfielders. Bang. One all and the quintupling of fear and trembling in Torquay.

Enter Jamie Ndah, the man we let go a few weeks back. That same calculating part of me had been, no, not gratified, but reassured to learn that he'd been substituted by Terry Bullivant mid-week and demoted to the bench today. Got that one right, I was thinking. Oh, yes? As panic further obliterated what traces of shape we still possessed, we surrendered another corner. It was high and to beyond the back stick. That didn't prevent last week's stalwart Ray Newland wandering off in half-hearted pursuit of it. His hands got nowhere near it. Nor did the heads of our two flat-footed centre backs. Jamie's did. His accurate nod back across gave Lee Howarth the easiest of headers into the open net and Jamie a very loud last laugh. End of our increasingly token defending. Completion of home team wilt.

Afterwards in the changing room Hodgie took our second-half performance apart even more devastatingly than Barnet. As he finished his impassioned, justified tirade he looked up to see one of his team smirking.

What do you do? You shower. You get dressed. You go home. Sod 'em.

Sunday 13 April

'It's not over yet.' The same thought that obsessed me last night, hounds me today. We're not yet sunk into that nightmarish grey area where we have to rely on the results of other games to rescue us. Our fate is still in the hands of our own feet. But mathematically, should we fail to pick up anything in our last three games, and others do, we can go. Down. Out. A long weary week lies ahead.

Somebody else who should sleep badly tonight is David Elleray. His failure to see that Chesterfield had scored a '66 World Cup goal (ball down from underside of bar to cross line) is quite pardonable. In real time (as opposed to the endless multi-angled slow motion television replays) it was lightning fast. If in doubt he had to err in favour of the negative decision.

His ignoring the linesman who had signalled a goal, however, is not to be condoned. And the Harrovian casuistry with which he afterwards attempted to justify this omission – earlier offence? What? Whose? The recording shows none committed – is precisely the sort of equivocating that brings the game and public schools into disrepute. 3–3 then, and not victory to the side already boldly going further than any other lower divisioned side.

Tuesday 15 April

We trained hard yesterday. If we'd won at the weekend it would have been a day of rest. Hodgie and I would have been considering which of those youngsters we'd give first-team experience to – a forward-looking policy that ideally we'd have liked to have put in gentle motion five weeks or so ago. Forward-looking in a larger sense is what we've got to force ourselves to be. The only way to proceed is to assume – to *believe* – that we'll be part of the Nationwide next season. Such power of positive thinking implies two immediate things for me. One: I've got to think in terms of playing next Saturday. Two: however far back in the transfer market queue we may be, I've got to resume scrutiny for that hidden gem. Putting these together sees me come evening being chauffeured by a fan el-cheapo style towards Wycombe Wanderers' enviably state of the middle-class art ground. As a passenger I can keep my right leg in the recommended straightened position: as a spectator I can clock Burnley's second choice keeper, Wayne Russell.

Is it to laugh or cry, I'm soon asking myself. In the first half the focus of my attention has retrieved the ball from his net four times. And I'm still scarcely the wiser. Twice a storming Wycombe have been awarded very questionable penalties: umpteen times the slowest, limpest back three I've seen in any game this season have left the relative novice behind them totally exposed. His body language is jittery in the extreme. But it's got every right to be.

Wednesday 16 April

More of the same. Charlton Reserves v Millwall Reserves. A couple of the Millwall lads catch my eye. New Den, new economic policies will probably see them listed any day now. In Torquay terms, though, their price tags are likely to be the sort you look at and then let go of at once.

In the evening Brentford v Woking. Another stiffs fixture. Joe Omigie, focus of my rapidly diminishing interest, turned in a definitively poor performance. He wasn't the only one. The game was awful. Sole consolation was the West London proximity of Griffin Park to the M4. The half-time boardroom cuppa didn't long delay my opting for the fast lane home.

Thursday 17 April

A day of rearranging the deckchairs as we bear down on the next iceberg. Against Hereford Danny Hinshelwood steps down to the subs' bench to make room for Paul Mitchell back from Lilleshall with a clean bill of health on his hamstring. A test today will establish whether I play. I train cautiously, gradually demanding more of my knee. Sufficient unto the day is the pain thereof but it's bearable. The knee will do a job and I presume to think, come Saturday, I will too.

Friday 18 April

With thoughts of Saturday coming, Friday is normally a light training day. Punches are pulled. There's no sense in risking a strain or a knock at this late stage. Today, though, is an exception. The first-team squad go into a North v South eight-a-side game and in no time the tackles are flying in and the running is flat out. I take a calculated risk and let things continue as they are. Over-aggressive it may be but it's a good sign. It's what we want tomorrow. Let's gamble no-one's injured. No-one is. More of the same tomorrow, lads.

Later in the day comes an off the wall instance of cause and effect – indeed, of another gamble. I'm back home writing out the headline instructions that tomorrow I'll fly-post in the changing room. At my elbow is the local paper. In it is a critical letter from a Torquay supporter. He's bemoaning our recent form and style. We're all kick and rush, he says, no longer playing it through, and to feet; our corners go for nothing; etc, etc. The letter's critical but not hostile. It isn't a loudmouth's rant but the comment of a concerned fan trying to help. He doesn't appreciate we haven't got the inner, let alone technical resources, at present to play prettily but in an ideal world he's more right than wrong. Because of this I don't dismiss the letter entirely out of hand. Certainly we've converted no more than a couple of corners ...

There's actually a speedily reached limit on what you can do with a corner. Near post, far post; in-swinger, out-swinger; play it short and vary the angle. We've worked variations on all these. The only thing we haven't done ...

On impulse, I decide to switch the personnel around. Instead of being on the near post for the flick on, Andy McFarlane can go deeper to attack the ball. Alex Watson will now move forward to do Andy's job ... I almost improvise a new line-up. Its key aim is to get Stevie Winter and Charlie Oatway in at the heart of the action. Not tall men, granted, but neither are the least backward in coming forward if there's a chance of getting on the end of something.

Besides, going over this tomorrow will be useful diversion therapy. It will help take everyone's mind off the awesomeness of the six pointer.

Saturday 19 April

No joy for Friday night's newspaper correspondent when the game got under way at Edgar Street. The pitch – surely not by intent! – was bobbly to a fault. Even the grass was uneven tuft to tuft. Not an unknown hazard to visitors trained up on Torquay recs but a killer to any residual thoughts of playing to feet.

Yes, score one for Centrax. We found our feet right away and, bar a couple of reasonably routine scares, grafted out a good, gritty first half performance – in which regard the crowd's chanting 'Cambridge 1, Brighton 0' was pretty even-handed encouragement to both sides.

The one downer to the half was that after just six minutes Paul Mitchell had to go off with another pull. It wasn't the end of our day. Jamie Howell came on and proceeded to play intelligently well for the long rest of the game.

In the 45th minute we won a corner. Up stepped the new Torquay formation dancing team. Over it came. Attacking the ball well Dean Chandler jumped high and crashed into a no less determined defender. Down they both went. More often than not this provokes a free kick (never a penalty) but no whistle sounded now. The ball's trajectory, unaffected by the collision, missiled into the head of unmarked Stevie Winter. Now the whistle blew. For a goal! Score another one for the improvising player-coach – and half-a-dozen for the local letter writer.

1–0 at half-time. Barnet all over again. We force-fed the same diet of changing room instructions to the team – 'Nearly there! Don't relax! Defend from the front!' – as last week. The last words of wisdom as we got to our feet again were: 'They'll have had a right rollocking in there and be really up for it. You be ready for it!' As we ran back out I had the strongest feeling of foreboding: we've been exactly here before and I'm not going to like what happens next.

One consolation of falling behind on the strike of half-time is that you can regroup in comparative calm. Graham Turner sent Hereford out for the second half in a 3–4–3 'go for it' formation. Stevie Winter and I consequently tucked in more to give us virtually a five at the back. It wasn't entirely for the best. Our midfield three tended to find themselves playing in the spaces between their midfield four. Hereford began to dominate. In came another 'hit and hope' ball high into our box. We failed to clear it decisively. A second attempt smashed into a Hereford face and as bodies fell, obstructions abounded and confusion reigned, Hereford scored. 1–1. Barnet again with a vengeance.

I looked around. Glazed eyes betrayed confidence draining and nerves and knees alike distraughtly dissolving. 'Here we go again' was etched on every drawn face. A look to Hodgie. 'Right. Stevie to go to right-side midfield. We're switching to 4–4–2.'

With me as an out and out left back that's how we fought it out. It was always tense, never at all comfortable, but this time we did defend well. It wasn't the story as before. The referee played hours of injury time – something of which, having done no stamina training for a good fortnight, I was highly conscious of myself. When the whistle at last went my arms were up with everyone else's pumping the air. I rushed to embrace, in twos, threes, fours my huddling, cuddling team-mates. Another precious, golden point. Hereford kept at bay. It should be enough to see us safe if ... as my tired mind tried to remember the numbers, do the arithmetic, the tannoy cut in on my struggle 'Cambridge United 1, Brighton 1' Yes! We had to be safe now. I punched the air again and counter-applauded as the travelling Torquay faithful broke into choruses of 'Staying up ... ' The Hereford players were quicker leaving the field and as they disappeared from view their shoulders were drooping. The changing room was all whooping and hollering and back-slapping and rebel yells. No villains now, all heroes. A team. Edgar Street still has a communal bath and our sense of solidarity was warmly enhanced by the 'all in this together' feeling. Relaxed at last, the apprehension of weeks past siphoned away, I let my mind float free. Then in my mind's eye I saw those drooped shoulders again. I all but shuddered. Looming ahead potentially for Hereford is arguably the most nerve-racking, sudden death shoot-out of a single game in the Football League's history. Unusually, this year there's no chopping block side a dozen points adrift making Division Three safe for all others. A fortnight hence Hereford are home to Brighton, last club at the moment but only three points behind and with comfortably more goals scored. Both sides will run out looking down the barrel of the Conference shotgun. For the winners, survival: for the losers, oblivion. I'm *really* glad I don't have to foot and mind slog through those two forthcoming weeks. I'm *really* glad I won't be sitting in either of those nerves-strung-up-to-piano-wire-tenseness changing rooms at 2.55 pm on Saturday 3 May.

On the returning coach Hodgie foamed open the Champagne with which we could celebrate our safe, however belated arrival, in the comfort zone. But by now the mood had changed. A beady-eyed awareness of reality had come seeping back in to dissolve away our euphoria. When our eyes met now it wasn't to signal triumph but guilt. We all knew that, a millimetre below the surface, this was a phoney, 'me-too' celebration. We were just playing at imitating the teams with something genuinely worthwhile to get excited about.

What had our achievement been? To get to the first base of survival. To avoid the ignominy, the economic disaster of being the last of the last and relegated. True, through freakish reasons that is where we had set out from but our avoidance of humiliation could all be traced to our bright start over the season's first three months. Thenceforward we had been, in statistical truth, the division's saddest squad – an undeniable fact born stark testimony to by our immediate 'previous' of one win from 16 starts. This was no champagne moment. No heroes us, but merely survivors. We were drinking now not to celebrate but out of sheer bloody relief. All the same, we now drew a formal line under survival with a season's first. We told our players their peerless services wouldn't be required until Thursday next. Peace for the wicked at last.

A relaxing, fear-banished day. Until bedtime. As I stretched out my mind went into warp speed – that overtired, racing-round, milling about sort of white mode when thoughts pile in to your awareness uninvited but with exaggerated clarity. So many things to sort! The lack of training facilities. New players to acquire. Youngsters – better late than never – to blood. Contracts to renew. Him. Him. Lads we have to let go. Probably as much for their own long-term good as the club's ... Him. Him. Fuelling this utterly unwanted burst of mental energy was, I knew, one fundamental realisation. Unless very significant team changes were made to the Torquay United way of doing things, Messrs Hodges and Nelson had done no more than postpone the inevitable. Next season, once again down among the nearly dead men, we'd have it all, yes, to do again ...

DREAM ON

Monday 21 April

In early but not as early as Hodgie. His smiling, relief-showing look of Saturday had already been replaced with a crestfallen look of doom. The reason was soon clear. He'd just come from an informally formal meeting with the chairman. In a nutshell Mike Bateson had declared that, in his book, the 1996/97 season had been a financial disaster and he wasn't prepared for the moment to divulge what monies, if any, might be made available for new players bringing in for the use of: no doubt about it, the club and coaches would have to err on the side of caution at the beginning of the new campaign ... The inevitable, then, I thought at once, wasn't likely to be postponed for long.

We agreed, Kevin and I, to tackle the chairman on this more formally next week.

Meanwhile hope for the best, work as if it's going to happen. All right, in concentrating on survival we've sacrificed valuable scouting-recruiting time. But all is not lost – not if we set up a trial game for

Wednesday week and issue a speedy crop of invitations. And not if – pull over, Villeneuve, we're coming through – we take in Villa's stiffs against the Owls this extended Monday night.

Wednesday 23 April

The scoutathon continues unforgivingly. Last night Middlesbrough were (semi)finally able to make their money talk against splendidly game Chesterfield, but my spectating treat was to watch Watford's stiffs take on QPR's. Today more of the same: Millwall Reserves versus Luton's. My eye was on Lions' midfielder Stephen Roche. My ear was being steadily bent by erstwhile team-mate Alan McCleary using his insider knowledge to mark my card as to who was likely to be culled from the new Den when the keepers next took stock.

Onward, then, and downwards to the south coast to watch Southampton's Paul Tisdale, already under our microscope before, already a trialist with Burnley and Bristol City, playing for the latter against Portsmouth. Of no less interest was my former Brighton team-mate Paul Wood. Injury has sidelined Paul for virtually the entire season and Pompey are releasing him. Tonight, though, confirmed he is back to match fitness and access to his multi-positional versatility would be a huge plus for Torquay. All this painstaking attention to detail on St George's Day.

But not, as my VCR was ultimately to update me, St Alex's. There were insufficient Englishmen in United's side this evening to slay the Borussia Dortmund dragon. Giving away the softest of goals early on at Old Trafford, Man U found themselves needing to score three to reach the European Cup final. They carved out opening after opening against opponents now backpeddling far too readily but – Cantona and Giggs the worst culprits – their finishing was as woefully inept as their form last Saturday. 0–2 on aggregate, then, and fantasies of world domination destroyed, the United faithful were left with nothing to do but eat, drink and sleep Jurgen Kohler.

Thursday 24 April

The reconvening of the Torquay troops. The essential trick was not to undo the goodwill generated by the unique first half of the week break by coming on too heavy-handed. The solution we served up was a fairly strenuous warm-up followed by a fun five-a-side. The session marked the end of involvement in our season of loan-signing Danny Hinshelwood.

By *News at Ten* time an end to English hopes in Europe. On aggregate, Paris St Germain 3, Liverpool 2. Take the pick from the combined Anfield and Old Trafford squads and you might produce a side capable of taking on the best in Europe. Winning 2–0 at home tonight, Liverpool at least had some shooting boots on. But their ability to hit a telling pass or cross in the last third of the field was no better than Torquay's on an average day. English football has to stop trying harder and start being cleverer.

Saturday 26 April

A day of displacement everywhere you looked. To begin with the time of today's home kick-off against Wigan. 12.15, would you believe? And whose stupid idea? The Devon and Cornwall Constabulary's, that's whose.

Blessed with the intelligence – I use the word in its cloak and dagger sense – that around 1,000 dirty Northern bastard fans of table-topping Wigan would be descending on the Torbay fold like Assyrian wolves, our brave guardians of the Wessex peace opted to generate an aura of tension where none would otherwise have existed. What else is flooding the Plainmoor precincts with a plodding army in blue likely to achieve? It seems not to have crossed their jobsworthy minds that the Wigan horde might consist of typically decent footballing fans asking for no more than a modicum of respect and good humour – qualities best reflected in a low profile routine police presence rather than shriekingly intimidating overkill. Nor does any decision-maker seemed to have registered that with nothing much on the result (Wigan already up, Torquay safe) the inherent potential for violence was minimal. No doubt they *did* clock that it would be cash-strapped Torquay and not their own copper coffers that would be stuck with the overtime bill for their gross over-reaction.

This last economic factor was GBH added to gate-receipt injury. Tasked with an extra ticket-buying trudge to the ground at the end of, face it, another 'nothing' season, a high proportion of our fans, loyal to a mediocre fault though they might generally be, opted to vote with their bums on couches. I came into the ground forewarned they were staying away in droves and that the Wigan fans would probably outnumber ours.

Then I encountered a further warp in the normal scheme of things. The chairman's latest programme notes made it abundantly clear that, for him, with or without a police presence, the game couldn't be over too soon. This time the words from our sponsor read:

'It is fairly common knowledge that I am seeking a buyer for my majority shareholding in Torquay United. After the trials and tribulations of the past few years it is becoming increasingly difficult for me to conjure up the enthusiasm and optimism which is a prerequisite of running a football club.'

Not to mention resilience! Not yet midday and my hold on reality was already on the receiving end of a left to the jaw and a right to the solar plexus. That, at any rate, is my after-the-event excuse for what was soon to happen.

Thinking that in the interests of complete autonomy the Devon and Cornwall Constabulary might like to buy out the chairman, I made my way to the relative tranquillity of the treatment room, there to complete my pre-match briefing notes ... *This is what you do here* and all that. A footfall made me look up in mid-scrawl. Charlie Oatway, the star performer of yesterday's finishing session, had just entered. Instinctively I sensed that Charlie was probably the nearest thing we'd have to an edge today. I seized on the moment to restore my pancake-flat morale by boosting his.

'Chas,' I said in my fluentest football speak, 'I want you getting into the box as often as possible. It's got to be your top priority. Leave your runs to late and your heading ability can do it for us. When we get a set-piece I want you really attacking the ball. Last week it was Stevie Winter from a corner. No reason why today it shouldn't be you.'

Charlie had been taking in my every word with a thoughtful, dead-pan expression. Now, though, he was less than straight-faced. His broad grin was bordering on the impertinent.

'There's a very good reason why it won't be me, Nelse,' he presumed to say.

'Oh? And just what might that be?'

'Just that I'm suspended. Good enough?'

Of course! Gulp! I stood there like a wrong-footed Captain Mannering ('Well done, Oatway. Just seeing if you'd remembered!') Like myself Charlie was another displaced element in the normal Saturday scheme of things. I'd known that ... just as I now knew with unmistakable clarity who would be the wearer of this week's yellow jersey. Of course, it had passed just between the two of us ... No. Dream on. I could hear him now.

'Oi, lads, guess what –'

There were no fires on the terraces, no riots, when Player of the Year Alex Watson led his team out in front of a pitiably small crowd and needlessly large police contingent. In mid-October, we had taken Wigan, already a Division Three front runner, all the way to the last minute at Springfield Park. Now we picked up where we'd left off. My pre-match notes must have counted for something. For the first 25 minutes the sparse crowd were treated to two teams both excellently on song.

Gradually, thenceforward, Wigan began to pull away. From the whistle we'd been at full stretch. They, though, still had another gear. The unremitting strain of trying to harness 100 per cent intelligence to 100 per cent physical effort had taken its toll on us. Gaps appeared between our intention and execution while Wigan continued to operate on the smoothest of automatic pilots. Inexorably they proceeded to quantify this superiority with three goals. Twice they scored when our Player of the Year celebrated his (thoroughly deserved) award by granting his man the freedom of Plainmoor's six yard box. Graeme Jones added goals four and five to his season's tally against us alone.

That completed the day's full house in displacement tendencies. Close to the outset of this season Wigan paid Doncaster a reported £150,000 for this particular Jones boy. For us, scrabbling around at the bargain basement bottom of the barrel, five acquisitions would probably be needed to justify such expenditure. Backed by David Whelan's millions, however, Wigan could afford the luxury of speculating to accumulate with a focused single-hit purchase. Not that single hit is the right expression. Wigan's promotion has been won very considerably courtesy of a Graeme Jones' scoring rate that will see him with nearer to 40 than 30 goals to his credit in a week's time.

Sunday 27 April

A quiet day at home gives me a chance to mill over Mike Bateson's going public yesterday on the decision he flagged up to board and management last November – his intention to step down as chairman. The short- to medium-term implication of this, today's calm perspective tells me, is that nothing will change. Like it or lump it, Mike is saddled with the club.

There are, as it happens, some nine other directors on the board. But compared with Mike's investment in TUFC, their shareholdings are minuscule. He is the one taking the loss week after week as he subs the club out his own pocket.

'We've got to change things,' another director might hypothetically say at a board meeting. 'We've got to bring in some new players.'

'OK,' Mike Bateson might reply, 'how much are you all willing to put into the pot? Shall we say £10,000 a head?'

Such an equally hypothetical (but totally justifiable) question would be met by silence and glances kept bashfully down on the boardroom table. No other director is in Mike's financial league. He needs to find a Sam Hammam.

I can very much sympathize with his present attitude. Mike is a self-made millionaire accustomed to success and managing that success. Other than the false dawn of his first season at Plainmoor, he has found success in the soccer world not so much elusive as a mirage. It's not happened for him after seven years in the chair and he's not the type – why should he be? – to remain content with a football club simply for its own sake. Like most of us he'd welcome a 'result'.

In fiscal fact – set aside the new running financial sore of Jon Gittens' salary – TUFC are not in that parlous a state. A canny transfer deal – bye, bye Rodney – would put the club as near as damn it in the black. If Mike is prepared to take a loss on his holding, somebody might be picking up a bargain.

Meanwhile, like all the rest of us, he has little option other than to keep on keeping on.

Tuesday 29 April

The start of something big and, as it is unavoidably going to prove, considerably unpleasant. Lists in our hands of the players we want to retain for next season and to let go, Kevin and I closet ourselves with the chairman. Initially there are four to whom we definitely won't be offering new terms and three with heavy duty question marks against their names. Whether any of this second group eventually stay very much depends on what at the moment is a grey area verging on a total unknown – the amount of funds the Torquay board will make available for new players.

Unfortunately the day was characterized by a parallel agenda – Mike Bateson had chosen today to follow up his programme announcement that he is (ideally!) resigning his chairmanship and will not be at the Torquay helm next season. Homing in on this 'the world is holding its breath' news item, covens of television crews drawn from the four corners of stringer land – 'Mike, if you could just angle your chair towards this light' – interrupted the meeting with the frequency of Nick Hancock's auto-cued ad-libs. Serious privacy, sustained dialogue, became impossible. The war chest allocation remained a mystery and the start had proved to be a false one.

The one positive – as far as it went – element we came away with was Mike's consoling pledge that faced with the complete absence of any interest in his Torquay shares, he would not cavalierly pull his finger from the fiscal dyke. Given no take-over from outside he would promote a successor from among the current board. The new chairman would deal with day-to-day administration while he himself continued cats-cradling the purse-strings. *Plus ça changera*, as we say in Chudleigh.

Wednesday 30 April

England 2, Georgia 0. The team with greater self belief beat the 11 with better skill while, in front of their monitors, the Italians grinned from ear to ear.

In the Plainmoor book, though, this was all after the Lord Mayor's Show. That afternoon we had repeated our experiment of inviting 18 or so trialists from all over the country – Carlisle, Bolton, Derby, Liverpool, London, Swindon; all either released YTS lads or senior squad players recently notified they were not being retained – to take part in a trial match. The key stipulation, understood by all, was that they would be participating entirely at their own expense. The best we could offer them would be a warm welcome and a cup of tea.

Two sides (one including our still aspiring to trade places physio Damien Davey) were selected and a full by-the-book 90-minute match was meticulously scrutinised by the three Torquay coaches from various vantage points. From our point of view, whatever measure of blind faith went into its cobbling together, the exercise more than justified itself. Inevitably the majority of the participants had to wearily wind their way homewards with, if not a flea in their ear, another bruise in their hearts. But one, Jamie Robinson of Carlisle, was asked to stay on for a few further days' training and another three will be asked to join us for the pre-season shape-up come July.

Thursday 1 May

May Day indeed! One way or another Ferguson will be going back to Europe over the next few months but Major won't. Today the Conservatives reaped the whirlwind that Margaret Thatcher's Victorian opportunism ('My country right or wrong. My husband drunk or sober') sowed and the nation gave a free to snouts in the trough culture. 'Bye, bye, David Mellor. Hello, Tony Banks.' Let's hope the BSkyB and Premiership boys get the message. Let's hope the prices at the Bridge come down.

A candidate wondering about his Plainmoor chances of being re-elected was Ray Newland. He came into the office today seeking to establish where he stood regarding new terms. The truth is that Hodgie and I have a pretty definitive knowledge of what his prospects are. But not only was Ray jumping the official gun – clubs aren't obliged to declare their intentions about retaining or releasing players until the third Saturday in May – we were concerned not to set a precedent. Particularly with one game still to go we did not want to trigger a stream of players banging on our door to ask if their Torquay licence was being renewed. Not altogether disingenuously we told Ray that, thanks to the interruptions of the TV crews to our budget discussions we didn't yet know what we'd got to play with either money-wise or squad-wise.

Friday 2 May

A couple of (temporarily broken) straws in the wind. Conspicuously to hand today were Rhys Wilmot and assistant physio Paul Maxwell who following recent operations have latterly tended to absent themselves from Plainmoor proceedings. They were respectively hinting at and requesting their inclusion on the team bus's final trip of the season tomorrow. I find this disturbingly symptomatic. I don't think either are straining at the leash to see a potential epic. I suspect that, like the selected team itself, their minds are less on Doncaster Rovers than the prospect of a school-is-out piss-up on said bus's run back south. We'll have to see about that. The return trip might be just the occasion for bringing us home not only the squad but the truth that, despite the attitude of some of its members since our achieving safety, Torquay United FC is not a social club.

A straw in the goalmouth wind tomorrow will be Matthew Gregg making his seasonal league debut. Belatedly, three other YTS lads will be on the bench and very likely to get a run.

Saturday 3 May

If not in hope we travelled north in relaxed, up-beat mood. By 3.12 today nothing of that remained. Scarcely able to believe their luck, I'm sure, the roving Doncaster forwards had pulled our back three every which way to collect two gift-wrapped goals and net a disallowed third. Reshuffles don't come any quicker. We went to a more orthodox, increasingly less fashionable, 4–4–2 and managed some sort of adequacy up to the half-time whistle. But I remained deeply unhappy.

In the changing room I didn't pull any end of term punches as I tried to brace and motivate the delinquents for their last labour-intensive 45 minutes of the season. They were playing, I pointed out, like de-mob happy drop-outs. Their minds were clearly on things other than the match and its demands. Specifically, they seemed already to be on the mobile bar they saw themselves soon departing in. Well, they should take thought for the morrow, I said, opening the door part way on chill reality. In four days' time each member of the Torquay squad would be up for his individual appraisal. On next week's sheep from goat separating assessments would depend continuing employment, perhaps, even, livelihood. Called to account, asked to comment on the almost countless (but clocked!) cock-ups, the many disappointments all of them, I was confident, would say 'Not down to me guv. I always gave it my best. It was all them other fellas.' Well, I continued, next Wednesday for some, for many even, would demonstrate there was no safety in numbers. There was something else to think about over their next 45 minutes in a Torquay shirt.

To a small degree my assault worked. Gaining just reward for his own fully committed performance, YTS forward Tony Bedeau scored his first ever Nationwide League goal. But this was the only particle of nourishment to be picked from the bones of another dispiriting defeat. After the end of game detour to pay final, supremely deserved tribute to our loyal handful of travelling fans, the team returned to the changing room to be confronted with some more facts-of-life home truths.

A season's record of played 46, lost 22 had secured us 21st place in the division. Out of 24. A few of those fans outside might just be inclined to celebrate this improvement on the previous year's rock-bottom performance, but the Torquay management would see no cause for comfort in the final league standings. The league tables don't lie. In the autumn we'd been fifth in the table. From 28 games we'd collected 40 points. We'd finished on 50. I left it to them to do the arithmetic that told the story of how in three months of self-inflicted wounds we'd converted ourselves from born-again believers to lost-soul losers. We'd replaced misty visions of a play-off Wembley for – over too long a period of agonising uncertainty – the sharpest of images of the door to the Conference standing wide open and waiting.

I had some more facts to conclude with. On the way home tonight there would be no stop at a road-side pub. Alcohol quota for the journey would be one crate of beer. Next season this would be standard operational procedure after all away games lost. Meanwhile we still had a game to prepare for – the Devon Bowl final against Exeter on Tuesday.

On the homeward journey the benefit of access to a double-decker coach became sharply apparent. Intentionally – even with malice aforethought – Hodgie and I opted to travel downstairs leaving the disgruntled team to stew in their own sullen juice as they eked out the crate of beer on the upper deck. Left on their own to gripe away in this position of temporary eminence they would be paradoxically better able, we well knew, to drag our names through the mud.

Always emotionally inclined to be one of the lads rather than the management, Damien joined us below. He wanted to register his disapproval of our exercise of schoolmasterly discipline which he considered petulant and counter-productive for team spirit. Fair dues to his standing up (well, sitting down, actually) to be counted but we continued to disagree. By degrees the conversation broadened to a wider, deeper analysis of where Torquay United might be getting it wrong off the field. Abruptly, the end of term mood loosening his tongue, Damien passed on an observation that sent waves of protest shooting through me. The lads, he courageously let hang out, resented that Steve McCall and I were automatic selections every Saturday despite not participating in every training session.

A welter of overlapping but all indignant reactions came close to leaving me speechless and, in fact, I didn't make a meal of leaping to my own defence. Had I done so, though, I'd have been hard put to know where to begin. I hadn't, after all, started the season as an 'automatic' selection. Early on I'd several times been on the bench. I'd become automatic on merit and the rest of the squad might like to reflect on whether they'd have enjoyed going through the season without me. All of that went for Steve. Part of our post-Christmas slump was attributable to his prolonged absence (or only half-fit presence) through serious injury.

The heady days of our good start had been sustained by Messrs Baker, McCall and Nelson providing an armature offering stability to the rest of the side.

Did they think we didn't *want* to train? If so, they were welcome to swap their own leisure activities – clubbing, golf, quality time with their families – for our reams of paperwork, endless miles and hours of scouting, emotionally wearing and tearing decision-making. Not only carrying a knock but less fit overall than I liked to be, I'd gone out for the last dozen games of the season knowing I would be playing in pain and having to count on adrenalin and will-power to get me through the last 15 minutes. Was that my *choice*? Jesus, filling in as a debutant wing-back because economics had stripped our left side bare, I'd come up with the performance of which, out of all my appearances this season, I'm most proud of. And that with – as Damien of all people had to know – my right knee giving me start to finish grief. In that last memory, as the coach lumbered on, was some food for thought that I might find very difficult to digest. Overall in the course of my career, I'd been amazingly lucky, all things considered, when it came to heavy-duty injuries. Now … well, the law of averages was finally evening the score. Prolonged rest, the consultant had stated, was the only 'cure' for my slack, permanently split tendon. But, being realistic, what sort of 'rest' could I expect to sink back into without prejudicing my overall fitness? Pre-season would be on us all again in eight weeks. Which was to say tomorrow … I felt cold blood crowding my heart. This could be it, after all – the career-ending, terminal injury. As early as next July, my player's boots hung up, I might be wearing only one hat. Next season I might be a lumbering coach myself. Well, for the sake of those who considered that Steve and I had pulled rank to get on the team sheet – the idea! – it was very much to be hoped my sour mood evaporated before then.

What really got under my skin, though, was turning the allegation on its head. Had a fit Steve and I withdrawn our Saturday service towards the end of the season when things were getting desperate, the message would have come through loud and clear (and in no time at all) that we didn't fancy it. *We'd bottled out* … My sad conclusion has to be that when it comes to the job of player-coach, this is a situation from which, if your name isn't Gordon Strachan, you just can't emerge as a winner.

It's another aspect of the job and the season that has made me a sadder, not much wiser, man. I did have one specific point to put to Damien. It happened that there were five YTS lads on the upstairs level and on the threshold of their careers. It didn't seem appropriate to me that after a year in which we had achieved bugger-all, they should be given the signal that the season's end was, of itself, licence for an all-systems-go piss-up.

Sunday 4 May

A chance after all the blood, sweat and tears of the season to contemplate the final Nationwide League tables in – 'Chris! Carly! Will you for Pete's sake stop that racket!' – tranquillity.

Like most pros, I'm certain, I shed a little mental blood in sympathy with relegated Hereford but this fellow-feeling was far outweighed by my unstinting admiration for Steve Gritt's organising and nurturing of Brighton's great escape. Inheriting a 12-point deficit he timed his run to the finishing post as well as any Piggott. No doubt when the Manager of the Year award is announced it will go to one of the cheque-writing Premiership endorsers of their club's scouting systems. But for me this year it's a three-horse race: Gritty, David Jones, mastermind behind a Stockport that ate up promotion and nearly got to keep their Cup cake too, or John Duncan whose taking Chesterfield as unprecedentedly far (for a Division Two or Three side) as an FA Cup semi-final replay is said to have put a new twist in the old town spire. God, we're told, is on the side of the big battalions. I suppose that's why I'm on the side of the small.

Monday 5 May

Sprung already fully formed from their forehead, it seems, Deloitte and Touche have produced a Football League-commissioned report advocating that 14–16 Conference sides be co-opted into the Third Division and that, the clock being put back the length of my lifetime, it be split into north and south sections. Given their usual dearth of Monday morning sports copy, some papers have written this proposal up as if it were already a law set in concrete rather than a white paper. They may well thus have given poor Hereford false hopes of an instant reprieve. The Football League has made it clear that, if at all, the suggested restructuring will not be put in train until the season after next. The key pro arguments are that 'overnights' will cease to be a ball-breaking expense to cash-strapped minnows and that there will be a higher density of local derbies. Immediately against that has to be weighed the loss to every club of six home games and the actuarial certainty of drawing crowds down by at least 500 on current gates. There's a deal of knee-jerking reaction going on all over the shop as I write, but two somewhat long-range thoughts most occupy me. A cynic might suppose that in broad terms this is another attempt by the bigger clubs to marginalise the small. In quality terms it certainly strikes me that given the anatomy of football in Britain at the moment, this has to be seen as the Third Division potentially dropping down to meet the standards of the Conference rather than the Conference stepping up. Deloitte and Touche, mind you, earn their corn by being where the money is. I don't suppose we've heard the last of this one.

Tuesday 6 May

More than a little aghast the squad was called in today for training. The chance to win some highly prestigious silverware still beckons – from Chudleigh to Bideford, nothing rates higher than the Devon Bowl. Not, though, it transpired to all our squad. Reactions to last Saturday's fit of managerial Puritanism may be lingering longer. Several of the virtually ever-present stalwarts from our league campaign reported that injuries – to body? to psyche? – ruled them out for tonight's game with Exeter.

They were close to doing us a favour. While we had no choice other than to field virtually a YTS side, it was something that in terms of feeding youngsters through, Hodgie and I were already half inclined to do. We had the opportunity also of including two guests. Jamie Robinson came all the way back down from Carlisle to parade his skills again (no small commitment this) while from Colchester we obtained temporary use of Paul Gibbs. A left wing-back, Paul was the lad obliged to make way for one Scott Stamps. My instinct is that, more aware of what's going on around him, he's the better long-term prospect.

The game was something of a triumph. We lost 1–2 but it was against a full bore Exeter side who only notched their winner in extra time (the 111th minute). Not only did the two newcomers fully justify their journeys but also our own lads – especially full-time pros to be Tony Bedeau and Wayne Thomas – delivered a positive performance.

Meanwhile the Premiership season was ending not with a bang but a whimper. Also tonight when only wins would help keep their title ambitions alive, an incredibly limp-wristed Liverpool and a notably flair-lacking Newcastle contrived to lose and draw respectively. The currently stuttering Manchester United are champions by default. In English terms they have to be described as worthy winners – just. Whenever this season, home or abroad, they faltered, they revealed sufficient strength in depth, sufficient character to return to winning ways in fairly short order. But judged by international standards that only makes them the best of an indifferent bunch. They're a young side. They have the potential to mature. As they turn immediately again to Europe they should be issuing themselves the same interim report as all the rest of us: must do better next time.

Wednesday 7 May

Judgement Day. Hatchet wielding day. The day when in the interests of quality control the squad must be culled and the Retained/Released verdicts handed down from the managerial bench. No yellow jersey fooling around now. This is all about men's livelihoods – and their hopes and dreams as well.

It had come late in my career. Seventeen years late. That didn't stop it still hitting me with all the force of a Stuart Pearce tackle. That early morning rendezvous, Alan Curbishley a little uncomfortably formal behind his desk and me on its other side; the downer of going out of the play-offs the night before still heavy in the forefront of both our minds. Then, speedily, Curbs' version of the words every professional footballer hopes never to hear.

'*Sorry, there's not going to be a contract for you next season.*'

There I had it. No Wembley. No work. All well within 24 hours.

And now, scarcely any time longer – a year is a short time in football, Brian – the Predator was on the other foot. I was about to experience my first D for Decision Day session from the bosses' side of the fence. It promised to be not in the slightest bit more enjoyable.

The occasion found me behind my own desk earlier than on any other 'admin' day since I'd arrived. Trying to be as civilised as possible (the prospect of the players arriving altogether and milling around in an uptight, speculating bunch was insupportable) we had given all of the pros appointments staggered through the day in broadly alphabetical order. As I braced myself, however, before the first one at 8.30, I felt anything but civilised. Knowing that to be kind to Torquay United FC we were going to have to be bloody mindedly cruel to not a few individuals, I was already feeling a bit of a shit. I tried calming my nerves by glancing again at the list of players – McFarlane, Jack, Watson, the most prominent names – still in contract and thus not obliged to put their heads on the block this time around. It wasn't a long list, I was thinking, when there came the first knock knocking on what, given the prevailing Plainmoor circumstances, nobody would be inclined to regard as Heaven's door.

First up and enabling Hodgie, Steve and I to play ourselves in gently was Paul Gibbs. For once Fate had elected to make life easy for us. Paul has a girlfriend in the Wrens based at Plymouth. Coincidence and geography were thus on our side and the early indications are that he would be as happy to join us as we to sign him. Albeit what overall budget we have to play with remains an unknown quantity, the terms Paul is seeking should certainly not be beyond the Plainmoor pay-structure pale.

Paul departed to catch an early train and was succeeded by Lee Barrow to whom we were very happy to offer a new contract. The unknown factor here is simply whether, given the offer's modest scale and given his solid reputation, Lee might prefer to take freedom of contract and put up the 'Have Boots, Will Travel' sign. He'll let us know.

Next in line was Ian Hathaway, our first victim. Despite turning in an excellent end to his season Ian was released. So, too, was the man following him into the office and out of the club, Mark Hawthorne. The combined talents of the two in one would constitute an admirable midfielder. Into no-man's land now stepped Jamie Howell. In his loan period he had not done badly for us, yet to me – that classic expression once again – he doesn't promise to give us anything beyond what we've already got. Thus we did not feel able to offer him a contract. We did, though, leave the door fractionally ajar. We mooted the possibility that if he failed to find a berth elsewhere he could join us for pre-season training and trials on a similar non-contract basis.

Paul Mitchell presented us with one of our most difficult decisions. As person and player we distinctly like him. But allowing him to play in less than half our fixtures this year, his fitness has been consistently suspect. This past season he was one of our top-paid players but the relative sparseness of his appearances makes him a thorough-going luxury in such a small squad and for a club with our stretched-thin resources. Again we didn't slam the door right in his face. We don't dare offer him terms equalling those he's been on and he consequently automatically picks up a free transfer. If, though, he now fails to get the nod from another club – and I think that's a very open question – the situation could develop where a fully fit Paul is invited back to join us for pre-season and, that fitness maintained, get paid for playing football.

Ray Newland did now finally discover his fate. He too put in another goodish finish to the season (and my conscience tells me that perhaps we were late giving him a first-team run) but the verdict still had to be another thumbs down. There was both anger and apprehension in Ray's initial reaction. It's likely to be very tough for him out there and he knows it.

Charlie Oatway, like Lee Barrow, was offered a one-year contract at the same money. His response was commendably impersonal and hence disconcerting. He said that what was going on was purely a cost-cutting exercise; he had no confidence we'd be given money to get players in and we'd end up without a side worthy of the name. Where would that leave him? He'd be looking forward again, presumably, to another season of constant struggle. He'd let us know.

It's an ill wind. Sometimes. The next man limping to judgement was Michael Preston – he who in February sustained a career-threatening knee injury. Had he remained unscathed he would almost certainly have been given a free. That, though, would now be to cast out into the 'Released' pool a man with no prospect of being anywhere near fit until around the end of the year. *Noblesse oblige* time. We offered Michael a renewed and identical contract that, lasting a year, would give him a full, unpressured opportunity of coming all the way back. Taking the size of our squad and budget into consideration the decision has to be seen as magnanimous and doing credit to our disenchanted chairman.

Mutual admiration is the current mode we find ourselves in with the next man, Jamie Robinson. We certainly like him and, having delayed his epic trek back to the far north for a day, he was now telling us that he'd been impressed by the Plainmoor set-up, especially – no mean endorsement, this, from a former Liverpool lad – the coaching. He's definitely interested in joining us. But ... Our matching interest now received a severe kick in the teeth as Jamie outlined the terms he was looking for. On the Torquay scale they were on the far side of exorbitant. Our starting positions are poles part. To be continued.

None of the coaches was relishing the thought of our times three encounter with the last letter in the Torquay alphabet. First in was veteran keeper Rhys Wilmot who, had he been fully fit at the outset of the season, would undoubtedly have put pen to paper on a two-year deal. In fact he reported for the pre-season in pain and with the vertebrae-fixing operation he'd undergone leaving his mobility significantly restricted. In the circumstances the best we had dared offer him was a month to month contract which, as his back somewhat improved, escalated to one running up to now with the understanding that, should he do enough of a job, it would be extended for another year. In the event, though, we often found ourselves running out for a game with a below par goalkeeper and, as we now told Rhys, we couldn't feel that he'd ever shaken off his disability sufficiently to warrant that renewal. There was both ice and fire in the way he received the verdict. He and the three of us are all the same generation. Nevertheless his three contemporaries were rejecting him. The hostile silence hung heavy. Then he went quietly. Sooner or later, he knew, he had to.

Stevie Winter must have come through the door with reasonable expectations. Having never previously managed a league goal he finished this season our third highest scorer – after Rodney Jack and myself – on six. Two of these, though, were penalties and we felt that overall this past season – and not only on the field – he'd rather underachieved. The news he was being handed a free did not leave him leaving us best pleased.

Last was the most difficult – being the most borderline – decision of all. Last Christmas having just been told he was being awarded a contract, Matthew Wright had floated out of this same office on Cloud Nine. Now we had to tell him the contract wasn't going to be renewed. It was a particularly hard decision for Kevin and Steve who have worked long and hard with him and got results. He's done nothing wrong It's the recent emergence of Wayne Thomas that has seen him pipped at the post by a (finally subjective) eyelash. Many clubs would be happy to keep both on but in our case the likelihood of our soon having to cut our budget denies us the luxury of doubling up. It hit Matthew hard. Unable to come to terms with the turn-down he sat silent for a small eternity unable rather than unwilling to move from the seat. I don't think he took in our assurances that his talent and attitude positively guarantee him earning a living as a professional footballer. The decision to let Matthew go may well come back to haunt all three of us.

Knowing the frequently grim day would take its toll on us, the three coaches had allowed themselves a small treat to conclude on. Three now played three as we called in YTS lads Tony Bedeau, Wayne Thomas and Matthew Gregg together. Grins split their faces at the good news they would all be offered a year's contract, all on identical terms and footing. We made clear our opinion they were all more than capable of successfully featuring in our team next year.

The season's bottom line, then, for our first-team squad and for one or two, perhaps, the end of the line. The savage pruning leaves the club out on its own precarious limb too. Seven first-team players let go. The number remaining constitute a squad that could, in a moment of the wildest optimism, be described as threadbare. The nearest we have to the silver lining of any sort of plus side is that we are in negotiation with five or six lively, promising professionals who have expressed (varying levels of) interest in joining Torquay.

Charlie Oatway's concern that our wielding the knife was for the wrong, cost-cutting reason was repeated by other members of the squad. We were at pains explicitly to refute this charge. The wages bill does come into it, of course, but our action now is with a profounder end in mind. I have to hand an 'anorak's' book detailing all the results, statistics and final league positions achieved by TUFC in the course of its history. Essentially, if your eye isn't immediately drawn to us as the club propping up the League's lowest division, then, excluding only the most occasional positive blip, looking just a couple of places higher will find us. Year after year after year. This has got to stop. Tinkering with an inherited squad in mid-season run is never going to come close to being the answer. What we need to do, are setting out to do, is radically change the club's *culture*. We need to establish a core of players not mentally browbeaten into the mind-set of expecting to lose every time they run out and considering a draw a result. The need is for new faces who as part of their baggage will bring along an enthusiastic appetite for the game that will last well beyond the pre-season and September honeymoon period.

Thus our intention. Hence our lack of compassion towards many of the old faces – most of them on the shoulders of thoroughly good blokes.

Thursday 8 May

After yesterday's blood-letting a black, black day. The chairman (and ongoing purse-string holder, whatever) has indicated that there are minimal monies in the kitty for attracting new players and filling their weekly wage packets. The day after we have released seven players he has informed us that we must now go to market with the princely sum of £1,500-a-week's worth of wages to dangle under the noses of those we'd like to replace them with.

Fifteen hundred pounds a week! It might allow us – just – to run to four low profile 'frees'. The translation of that into reality is that we might find a couple of old lags, a couple of unknowns willing to put on a Torquay shirt every week in return for receiving the near derisory sum in their pay packet of £350 to £400. None of them will think that adds up to enough money – 'What! I'm supposed to run my heart out for this!' – and, since we can guarantee that the calibre of player such a wages allocation will attract will be no better than that of those we've let go, the overall numbers don't add up, either. As an absolute minimum we need to bring in six new men. The chairman has set a figure, in fact, based on faulty arithmetic.

In our meeting today he told us that his base for arriving at the grand and a half was the calculation that we already possessed a first-team squad of 13. The sight of my jaw hitting the deck must have told him at a glance that I considered this cobblers, but I was discretion itself in allowing him to explain himself.

'How do you arrive at that?' I restricted myself to saying

He spelled out where he was coming from and I was right. It *was* cobblers.

'Bateson's Thirteen' (unlucky for some) included to begin with Torquay's three coaches, Messrs Hodges, McCall and Nelson. Apart from the general truth that we are all so on in years you can fairly expect to find 'Wells Fargo' embossed on our butts, our individual playing potential for next season has to be weighed against these unquestionable facts.

Hodgie played 20 minutes this season as we killed a game off. He played all of one whole game the previous year. He'll be 37 next month.

Steve McCall's mind is as acute as ever but he's already had two major operations on his Achilles and it's unlikely ever to let him find space, hit those canny passes that have long been his trade-mark, in the way he was able in the heyday of his career. Next season could well see him permanently invalided out of the game.

Exactly the same could apply to me. The splitting apart tendons alongside my knee continue to give me low level but constant grief. Their condition has to be considered as permanent and, for as long as I'm playing week-in, week-out, inoperable. They've already inhibited my game these past two or three months and the cold-blooded assessment has to be that I'll do well to manage twenty or so games next season. When I do play it's not going to be up to the standard I've come to set myself – the standard, dammit, at which I enjoy being involved.

So much for the veteran 'backbone' of the team. Ten Bateson bankers to go.

Make that nine. Mike Preston won't be able to train with anything like seriousness until the New Year. If he gets back to where he was, he'll still be struggling to merit first-team consideration. This isn't true of the three lads newly promoted up from YTS status but, by definition, however keen, whatever their potential, they've all got a way to go yet on the learning curve. On the law of averages at least one might plateau out sooner rather than later. It could be the one goalkeeper we've currently got on our books.

Lee Barrow and Charlie Oatway, by contrast, have provenly reached a very satisfactory standard. Both in my book are more likely than not to turn their current contract offers down.

That leaves a sure-fire three currently legally obliged to run out for Torquay in three months time. Well, when I say 'sure-fire' ... Rodney Jack may well have to be sold on to up the petty cash flow. It's not inconceivable the same will prove true of Alex Watson. Andy McFarlane is more likely to stay. But, then again, our end of season word to the wise with Andy was very much along the lines of 'Must try harder... '

So. Depending quite where you draw the line, the reality as far as I'm concerned is that at the moment we're looking at a viable squad that adds up to just over half a first team. If that. Mind you, according to the chairman, we've got one other trump card to play. Executing a screeching U-turn Mike Bateson is proposing that if we have to pay Jon Gittens, we should play him.

My instant retort to this was twofold. Reconsidering Jon Gittens as a selection option would put back at the centre of things a player whose influence on the team we knew from extended experience was divisive and counter-productive. Further, re-including in our plans a player we had publicly ruled out would put the coaching staff on the back foot from the first minute of Day One of the pre-season.

Hodgie, Steve and I came away from today's meeting feeling we were very much on the back foot anyway. It was not that the events of today and yesterday had occurred in the wrong order. The chairman's 'thus far and no further' figure of £1,500 a week had been arrived at after he'd learned who was being let go and the savings there would consequently be to the wages bill. And in any case, all three of us remained convinced that the 'clean sweep' attempt at a change of culture was the only way to change Torquay's long-term losing game. What now dispirited us was the discovery that, after backing our hand over all kinds of smaller and not so small issues, our self-confessedly disillusioned chairman was now

281

putting the block on the most important initiative of all. We had made it clear that we were thinking not only in terms of six new signings but that in terms of class they should be a notch or two up from bargain basement bottom. Six useful players into £1500 a week doesn't begin to go.

I drove home thinking that this Battle of the Budget would have to be refought and in the very near future at that. Without the coaching staff achieving the victory there would be absolutely no chance of Torquay United winning anything amounting to a battle or a victory in our next season. One way or another, the weary certainty came to me, there would be tears before bedtime.

Friday 9 May

Not so much a labour of love but more an unalloyed pleasure and a privilege. Mind you, it was made a whole lot easier by the fact that for me a return to my roots and to Roots Hall is virtually one and the same. My father still lives in the house just over the road from Southend's ground where I spent three years of my childhood growing up. I could nip in beforehand to enjoy the home comforts of a decent cuppa and some toast and go on to the game happily conscious I'd be a minute's walk away from a bed for the night.

The occasion? A testimonial game for my long-ago mentor the Shrimpers' Youth Team guru, Frankie Banks. Southend versus an All Stars XI – Hoddle, Wilkins, Whelan, Blisset, Peter Taylor and so on. Where you find stars, there you'll find extras. As a Southend old boy I was promised the second half run-out which I was sure, the tackles not going to be flying in, my partially rested knee would be up to managing

With some deft engineering – and the frequent use of 12 men! – the good guys shaded it 5–4. That, though, was incidental to Glenn Hoddle conjuring magic out of the night with a juggler's repertoire of touch, outrageous dummying and inch-perfect passing. Matching the precision of the latter was the sorcerer's apprentice, Dean Wilkins's brother, who weeks after announcing his retirement scampered hither and yon like a teenager and capped a vintage evening's work with an exquisitely flighted scoring chip. For Frankie a richly deserved nice little earner. For me the warming psychological comfort of sitting in the changing room afterwards and exchanging job experiences with the great player England inexplicably failed to construct the national side around 15 years ago. So how were things in the England camp? Were they all getting their

Shredded Wheat? And at Torquay, Nelse? There was a warm gleam of understanding sympathy in Glenn's eyes as I marked his card. Actually, I was able to put him right on quite a few things. Oh, he may have the pick of the nation's talent to select from, play in the world's finest stadiums, travel first class wherever he goes, have assistants at his disposal with the sharpest brains in the English game. The Football League may frequently alter their plans to fit in with his. On a personal level he's long been past the point of ever having another financial worry. But what's that at the end of the day? As a seasoned old hand I felt it only right to point out there's a hell of a lot more to football than that!

Saturday 10 May

A Saturday. Otherwise, catching the 9.10 for Liverpool Street, I might have been mistaken for any middle-aged City commuter. No scrambling for seats today, though. Just as well. Forty-five minutes at less than full throttle last night and my knee was giving me gyp again. Anywhere would do. I shoved my over-nighter down on a seat and, as I settled back and took a relaxing breath, I was delighted to find the sense of well-being I'd taken away from Roots Hall last night still rode with me.

It was an 'off the hook' feeling. Relegation issues, play-offs, the Cup Final, the Grobbelaar replay, the Bosman saga, England away to Poland – all remained to be fought out to their bitter and triumphant ends but I found myself strangely uncurious as to what those ends might be.

It was a broader, softer-edged version of the relief which had swept through me after the draw at Hereford. It was the negative relief that, simply, the Torquay season was over: that we'd got through to the end and it had turned out at the (near)death an end that wasn't a total disaster. For the moment it seemed like coming to the end of one of those psychologically interminable away-game trips to Hartlepool or Carlisle. When the coach comes to a final halt, no matter where you are or what mullering imminently awaits you, the only possible instant response is to be glad it's over at last.

On that long, long ride you'll have played cards – brag, poker, euchre, whatever. You may have lost a few bob or won a few bob. The difference will have been down to a mixture of your skill and the cards you were dealt. That's not a bad comparison in miniature with how you got through the season.

Sweep the million and one details of the last 10 months up, sort them, pigeon-hole them in the memory's inexhaustible data banks and, as ever, you're left confronting that most basic of questions: did we do the best we could?

The answer, of course, is 'no'. No-one ever does. Not Pele, nor Platini, were ever perfect. Did we, though, try to do the best we could given the way things seemed to us at the time? I think the answer is 'yes'.

Newcomers, Hodgie, Steve and I no doubt made close to every mistake in the book – where, that is, we had the luxury of choice in the first place – in terms of squad and team selection, loan deals, individual person-to-person relationships, tactical emphases and, since we're talking Torquay, car maintenance. More than once we found ourselves putting earlier initiatives into reverse.

But viewed from this new-found moment of tranquillity, the mental caning we'd latterly been giving ourselves was probably excessive. It can fairly be said that it was an inherited bad job that we were trying to make the most of; that our energies were about as unflagging as flesh and central nervous systems ever allow; that, whatever their consequences in terms of points and gates, those intentions were always good.

Well, we all know where good intentions are supposed to lead. I don't think Hodgie and I have quite arrived there yet. Or, indeed, taken Torquay. The record shows that working with substantially the same squad we coaxed the Gulls a few vital inches away from toppling off the Nationwide perch and plunging in almost certainly irreversible free fall down the precipice of non-league football. The season's bottom bottom-line is on the plus side of the register. Briefly, when it mattered, we made the leaky boat that is Torquay a fractional degree or two more watertight. No more than a tiny achievement. Not, we can all readily agree, a major boast with which to bore our grandchildren one day.

And now we had it all to do again. Only more so. As the train hammered along it came to me that, as the chorus girl said to the curate, there was no guarantee it would be easier the second time, and the Torquay of May '97 were in many respects in direr straits than the wooden spoon team of a year ago. Then, league status assured, there had been the left-handed knowledge that whatever happened in 1996/97 it couldn't be worse; there had been a full complement of apparently able first-team players in fact and not only on paper; there had been a bit of money floating about.

And, of a kind, there had been hope.

Innocence, I could see now, hadn't been the word. Ignorance had.

Underneath the token, obligatory cynicism, Hodgie and I had gone into last year's pre-season wide-eyed with, well, great expectations. How we'd turn things around! Staring at the hot plush of the train's upholstery without really seeing it, I winced as I recalled grand plans to throw a centre back forward when we were (ha!) three up and hence grab a goal-difference improving vital last minute score or two. How flexible we'd be! Diamond formation, Christmas tree, three-two-bloody-five – we'd bob and weave week by week and nobody would have a chance of anticipating the next change we'd ring ... Yes, I wish I was a little bit younger and knew what I know now ...

The plush was a dusty shade of electric blue. As I finally clocked this it came to me that the strange feeling of calm I was experiencing was due to a very basic reason. I was drained. Exhausted. Deeply tired. The lack of curiosity I was feeling as to how the season's unfinished business might turn out was closer, truth be told, to complete indifference. Not really like me. Usually, however how demanding, disastrous even, the outgoing season has been, within days of it finishing I start to get the first intimations of positive vibes. My enthusiasm swells and then the fantasies. The next campaign will all be different. This time we'll get the rub of the green. I'll go through the season niggle-free. My personal goals tally will shoot up. Roll on July.

This time – and for the first time – I feel none of that. I'm in a state of recoil. The thought of 'Having it all to do again' is in my face. Because it means exactly that. Doing it all again from Day One and Square One. The training – in which I'll have to push myself as hard as anyone because they'll all be looking to see whether the old git can practise what he preaches. The tactical drills – *This is what you do here* – over and over again. Quite likely with players missing the object of the exercise along with the ball. All on council recs as our own groundsman digs in his heels over us using the Plainmoor pitch. The renewed discussions, confrontations as they're now almost certain to be, with the chairman (whoever that may be, glove puppet or not) over money. And the scouting missions. I suddenly realised that these were what I was dreading most. Journeys to check out various unknowns playing at various obscure locations which, since my base was Torquay, would overwhelmingly tend to be a minimum of two hours up the M5 and then all the rest, necessarily far from a West Country that has been denuded of native Avon Combination Games. And then, the occasional hint of a golden boy discovered, what ...? Overwhelming odds that there wouldn't be enough

285

Torquay cash in the kitty to attract him down to Plainmoor. Total certainty any other club interested in us would outbid our feeble effort.

The upholstery stared back at me. 'Whinger' it contrived to convey. 'That's your job, remember. What you get paid for.' It had a point, I had to concede. I told myself that in a couple of days the feeling that the Chinese-style Torquay water torture had got to me, the sense that I'd shipped one body blow too many and it was nicer to stay down here with my head on the canvas, would pass. I was letting the virtual certainty that my days as a player out on the park were numbered get to me. That was no longer my primary job and it behoved me now to tighten my coaches' cap. Yes, no question, a couple of days or so more and I'd be on the case again looking to help the club improve on its 21st finish, 20th next year, perhaps, 19th. Yes, it was what I was paid for and, given that, it was down to me to keep on keeping on. It was the one victory that, however bad the immediate setbacks, was totally in my power to win. I owed it to Torquay, to its fans and above all, looking ahead to all the years of looking back, to myself. After all, Brian, as the man almost said, what will survive of us is work.

The train rattled along through the sunny morning. Southend to Torquay. A half day's journey. And half a lifetime's too.

AFTERWORD

In the second week of May, 1997, Brian Marwood, the organisation's commercial executive, gave the PFA the statutory one month's notice of his leaving. Within a few days Garry Nelson was asked first informally and then formally by PFA officials whether he was willing to allow his name to go on the short-list of those being interviewed to fill the vacancy. His answer was that he was and within a week, following an interview at PFA Headquarters, he was chosen as the new commercial executive. The appointment was made public on 21 May, following the discontinuation of his Plainmoor contract the previous day.

Thus ended a playing career stretching from 1969 to 1997. In the course of these 18 seasons Garry Nelson played in 753 first-class games scoring 156 goals. Never playing in either the old First Division or the Premiership, he won (other than club Player of the Year/Man of the Match awards) just one tangible honour – a Fourth Division Champions medal. In 1988 he was selected by his fellow professionals as a member of the PFA Third Division all-star team. His career embraced one relegation and three promotion seasons. He was twice involved in unsuccessful play-off campaigns. He was sent off just once – for dissent. Among the many venues he played at are Highbury, Anfield and Old Trafford. He never played at Wembley nor at Goodison Park, the ground belonging to the team which he has supported from childhood.

In mid-June 1997 Mike Bateson resigned as chairman of Torquay United to be succeeded by 66-year-old Mervyn Benney. Mr Bateson continued to hold an 80 per cent interest in the club.

Early in July the Torquay squad assembled for pre-season training. Among their number was the still under contract and now reinstalled Jon Gittens.

In the same week, starting work at the PFA, Garry Nelson turned the page upon a new chapter in his life in the capacity of, to quote from his daughter, 'a briefcase man'. On the way to his first day in the office he was climbing the second of the Piccadilly Line Underground's long, steep escalators when his knee gave way and sent him sprawling. Among several concerned commuters who helped him to his feet and to regain his briefcase was an elderly woman.

'You should slow down, young man,' she told him. 'You've still got a long way to go.'

Garry Nelson's reply is not on public record.